HEROINES

of

MERCY STREET

HEROINES

of

MERCY STREET

The Real Nurses of the Civil War

PAMELA D. TOLER, PhD

LITTLE BROWN AND COMPANY
New York Boston London

Little, Brown and Company
Hachette Book Group
1290 Avenue of the Americas, New York, NY 10104
littlebrown.com

First Edition: February 2016

Little, Brown and Company is a division of Hachette Book Group, Inc. The Little, Brown name and logo are trademarks of Hachette Book Group, Inc.

The publisher is not responsible for websites (or their content) that are not owned by the publisher.

The Hachette Speakers Bureau provides a wide range of authors for speaking events. To find out more, go to hachettespeakersbureau.com or call (866) 376-6591.

ISBN 978-0-316-39207-5

Library of Congress Control Number 2015953905

10 9 8 7 6 5 4 3 2 1

RRD-C

Produced in collaboration with Booktrix

Printed in the United States of America

Contents

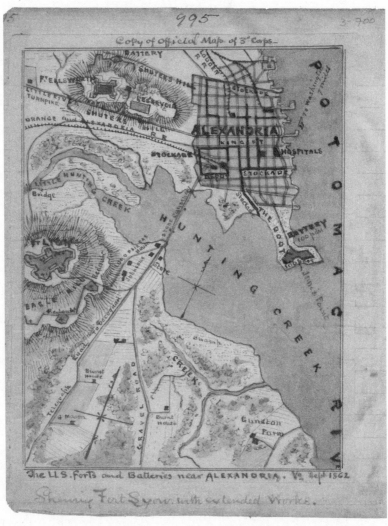

Map of military installations around Alexandria, Virginia, in
September 1862, from the Civil War memoir of Union soldier
Robert Knox Sneden, whose 500 watercolors, maps and drawings are
the largest collection of soldier art to survive the war.
Library of Congress, Geography and Map Division/
Virginia Historical Society, Richmond, VA

Foreword

The Civil War lives on in our imagination as a series of black and white photographs; stoic young men in uniform, fields strewn with bloated corpses, the smoldering ruins of a once proud city. It is a silent, static world, as if stilled by tragedy. But if our modern world is anything to judge by, war is vivid, chaotic, and noisy. It is above all a human experience filled with passion, tragedy, heroism, despair, and even, at times, unexpected humor. That is the story we went looking for.

The series *Mercy Street* was largely inspired by the memoirs of doctors and female volunteer nurses who were in many ways the unsung heroes of the Civil War. For every soldier wounded in battle, there were dozens of caregivers behind the front lines selflessly trying to repair the physical and psychological damage. That job was all the harder during the Civil War because medical science was in its infancy and nursing was relegated to convalescing male soldiers who were, for the most part, untrained, unsympathetic, and far from gentle. Female volunteers were initially unwelcome in Army hospitals, and yet they were sorely needed. Where medicine fell short, "sympathy and a friendly face" (as our Emma Green explains) made an enormous difference, even if it was simply to help a dying soldier find peace of mind.

Mary Phinney, Baroness Von Olnhausen, was a historical figure. Her memoir provided an ideal setting for our series: the dysfunctional world of Mansion House Hospital in Union-occupied Alexandria, Virginia. Mary wrote about the place with so much detail and wit that it needed little embellishment. Most of our hospital characters are based on the people she described: the cranky chief, the empathetic chaplain, the corrupt steward, and the long-suffering matron. Our Mary is very close to the real Mary with a few added attributes borrowed from another woman we admire, Louisa May Alcott. Louisa worked as a nurse during the war and wrote a book called *Hospital Sketches* based on her experiences. Her ability to balance drama with humor inspired us to do the same. We also gave our character her Concord roots, abolitionist politics, and feminist views.

Mary's rival, Anne Hastings, is based on Anne Reading, an English nurse trained by Florence Nightingale during the Crimean War. Her memoir reveals an independent woman defined by her vocation. It must have taken exceptional courage to travel across the Atlantic to volunteer in a war in which she had no stake. She was truly one of the first professional nurses, someone whose primary goal was helping others and not simply doing her patriotic duty. However, some of Anne's quirks and vices also find their way into our characterization.

The Emma Green character in our story is initially drawn to nursing as a way to help wounded compatriots and rebel against her parents, but she soon discovers a greater purpose. Her personality is drawn from accounts written by Confederate nurses like Kate Cummings and Sarah Morgan. The real Emma Green did not volunteer as a nurse, as far as we can tell. What we do know is that her father, a successful businessman and Southern loyalist, owned Mansion House Hotel and that she and part of her family remained in Alexandria throughout the war, living right beside the hospital.

Where the written record falls short we have filled in the blanks with the help of historians and our imagination. Our series is fiction after all, and we must thank the ladies of Mansion House Hospital and the thousands of women who volunteered during the war, be they Union or Confederate, white or black, for inspiring us with their remarkable stories.

—Ridley Scott, Executive Producer,
Mercy Street

HEROINES

of

MERCY STREET

Introduction

It is impossible to fully understand the American Civil War without looking at the role of medicine, both its triumphs and its failures. The death toll was high at more than twice the number of American soldiers who died in World War II. The new mass-produced weapons of the industrial age created mass-produced deaths on the battlefield, but even the new Gatling guns and rifled muskets could not compete with older killers: gangrene, typhoid, pneumonia, yellow fever, malaria, and dysentery. Disease counted for two-thirds of all Civil War deaths.

When the war started in 1861, the Union army's Medical Bureau—made up of thirty surgeons, eighty-six assistant surgeons, and a surgeon general who was a veteran of the War of 1812 and took office in 1836 under the administration of Andrew Jackson—was unprepared for the carnage that would follow. American medicine in general wasn't up to the task.

Europe was in the midst of a medical revolution, based on the application of scientific techniques of observation and measurement to medical questions. New instruments, such as the stethoscope (1816), the laryngoscope (1854), and the ophthalmoscope (1851), allowed physicians the opportunity to study a disease the same way the period's naturalists studied the structure of plants and minerals. In France, unfettered access to corpses for dissection gave doctors a more profound understanding of the relationship between nerves, muscles, organs, blood vessels, and bones in the human body. Medical scientists like Xavier Bichat and Pierre Louis supplanted the old medical theories of humors and temperaments with new ideas about how diseases worked—the first steps toward the development of the germ theory of disease. In England, physicians moved the techniques of observation and measurement beyond the human body to track the progress of a disease through a population, demonstrating the correlation between infected water and illnesses like cholera and typhoid. In the ten years following the Civil War, Joseph Lister would introduce carbolic acid as the first antiseptic, Louis Pasteur would pioneer the germ theory of disease and lay the foundations of the study of epidemiology, and Sir Thomas Allbutt would invent the first clinical thermometer—a revolutionary tool in light of how many deadly diseases initially manifest themselves as fever. But none of that was available to Civil War doctors and their patients.

In Europe, thousands of students went to Paris to study medicine, including young Americans interested in the possibilities of medicine as a science rather than medicine as an art. They attended lectures by noted physicians on subjects that included anatomy, physics, medical hygiene, surgical and medical pathology, pharmacology, organic chemistry, therapeutics, operative and clinical surgery, midwifery, diseases of women and children, and legal medicine. More important than the lectures was the clinical experience offered in the great Parisian hospitals. In addition to the benefits of following a physician on his daily hospital rounds, the sheer size of the Parisian hospitals meant that students could see a wider variety of the sick and the wounded in a matter of months than an American doctor would see in a lifetime in even the largest American hospitals. In 1833, for example, the twelve Parisian hospitals treated almost 65,000 patients, more than the entire population of Boston at the time.

By comparison, the United States was a medical backwater. Neither a license nor a medical degree was required to practice medicine, and many doctors had neither, instead learning the trade as apprentices to older doctors. In fact, a degree was no guarantee a doctor was well trained. The quality of American medical education went down in the early nineteenth century, as proprietary medical schools began to spring up in the 1820s in response to a rising population with a growing need for doctors. In most cases, the education provided by these schools consisted of two four-month terms in a two-year period; first- and second-year students attended the same lectures. There was no clinical work and no surgical demonstrations. Attendance was not required and examinations were minimal. Best described as entrepreneurial education, many of these schools were more concerned with generating fees than training doctors: a substantial "graduation fee" encouraged schools to allow students to earn their degree without regard to competence. Even the best American medical schools, often led by doctors who had studied in Paris, lagged behind European schools; medical students at Harvard, for instance, did not use microscopes in laboratory work until 1871.

Doctors relied on emetics, purgatives, bloodletting, and the painkilling properties of whiskey, which they administered to patients in the absence of anesthesia. (Civil War nurses often complained that doctors dipped into the whiskey supply for their own use as well. One Confederate nurse dubbed struggles between doctors and nurses over control of medicinal liquor the "wars of the whiskey barrel."[1]) Many of the medicines in common use dated from the time of Hippocrates, who laid the foundations for Western medicine in the fifth century BCE; some were the ancestors of modern wonder drugs, but others were close kin to the cure-alls made and sold by patent medicine charlatans. Opiates were widespread and legal despite the known dangers of addiction. Doctors had used ether and chloroform as anesthetics for twenty years, but dosages were still uncertain, and it was difficult to secure the necessary supplies on a reliable basis during wartime given the complexities of military logistics.

For the most part, neither doctors nor their patients had any experience with hospitals. Hospitals were charity institutions and existed only in the largest cities: New York, Boston, Philadelphia, Washington, DC. Doctors in smaller towns and cities would never have practiced at a hospital. Even in large cities, female family members attended the ill at home if at all possible, perhaps with the support of a visit by a doctor. If surgery was needed, doctors often performed the procedure on the kitchen table, which was probably cleaner than most hospital operating theaters and certainly cleaner than the surgical instruments used, which doctors carried in plush-lined cases that were germ breeding-grounds.

Only the poor and the desperate went to a hospital when they were ill. As one medical student put it shortly before the war, "The people who repair to hospitals are mostly very poor, and seldom go into them until driven to do so from a very severe stress of circumstances. When they cross the threshold they are found not only suffering from disease, but in half-starved condition, poor, broken-down wrecks of humanity, stranded on the cold, bleak shores of that most forbidding of all coasts, charity."[2] Infection and cross-infection were so common that some diseases were known as "hospital diseases"—not surprising since the same bed linen would be used for several patients. The smells were so bad that the rough hospital nurses of the antebellum world, who typically belonged to the same economic classes as their patients, inhaled the finely ground tobacco known as snuff to make working conditions more tolerable.

Nursing as a skilled profession barely existed in the mid–nineteenth century, with the exception of a few religious orders. Most women could expect to care for ill or infirm family members or friends at some point in their life. A few would serve as paid nurses in the homes of the well-to-do, as temporary domestic servants who performed the same services a family member might perform in a less wealthy home. Such work was for the most part the domain of American-born, poor, white, older women—often widows. Women who took up hospital nursing were a large step down the social scale from private nurses, cleaning, feeding, and watching over patients who were society's most marginalized people in an institution that many rightly feared as a death trap. British nursing advocate Florence Nightingale summed up the public perception of hospital nurses: women "who were too old, too weak, too drunken, too dirty, too stolid or too bad to do anything else."[3] Most of the limited jobs open to poor and working-class women in urban America—mill worker, seamstress, milliner, laundress, and especially domestic servant—required proof of a good moral character. Losing a job without a reference was an economic calamity. Hospital nursing was the penultimate step in a downhill slide: a job for women who had few options left other than the street. At Bellevue Hospital in New York, women arrested for public drunkenness or disorderly conduct were sentenced to ten days in the workhouse. Once they dried out, these "ten-day" women could be paroled if they agreed to work as nurses in the Bellevue wards.

The reputation of nursing as no job for a respectable woman began to change with Florence Nightingale's ground-breaking work in the Crimean War in 1854 and her subsequent publication of the best-selling *Notes on Nursing* in 1859. Her efforts in the war caught the public imagination, thanks to publicity from the new breed of war correspondents spawned by the telegraph, the steamship, and daily newspapers aimed at the middle classes. Using the benefits of her fame, Nightingale set out to change the perception of nursing, which she considered a calling rather than a job. She opened a nursing school in London in 1860. Students included not only "probationers," scholarship students drawn from the lower middle classes, but also "Lady nurses," higher-class (or at least wealthier) women who paid their own expenses and expected to become instructors and supervisors. Her example inspired young American women with dreams of glory. As one young woman put it soon after the beginning of the war, "It seems strange that what the aristocratic women of Great Britain have done with honor is a disgrace for their sisters to do on this side of the Atlantic."[4]

Nightingale's success also forced the army Medical Bureau to change its practices regarding nursing. Before the Civil War, convalescent enlisted men who were not yet able to return to their military duties performed any nursing required by ill or wounded soldiers, a system that would continue side by side with female nurses throughout the Civil War. The lessons of the Crimean War made it clear to at least some Americans that such ad hoc nursing was not enough. Nightingale's version of nursing could be seen as an exalted version of a woman's household duties. Recuperating soldiers did not have the domestic skills to ensure well-cooked food for special diets or meet the new standards of clean wards, clean sheets, and clean men. Female nurses, trained or not, would be needed to care for ill and wounded soldiers.

It turned out to be easy to find them. Thousands of women volunteered over the course of the war, though there was never any official call for nurses in the North. The largest number of volunteers came after the First Battle of Bull Run in July 1861, but women continued to volunteer well into 1864. By one estimate, more than twenty thousand women served as nurses during the war, not including an unknown number of uncompensated volunteers.[5]

The popular image of a Civil War nurse is a single Northern woman, old enough to be considered a spinster but young enough to have the energy for the work, from a middle- to upper-class family, with an inclination toward philanthropy or reform. In fact, they were as diverse as the new and expanding nation from which they were drawn: teenaged girls, middle-aged widows, and grandmothers; society belles, farm wives, and factory girls; teachers, reformers, and nuns; free African-Americans and escaped slaves; new immigrants and Mayflower descendants. Some worked from patriotic zeal or a sense of adventure; others took the work because they needed the money. (The Union army paid $12 a month plus board, rations, and transportation, when it paid at all.) What they had in common was the physical capacity to do the work and a willingness to serve

Heroines of Mercy Street: The Real Nurses of the Civil War will focus on one Union hospital and the nurses who passed through it. Mansion House Hospital was located in Alexandria, Virginia, which held the distinction of being occupied by Union troops longer than any other Confederate city. The women who worked at Mansion House can be seen as a microcosm for the medical experience of the war. Its nurses did battle with hostile surgeons, corrupt house stewards, dirt, filth, inadequate supplies, and their own lack of training. They fought to make sure their patients received the care they needed along with minimal comforts, wept for those they lost, raged at the enemy, and raged even harder against the indifference and inefficiency that left wounded men lying on the battlefield without care. They learned to dress wounds, bathe naked men with whom they had no familial relationship (not an easy adjustment to make at the height of Victorian prudery), and evacuate the building in case of fire. Worn out by the grinding nature of the work and exposed constantly to diseases, they themselves fell sick, often with no one to nurse them in their turn. At least one Mansion House nurse fell in love with a soldier and was forced to leave the service. Some lasted less than a month; others made the leap from volunteer to veteran. By war's end their collective experience, along with that of nurses across the country, had convinced Americans that nursing was not only respectable but a profession.

Chapter 1

Dorothea Dix Goes to War

"This dreadful civil war has as a huge beast
consumed my whole of life."
—Dorothea Dix[1]

"[Dorothea Dix] is energetic, benevolent, unselfish
and a mild case of monomania; working on her own
hook, she does good, but no one can cooperate with
her for [she] belongs to the class of comets, and can be
subdued into relations with no system whatever."
—George Templeton Strong[2]

The Civil War began at 4:30 a.m. on April 12, 1861, when troops of the two-month-old Confederate States of America fired on Fort Sumter, an unfinished red brick fortress built on a man-made granite island in the entrance of the harbor at Charleston, South Carolina.

The fort, held by sixty-eight Union soldiers under the command of Major Robert Anderson, had become the emotional focal point of the conflict between North and South in the weeks since South Carolina became the first state to secede from the Union on December 20, 1860. The small garrison was cut off from resupply or reinforcement, but the soldiers there refused to surrender the fort to Confederate control. Anderson, a Kentucky native and former slaveholder, was praised as a hero in the North and reviled as a traitor in the

South. President James Buchanan, at the end of his term of office, was unwilling to trigger civil war by attempting to relieve the besieged unit and equally unwilling to trigger a public outcry by recalling the troops from Sumter. "If I withdraw Anderson from Sumter," he said in late December 1860, "I can trail home to Wheatland [Pennsylvania] by the light of my own burning effigies."[3] He chose instead to leave the problem for his successor.

When Abraham Lincoln took office on March 4, the garrison at Sumter had less than six weeks of food left. Lincoln's cabinet told him it was impossible to relieve the fortress and urged him to evacuate Anderson's troops as a way of reducing tension between North and South. Popular opinion screamed for Lincoln to reinforce the "gallant band who are defending their country's honor and its flag in the midst of a hostile and traitorous foe."[4] With public opinion eager for action, and no sign that delay would improve the chances of reuniting the country, Lincoln chose to resupply the garrison but not send reinforcements unless the Confederates attacked either the fort or the supply ships, a compromise that pleased no one.

Shortly after midnight on April 12, with resupply ships on the way, the Confederate government gave Anderson until 4:00 a.m. to surrender. Anderson refused. At 4:30 a.m., the bombardment began. Although they had neither the men nor supplies to mount a meaningful defense, the Union forces held out for a day and a half before surrendering.

Almost before the echoes of the first gun shots died away, President Abraham Lincoln called for 75,000 militia volunteers to serve for ninety days, certain that would be enough time to put down what he described as a state of insurrection, not a state of war. The public's response was immediate and over-whelming. Men thronged the army's recruiting offices. The first two Massachusetts regiments marched toward Washington and Fort Monroe two days after the president's call; two more followed within the week. Individual states filled their recruit-ment quotas and offered more. The governor of Ohio, having raised the thirteen regiments requested, telegraphed the War Department to say, "without seriously repressing the ardor of the people, I can hardly stop short of twenty."[5]

Citizen soldiers were not the only volunteers to respond to the president's call. Even though Lincoln had said nothing about nurses—and had certainly not called for women to come to their nation's aid—Dorothea Lynde Dix, a fifty-nine-year-old reformer dedicated to improving the treatment of prisoners, paupers, and the mentally ill, set out immediately to volunteer her services to create an army corps of female nurses to care for wounded soldiers, modeled on the group of nurses who fol-lowed Florence Nightingale to the Crimean War.

A Useful Life

Dorothea Dix was born in 1802 in a small frontier settle-ment in northern Massachusetts (now a part of Maine). Her childhood was difficult and often lonely. Her grandfather, a successful Boston doctor, had purchased thousands of acres of undeveloped land with the intention of building new towns, and he sent her father, Joseph Dix, to manage the property. By the time Dorothea was born, he had carved out a small piece of farmland from the wilderness and built a plaster-chinked log house. It would have been a hard life even if Joseph Dix had been a dedicated farmer—and he wasn't. Instead of concentrating on farming and developing the land, he became an itinerant Methodist minister and was often away from home, supplementing his meager income by selling printed copies of his sermons. Dorothea had the hated job of cutting and folding the printed sheets and sewing them into pamphlets. Her mother was no help; she took to her bed after the birth of Dorothea's second brother and remained a semi-invalid who suffered from what sounds to a modern reader like debilitating bouts of depression. As the oldest of three children, Dorothea became responsible for much of the work of the frontier household at a very early age.

When Dorothea was twelve, she escaped to Dix Mansion, her widowed grandmother's home in Boston. Life was better with her grandmother, but the two Dix women soon butted heads. The senior Mrs. Dix was determined to turn her backwoods granddaughter into a lady, and Dorothea rebelled. After two years, Mrs. Dix realized she didn't have the strength to take care of a strong-willed teenager and sent Dorothea to her great-aunt Sarah in Worchester, forty miles west of Boston.

In a warm and loving environment for the first time, Dorothea thrived with her relatives in Worchester, but she was used to working. She needed more to do than the picnics, garden parties, and teas that occupied her contemporaries there. With her aunt's permission, she opened a school for young children in an old printing shop, where she taught reading and writing, Bible studies, and the kind of manners she herself had resisted learning in Boston. Dix was only fourteen, but the school was a success, with as many as twenty children attending at a time.

She ran the school in Worchester for nearly three years, until her grandmother, now seventy-three, asked her come back to Dix Mansion. In 1819, she returned to Boston where she made an unobtrusive debut in society, studied with private tutors, attended public lectures, and discovered the Unitarian religion, which flourished in Boston during the period. She also met Anne Heath, whose friendship would be a constant comfort for the rest of her life. In 1821, she convinced her grandmother to allow her to open a charity school in the barn behind Dix Mansion. When the school proved to be a success, she opened a second one within Dix Mansion itself, aimed at students who could afford to pay tuition. During this period she also began to write textbooks for children. One of these, *Conversations on Common Things*, published in 1824, enjoyed a surprising success; by the time the Civil War began, it had been reprinted sixty times.

Throughout the 1820s and 1830s, Dix suffered from respiratory problems, fatigue, and depression. Her poor health made it difficult to teach on a regular basis. In 1836, she suffered a serious physical and emotional collapse and was forced to close her school. Her doctor and friends encouraged her to take a restorative trip to England, where she convalesced for eighteen months in the home of fellow Unitarian William Rathbone. At Rathbone's home, Dix was introduced to a circle of reformers concerned with the social problems created by a half century of industrialization in England, among them utopian socialist Robert Owen, prison reformer Elizabeth Fry, and Samuel Tuke, founder of the innovative York Retreat, an asylum for the mentally ill that emphasized humane treatment, healthy diet, exercise, and productive work. Dix's involvement with the Unitarian congregation in Boston had already introduced her to ideas of liberal Christianity and social reform, but now she discovered a new way of thinking about social problems that utilized direct observation and data collection to argue for change.

Dix was not well enough to make the trip home until the fall of 1837, several months after the death of her grandmother. Between the money she inherited from her grandmother and the income she received from her books, she had enough money to allow her to devote her time to reform and charitable work. Being a woman of independent means would be a crucial element in her success as a reformer.

For several years after her return, she traveled in search of both a home and a cause. She found her true calling at the age of thirty-nine, when a friend asked her to take over his Sunday school class for women inmates at the East Cambridge Jail. On March 28, 1841, she arrived at the jail, prepared to lead the twenty waiting inmates in a Bible lesson, a prayer, and a hymn. When the lesson was over, she asked the jailer for a tour of the facilities, a standard activity among the nineteenth-century reform community. What she found shocked her, particularly the section of the prison where the mentally ill were kept in small cells without furniture and no stove to keep the inmates warm. When she asked why they didn't have heat in their cells, she was told it was unnecessary and dangerous: because they weren't in their right minds they didn't feel the cold, and, besides, they might start a fire and burn down the prison.

Outraged, Dix took the matter to the county court. Women were not allowed to speak before the court, but they were allowed to state their case in writing. Dix described the conditions she had seen and appealed to the court to at least provide stoves for the inmates. At first she was greeted with anger and disbelief, but she wrote letters to prominent Bostonians and finally caught the attention of Samuel Gridley Howe, who was doing similar work on behalf of disabled children, and of Boston legislator Charles Sumner. When they took up Dix's cause, both the public and the court listened. The mentally ill inmates of the Cambridge jail got their stoves.

While she campaigned on behalf of the inmates of the East Cambridge Jail, Dix began to investigate how the mentally ill were cared for elsewhere. For a year and a half, she traveled across the state of Massachusetts, investigating conditions in every poorhouse and prison, public and private, that she could gain access to. She quickly learned that the conditions at East Cambridge were not unusual; in fact, in many places they were much worse. The wealthy could pay for attendants to care for mentally ill family members at home or pay for them to be housed in private hospitals, but the poor had nowhere to go. In 1841, there were only fourteen mental hospitals in the country. Most of the mentally ill were housed in prisons and poorhouses, and even those housed in asylums were often brutally treated. Appalled, she set out to reform the treatment of the mentally ill in Massachusetts, replicating her East Cambridge campaign on a larger scale.

Dix had found both her cause and her mode of operations: painstaking investigations, dramatically written descriptions of conditions, and the help of powerful men to apply pressure on the political system. Between 1843 and 1845, she traveled more than ten thousand miles and visited hundreds of institutions, often at the request of concerned citizens in other states who wanted help in undertaking asylum reforms.

By the time the Civil War began, Dix had spent twenty years working to change the way people thought about the mentally ill. She traveled almost continuously at a time when few people traveled more than a few miles from home and women seldom traveled alone. Railroad companies gave her free passes, and freight haulers carried her packages to prisons, hospitals, and asylums at no charge. Most importantly, she had convinced politicians at every level of American government to support prison reform bills and to build insane asylums. She had even worked for reform at the federal level. In 1848, she lobbied for a bill to grant the states more than twelve million acres of public land to be used for the benefit of the insane, deaf, dumb, and blind. The bill passed both houses of Congress. President Franklin Pierce ultimately vetoed the bill, but Dix made important connections in Congress in its pursuit, a fact that meant her proposal for an army nursing corps got a fair hearing.

In the eighteen months before the war, Dix had spent much of her time on the road, touring mental health facilities, lobbying state legislatures for capital appropriations and needed reforms, and gathering local information about the national political crisis, hoping she would be able to use her connections on both sides of the political divide to calm the secession crisis. Her travels took her through more of the country than a nineteenth-century presidential candidate on campaign would have seen. She toured the deep South shortly after John Brown's raid in October 1859, then turned her attention north and west, where she visited prisons and hospitals for the mentally ill in the pioneer states of Illinois, Iowa, Missouri, Kansas, Wisconsin, and Minnesota. In the early months of 1861, she focused her attention on the border regions where the divisions over slavery, agriculture, and industry were most bitter, traveling from Kentucky, to Missouri, Tennessee, and back to Kentucky. As she traveled, she noted the nation's political dissension with apprehension. In February of 1861, she confided to her lifelong friend Anne Heath that she was grateful to be busy: "I thank God I have such full uses for time now for the state of our beloved country would crush my heart and life."[6]

During this period, Dix failed in her attempts to promote compromise, but she helped prevent a conspiracy to assassinate Lincoln. Her privileged position as a lady and a welcome guest in the South allowed her to overhear details of a plan to murder Lincoln on the final leg of his trip to Washington for his inauguration. In mid-January 1861, she met with Samuel M. Felton, the president of the Philadelphia, Wilmington and Baltimore Railroad; she laid out what she knew about a conspiracy to burn the railroad bridges, cut the telegraph lines, and sabotage Felton's railroad when the president-elect's train reached Baltimore as the first step in seizing Washington and declaring the Confederacy the de facto government of the United States. Felton had heard similar rumors for some time. He passed the information on to detective Allan Pinkerton, whom he used to police the railroad. Using Dix's information, Pinkerton's men confirmed the plot to assassinate Lincoln when he changed trains in Baltimore; spies from the War Department confirmed the story independently. Felton always believed that Dix had changed the course of history by this act alone.

Dorothea Dix Volunteers

Dix was taking a well-deserved rest with friends in Trenton, New Jersey, when she heard the news that Sumter had fallen. Without hesitation, she repacked her bags and left that afternoon for Washington, DC, on a trip that would be marked by troop movements, patriotic crowds, packed trains, wild rumors, and secessionist disruptions.

Her first stop was Philadelphia, which was full of rumors of secessionist plots to cut off Washington by destroying the railroad bridges. Fearing that she might not get through, Dix by-passed the cumbersome horse-car transfer system that took passengers from one railroad terminal to another and raced through Philadelphia at top speed in a rented carriage. She reached the terminal just in time to catch the last southbound train before Confederate sympathizers destroyed the Susquehanna River bridges and cut off the road to Washington.

She was not so lucky in Baltimore. Three hours before Dix arrived, the Maryland capital erupted into mob violence when the Sixth Massachusetts Regiment arrived in the city on its way to Washington. Cheering crowds and patriotic demonstrations greeted the Sixth at every station for the first three hundred miles of its journey, but railroad officials warned them they could expect a rough reception in Baltimore, which was strongly pro-South and had a long history of urban violence.

Each railroad had its own system of stations, which meant that passengers traveling from Philadelphia to Washington had to transfer from the Philadelphia, Wilmington and Baltimore Railroad station to the Baltimore & Ohio Railroad station; this process required teams of four horses to pull each car for a mile and a half along tracks from President Street to Camden, where railroad workers attached the cars to a Baltimore & Ohio engine. The regimental quartermaster had issued each member of the Sixth twenty rounds of ball cartridges before they reached the station and ordered them to cap and load their Springfield rifles in anticipation of trouble. The line of seven horse-drawn cars traveled only a few blocks before they attracted an angry crowd. At first the secessionist rioters limited themselves to yelling at the soldiers. The soldiers were anxious to retaliate, but their officers told them to hold their fire. When the crowd escalated to rock throwing and gunfire, an injured soldier in the rear car requested permission to fire back. Permission granted, the soldiers dropped to the floor of the car, loaded their muskets, and rose to fire out the windows. Once the car pulled into the safety of Camden station, windowless and bullet ridden, the mob attacked the horse-car tracks with crowbars and pickaxes, rendering the tracks impassable. The remaining four companies of the Sixth had no choice but to march in columns to the station through the narrow streets of Baltimore, surrounded by rioters. After four blocks of taunts, thrown bricks, and gunfire, the militia fired back. The orderly march turned into street fighting, leaving four soldiers and eleven civilians dead and dozens of soldiers, rioters, and bystanders wounded—the first casualties in a war that would claim the lives of more than 620,000 soldiers over the course of four years.

By the time Dix arrived at President Street station, the riot was over but its aftermath remained. She found her way to the Baltimore & Ohio station along the same route taken by the Massachusetts regiment several hours before—disabled tracks, bullet holes, broken store windows, and all. As she wrote to Heath the next day, "It was not easy getting across the city— but I did not choose to turn back—I reached my destination."[7]

Dix reached Washington that evening, several hours after the Massachusetts regiment arrived with news of the Baltimore riots. The city was on high alert. Pickets guarded public buildings and bridges. Soldiers were billeted at the White House in anticipation of a Confederate attack before morning. A less determined woman might have have hesitated, but Dix went directly from the train station to the White House, where she volunteered her services and those of an "army of nurses," yet to be gathered, to support the Union's troops.

If any other woman had appeared unannounced at the White House with such a scheme, she might have been turned away. But Dix, soft-spoken and physically fragile but mentally tough, was preceded by her national reputation as a humanitarian, crusader, and lobbyist. She was used to working with powerful politicians, and they were used to working with her. Even with the threat of the Confederate army at the door, she and her proposal received a warm reception. Lincoln's private secretary, John G. Nicolay, noted late that night that "we have been much impressed" by Dix's proposal.[8] The army's Medical Bureau would prove to be less enthusiastic.

Appointed and Undermined

Dix's offer to form a nursing corps was not at the top of the agenda for an administration literally under threat of siege. After two days of waiting, Dix sent a note repeating her offer to Secretary of War Simon Cameron, one of several cabinet members who served in Congress during her land-bill campaign. Rightly anticipating opposition from the army Medical Bureau, she promised to work "subject to the regulations established by the Surgical Staff," a promise she would find difficult to keep almost from the beginning due to efforts on the part of the Medical Bureau to undermine her authority. Further, she assured Cameron she had access to a network of the philan-thropically inclined and told him she sought "that *authority* which you as head of the Department alone can give" so that she could "call in such substantial aid as I can immediately affect."[9] It was one of the last times she would demonstrate tact or political savvy in dealing with the military's bureaucracy.

Overwhelmed and underresourced, Cameron accepted Dix's offer the next day, without taking the time to define what her position would entail or how she would fit into a military medical bureaucracy, which was itself in a state of transforma-tion. The official order of April 23, 1861, which initially approved Dix's proposal, was at best a vague mandate:

> The free services of Miss D. L. Dix are accepted by the War Department and that she will give at all times necessary aid in organizing military hospitals for the cure of sick and wounded soldiers, aiding the chief surgeon by supplying nurses and substantial means for the comfort and relief of the suffering; also that she is fully authorized to receive, control and disburse special supplies bestowed by individuals or associations for the comfort of their friends or the citizen soldiers from all parts of the limited states; as also, under the action of the Acting Surgeon General, to draw from the army stores.[10]

The Medical Bureau was in transition. The surgeon gen-eral, Thomas Lawson, had fallen ill after the fall of Fort Sumter. In his absence, Acting Director Colonel Robert C. Wood strug-gled with Dix over the nature of her authority and her relation-ship with the War Department.

Dix's offer to create an army corps of female nurses was revolutionary at the time, and several steps ahead of the Union army, which had not yet organized even its own medical corps for the coming war. Dix envisioned a nursing corps of respectable women similar to that pioneered by Florence Nightingale but on a much larger scale. She believed the development of such a corps would be a natural offshoot of her work with hospitals for the mentally ill. In fact, Dix had visited Nightingale's hospital in Scutari, now part of modern Turkey, during the height of the Crimean War and had spoken at length with her chief lieutenants, though she was unsuccessful in obtaining an interview with "the Lady with the Lamp" herself. She shared Nightingale's belief that a nurse should not simply be a doctor's assistant but a patient's primary advocate within the hospital, similar to the role she played on a wider scale for the mentally ill, an idea that would inevitably put Dix and her nurses in conflict with the doctors they worked with.

Wood, and almost all of the doctors in the army's Medical Bureau, opposed the employment of female nurses in military hospitals on grounds that included affronts to female modesty in the rough atmosphere of the hospital, lack of upper-body strength, and the simple fact that the army had never employed women before. He tried to interpret the vague construction of Dix's appointment in ways that would limit the direct involvement of women volunteers with the Medical Bureau.

His first effort focused on her authority to receive supplies donated by individuals and groups like the newly formed ladies' aid societies. The Medical Bureau's budget assumed a peacetime army of 15,000 soldiers; it was totally overwhelmed by the prospect of an additional 75,000 volunteers. Even the most

basic medical supplies—lint, bandages, clothing, and bedding—were in short supply. Wood hoped Dix could help fill
the gap. Two days after Cameron announced her appointment,
Wood asked Dix to provide the army with five hundred hospital gowns, a request that caused Dix some embarrassment since
she had exaggerated the scope of her personal network of potential donors in her correspondence with Secretary of War Cameron. Eager to appear useful, she bought the gowns with her
own money, but realized she didn't have the resources to help
the army secure basic supplies on a regular basis. Moreover, she
was ill-equipped to run a broad-based collection campaign for
medical supplies, a function that the then-forming ladies' aid
societies would fill in an exemplary fashion over the course of
the war. Instead of allowing Wood to maneuver her into serving as an unofficial adjunct to the quartermaster, the officer
responsible for providing supplies, equipment, and facilities to
the army, she adopted a tactic she had used in soliciting contributions for the asylums she supported: she concentrated on
canvassing her network of reformers, asylum directors, and
Unitarian congregations for supplies not provided for in the
standard military budget. One of the first items she requested
from her contributors was industrial-sized coffeepots for hospital kitchens.

Wood then turned to Dix's charge for "aiding the chief
surgeon by supplying nurses," a phrase that gave her responsibility without authority. On May 1, with the hope of prevent-
ing unwanted female volunteers from appearing unexpectedly
at military hospitals, he announced that all interested women
should contact Dix at her home. By making Dix accountable
for all nurses he could, as one contemporary advocate for

female nursing angrily described it, turn her into "a break-water against which feminine sympathies could dash and splash without submerging the hospital service."[11] Dix responded with a press release three days later asking volunteers to not travel to Washington until they received notice their services were needed.

Wood's bureaucratic maneuvering with Dix ended with the death of Surgeon General Lawson on May 15. Thanks to the seniority system then in place in the Medical Bureau, Lawson was succeeded not by Wood but by the elderly and intransigent Clement Alexander Finley, described by one of his younger colleagues as "utterly ossified and useless."[12] Finley was opposed to change of all kinds: he disliked the idea of an ambulance corps as much as he disliked the idea of female nurses. Secretary of War Cameron used the occasion as an opportunity to clarify Dix's role. In a letter to Finley dated June 10, Cameron both broadened Dix's authority and undermined it. Military doctors might oppose employing female nurses, he told Finley, but public sentiment disagreed. Hereafter, women nurses were to be "adopted or substituted for men nurses in the General Hospitals, whenever it can be effected." Dix, now appointed superintendent of women nurses for the Union army, the first federal executive position to be held by a woman, was given sole authority to select nurses and assign them to military hospitals, not only in the Washington region but across the country. On the other hand, Cameron equivocated that "it is of course, understood, that all women nurses are to be under the direction of the Surgeons in charge of the hospitals." Similarly, Dix had the right to visit and inspect military hospitals, and her suggestions and wishes were to be carried out "as far as is compatible with the order of the Medical Bureau."[13] In short, Dix had powers over nurses and hospitals up to the point at which her authority conflicted with that of local surgeons.

Selecting Nurses

Dix had outlined her ideas about nursing more than a dozen years before in connection with ongoing debates about asylum therapy for the mentally ill, stressing the mental and moral qualities required in a nurse. Now she applied these standards to choosing nurses to serve with the Union army.

Her standards were stringent and reflected her personal prejudices as well as the practicalities of nursing in the male-dominated environments of the war. She required two letters of reference that testified to an applicant's "morality, integrity, seriousness, and capacity for the care of the sick." She didn't bother to ask about an applicant's experience or training, as it was presumed that no reputable applicant would have nursing experience beyond caring for ill family members. Only women between the ages of thirty or thirty-five and fifty would be accepted. "Neatness, order, sobriety and industry" were required; "matronly persons of experience, good conduct or superior education" were preferred.[14] Dix wanted her nurses to be matronly, but she also wanted them to be strong enough to turn a full-grown man in his bed, a qualification that further thinned the ranks of acceptable applicants.

Possibly the most controversial of her requirements was the demand that nurses were to present a plain appearance, a dictum often interpreted, then and now, to mean that Dix believed nurses should be homely women. The wording in

Circular No. 8—the official statement of requirements for army nurses that Dix published on July 24, 1862, in conjunction with Surgeon General William Hammond, a full year after Cameron accepted Dix's proposal—does not support that interpretation. What is clear is that they were to wear brown, gray, or black dresses: practical choices given the inevitable exposure to blood, pus, vomit, and other filth in a hospital of that day and the heroic efforts required to do laundry in the nineteenth century. Bows, curls, jewelry, and especially hoop skirts and crinolines were forbidden. Again, a practical requirement. Hospitals were crowded and the aisles were too narrow for women in fashionably wide skirts to walk through. In at least one case, a wounded soldier is reported to have bled to death when the crinoline worn by a female visitor caught on his cot and tore open his wound.

In part, Dix's preference for the middle-aged, matronly, and plain (however defined) was intended to discourage candidates drawn to the perceived romance of nursing wounded soldiers—a fantasy nourished by several popular novels about the Crimean War—and to protect her nurses against charges of immorality or husband hunting. Instead doctors often dismissed them as ineffectual old maids, a position summed up by Dr. J. H. Brinton when confronted with the prospect of Dix's nurses being assigned to his hospital in Mound City, Illinois: "Can you fancy half a dozen or a dozen old hags, for that is what they are, surrounding a bewildered hospital surgeon, each one clamorous for her little wants?"[15]

Dix turned away many able applicants because she thought they were too young, attractive, or frivolous. Twenty-three-year-old Cornelia Hancock, for instance, was preparing to board the train to Gettysburg with a number of women many years older than she was when Dix appeared on the scene to inspect the prospective nurses. She pronounced all of the nurses suitable except for Hancock, whom she objected to on the grounds of her "youth and rosy cheeks." Hancock simply boarded the train while her companions argued with Dix. When she reached Gettysburg, the need for nurses was so great that no one worried about her age or appearance.[16]

Like Hancock, many of those she rejected found other ways to serve; despite the terms of her appointment, Dix never controlled all the nurses in Union hospitals. The United States Sanitary Commission, formed in June 1861 with the intention of improving sanitary and moral conditions in the Union army, maintained and staffed field hospitals and transit ships as did its St. Louis–based rival, the Western Sanitary Commission, and various unaffiliated ladies' aid societies. Beginning in April 1862, surgeons had the right to hire their own nurses and often did so. Some volunteers stepped outside the system altogether and nursed without official sanction from any person or organization, most notably Clara Barton, who formed her own support network and traveled the battlefields as an independent nurse.

"Dragon" Dix

Almost everyone, including Dix, assumed that her years of lobbying on behalf of the mentally ill gave her the necessary skills to manage the army's nursing corps. She had, after all, spent years working with administrators to improve conditions in prisons and hospitals. Her knowledge about the inner workings of public institutions, in both America and Europe, was intimate and encyclopedic. One important exception to this opinion appears to have been held by Dr. Elizabeth Blackwell, the first woman to become a certified doctor, who grumbled on hearing of Dix's appointment as the superintendent of women nurses: "The government has given Miss Dix a semi-official recognition as meddler general—for it really amounts to that, she being without system, or any practical knowledge of the business."[17]

It soon became obvious that Blackwell's assessment of Dix's administrative skills was painfully accurate. Dix had always worked alone. She traveled where she felt she was needed and addressed problems as they caught her attention. As a lobbyist, she knew how to work the political system. As a reformer, she knew how to inspire action in others. But she had never run an organization, and she didn't try to run one now. Instead she treated the nursing corps as a web of personal relationships with herself at the center. She interviewed nursing candidates, assigned them to hospitals, and occasionally escorted them to their new posts in person. She sent out appeals for relief goods and distributed them herself. She defended her nurses against hostile surgeons, helped them collect back pay, sent food to those who had trouble living on the allowance for rations, and maintained a house in Washington where nurses could live while waiting for their next assignment. She traveled from hospital to hospital, providing needed supplies and ferreting out abuses, including dishonest supply stewards and drunken or incompetent surgeons. She engaged in feuds with chief surgeons who resisted using her nurses, including the surgeon in charge of Arlington's Mansion House Hospital, and occasionally used her power to humiliate a surgeon whom she thought was wrong. While she was often right in her assertions, she was seldom tactful. When one enraged physician demanded, "Madam, who are you to dictate to me?" Dix, tall, thin, and straight-backed as any solider, drew herself up and answered, "I am Dorothea L. Dix, Superintendent of Nurses, in the employ of the United States Government."[18]

In her new position, Dix continued to travel at her discretion and with no thought for the schedules of others, leaving outraged members of the military or the Sanitary Commission and prospective nurses waiting for her return. She had no system in place for finding and approving nurses. With no organization to back her up, she handled every detail herself, and was seemingly incapable of distinguishing between the important and unimportant. George Templeton Strong, treasurer of the Sanitary Commission and definitely not a fan of Miss Dix, reported an extreme example in his diary: Dix once appeared at a meeting, breathless with distress because a cow was dying of sunstroke on the Smithsonian's grounds, "and she took it very ill that we did not adjourn instantly to look after the case."[19]

Sometimes called "Dragon" Dix by her detractors, she was protective of her authority and prepared to defend it against both hostile doctors and independent nurses, such as Clara Barton, who later founded the American Red Cross. She antagonized many whom she would have been wiser to conciliate. According to one contemporary source, "Unfortunately, many of the surgeons in the hospitals do not work harmoniously with Miss Dix. They are jealous of her power, impatient of her authority, find fault with her nurses, and accuse her of being arbitrary, opinionated, severe and capricious."[20] Members of both the Woman's Central Association of Relief in New York and its parent organization, the United States Sanitary Commission, found reasons to gradually dissociate themselves from Dix, despite the fact that their goals were closely aligned.

The personal cost of Dix's administrative failings was high. Her health, always fragile, suffered over the course of the war. Worn with constant bouts of malaria and lung problems, she lost weight, reaching a low of ninety-nine pounds by war's end. (Despite her physical problems she managed to outlast three surgeons general who opposed her.)

Possibly worse, from her perspective, was the constant erosion of her authority, which began almost at once. In August 1861, Congress passed a bill authorizing the formation of the nursing corps, including a salary of $12 month plus "subsistence" for official army nurses. That same bill allowed army doctors to hire nurses without going through Dix. It was the first in a long series of official decisions that appeared to bolster Dix's position while in fact undermining her authority. Circular No. 7, issued by newly appointed Surgeon General William Hammond on July 14, 1862, under the guise of giving "greater utility to the acts of Miss. D. L. Dix as 'Superintendent of Women Nurses,'" authorized chief surgeons at army hospitals to dismiss any female nurses found to be, in his words, "incompetent, insubordinate, or otherwise unfit for the vocation."[21] General Order No. 351, issued on October 29, 1863, by Secretary of War Edwin Stanton at the behest of yet another new surgeon general, Joseph K. Barnes, was presented as a compromise. Dix had argued for months that rules should be enacted that forbade surgeons from dismissing nurses without cause, and the order initially seemed to give Dix what she wanted: if a nurse was discharged, the hospital's chief surgeon had to offer specific reasons. The cost of that protection was high in terms of Dix's authority, though. That same order decreed that the surgeon general could now appoint nurses. Surgeon General Barnes immediately promised that he "both could and would appoint ladies at the request of a surgeon irrespective of age, size or looks."[22]

Despite all attempts to compromise, undermine, or otherwise limit her authority, over the course of the war Dorothea Dix appointed more than three thousand nurses, roughly 15 percent of the total who served with the Union army, and more than any other person or organization involved with nursing in the Civil War.

Chapter 2

The Army Is Unprepared

"During the entire engagement, I never received
a single order from either Colonel or other officer,
Medical Inspector, the surgeon of my regiment
or anyone else . . . It was like the days when
there was no King in Israel and every man did that
which was right in his own eyes."
—Assistant Surgeon William Williams Keen,
Fifth Massachusetts Regiment[1]

The first three months of the war after the fall of Fort
Sumter saw only minor skirmishes, but those were
enough to prove that the Union army's Medical
Bureau was not prepared to meet the needs of its 75,000 new
soldiers.

When members of the Sixth Massachusetts Regiment
injured in the Baltimore riots on April 19 arrived in Washington, DC, later that night, they had nowhere to go. The Medical
Bureau maintained a few army post hospitals in frontier states;
the largest of them, located in Fort Leavenworth, Kansas, had
forty beds. But there were none in the eastern states. The Quartermaster Corps, an independent department of the army, had
refused to build hospitals in anticipation of the pending war on
the grounds that "men need guns not beds."[2] With neither hospitals nor barracks available, the members of the Sixth, injured
and uninjured alike, slept on the carpeted floor of the Senate

chambers that night. The coming months would prove that men needed beds as well as guns.

The camps housing the new recruits were crowded and filthy, a cross between a garbage dump and a cesspool. Water was scarce, making it difficult for soldiers to keep themselves clean. Many gave up. As one surgeon noted, "It was a common subject of remark that men who, but a few weeks before, occupied positions in society demanding cleanliness and care for personal appearance, now disregarded it, and either from apathy or laziness neither washed their persons nor the clothing they carried upon them."[3] By June 1861, 30 percent of the army was on sick call as a result of outbreaks of infectious diseases, most notably typhoid and dysentery, both closely associated with poor sanitation.

In order to cope with the crisis of illness and minor injury among the first recruits, the Medical Bureau requisitioned buildings throughout the Washington area, primarily hotels and schools, for use as general hospitals. Many of them were run down, and most suffered from inadequate ventilation and poorly designed toilet facilities, which aggravated rather than ameliorated the problems of disease.

The largest of the Washington hospitals was the Union Hotel, where Louisa May Alcott worked in her brief stint as a Dix nurse. The hospital opened on May 25, 1861, and was soon infamous for its poor condition and worse smells. After the military and medical debacle of Bull Run, Cornelius R. Agnew and William H. Van Buren assessed the condition of the hotel for the United States Sanitary Commission. Their report, dated July 31, 1861, was negative but restrained:

The *Union Hotel Hospital, Georgetown,* was occupied as its name implies, until recently hired for its present use. It is considered capable of accommodating 225 patients, and at present contains 189. It is well situated, but the building is old, out of repair, and cut up into a number of small rooms, with windows too small and few in number to afford good ventilation. Its halls and passages are narrow, tortuous and abrupt, and in many instances with carpets still unremoved from their floors, and walls covered with paper. There are no provisions for bathing, the water-closets and sinks are insufficient and defective and there is no dead-house [a room or structure where dead bodies could be stored before burial or transportation—a grim necessity in a Civil War hospital]. The wards are many of them overcrowded and destitute of arrangements for artificial ventilation. The cellars and area are damp and undrained, and much of the wood work is actively decaying.[4]

Alcott, who would satirize the Union Hotel Hospital as Hurly-Burly House in *Hospital Sketches* (1863), a fictionalized account of her nursing experience, gave a more pointed description of conditions in a letter dated January 1863:

The air is bad enough to breed a pestilence; and as no notice is taken of our frequent appeals for better ventilation, I must do what I can. Poke up the fire, add blankets, joke, coax, and command; but continue to open doors and windows as if life depended upon it.

Mine does, and doubtless many another, for a more perfect, pestilence-box than this house I never saw,— cold, damp, dirty, full of vile odors from wounds, kitchens, wash-rooms, and stables. No competent head, male or female, to right matters and a jumble of good, bad and indifferent nurses, surgeons and attendants, to complicate the chaos still more.[5]

The hospital would be closed in May 1862, reopened in July 1862 to accommodate the heavy casualties of the Seven Days' Battles, and closed for the last time in March 1863, when its patients were transferred to other, less dangerous, hospitals in the vicinity.

It is not surprising that the Medical Bureau's first attempts at creating hospitals would be improvised on the cheap. Surgeon General Lawson's twenty-five years as the bureau's head were shaped by the need to make the best use of the minuscule budgets allotted to the medical service of the peacetime army. As he wrote to Zachary Taylor, then commander of American forces in Florida, "Finery and furbelows cannot be tolerated in field hospitals or other sick stations."[6] Certainly there were neither at the Union Hotel Hospital. Lawson's successor, Clement A. Finley, also spent many years managing with limited resources and did not grasp the magnitude of the problems facing the army after the fall of Fort Sumter. He reported with pride that the Medical Bureau spent less than it had been allocated for the fiscal year ending June 30, 1861.

His pride was misplaced. The first major battle of the war, fought only twenty-one days later, on July 21, 1861, found the medical service, like the rest of the United States Army, unprepared.

"The Great Skedaddle"

General Irvin McDowell was certain his army was not yet ready to take the field, but the political pressure to do so was strong. Many of his men were three-month volunteers who had signed up after the fall of Fort Sumter: untested troops who had never taken a long march, let alone experienced combat. But their discharge date, and the end of President Lincoln's estimate of a ninety-day war, was rapidly approaching. On July 16, 1862, McDowell led the Army of the Potomac out of its mired and disease-ridden camps outside Washington, DC, and marched them toward Centerville, twenty-seven miles to the southwest, where the Confederate army was encamped under the leadership of General Pierre G. T. Beauregard, the commander who had taken Fort Sumter in April. Their behavior as they marched confirmed McDowell's fears, and he later complained, "They stopped every moment to pick blackberries or get water. They would not keep in the ranks, order as much as you pleased."[7]

McDowell's uncertainties about the abilities of his newborn army were not widely shared. On July 21, a sweltering day by anyone's standards, hundreds of Washington civilians, including two senators, at least fifty reporters from Northern newspapers, and what one Confederate observer described as "gay women and strumpets,"[8] packed picnic baskets, opera glasses, and bottles of champagne and drove out from the nation's capital to the Virginia city of Manassas so they could cheer the Union soldiers on to victory, as if the coming battle were a match between opposing baseball teams. Instead of victory, they watched the defeat and subsequent rout of the Union forces from their carriages.

For the first few hours of the battle, the popular confidence in McDowell's troops seemed justified as outnumbered Confederate forces retreated before the 35,000-man Army of the Potomac. (The *New York Times* was so certain of victory that its headlines proclaimed the battle won before it ended: CRUSHING REBELLION, THE GREATEST BATTLE EVER FOUGHT ON THE CONTINENT . . . THE REBELS ROUTED AND DRIVEN BEHIND THE MANASSAS LINES.[9])

In midafternoon, the battle turned against McDowell when Confederate reinforcements, among them a brigade of Virginians commanded by Thomas J. (soon to be "Stonewall") Jackson, reinforced the collapsing Confederate line. According to later reports in the Richmond newspapers, Jackson told General Barnard Bee, who led a Confederate brigade at Bull Run, that he would stop the Union advance with bayonets if necessary. Bee then called out, "Oh men, there are Jackson and his Virginians standing behind you like a stone wall! Let us determine to die here, and we will conquer, follow me." The sight, and sound, of several thousand screaming Virginians bearing down on the Union line changed the course of the battle. What began as an orderly retreat turned into a rout as the inexperienced Union soldiers panicked. Men became separated from their units and their officers, and soon the fleeing soldiers became tangled with the equally panic-stricken spectators. The *Saint Paul Daily Press* told its readers that the retreat was "horrible to look upon. Congressmen and gentlemen politicians, hurrying from the scene of danger; ambulances, wagons, wagon and artillery horses, with harness and from one to three men on their backs; the worn out and fatigued soldiers, many having lost or thrown away their guns and knapsacks, bare footed, bare headed, and some nearly naked, having their clothes literally torn off from them in hand to hand fights, with hands torn to pieces, arms broken and any quantity of flesh wounds, all winding their way, with heads down and as silent as mutes; none with comrades."[10]

The Southern press simply dubbed the retreat "The great skedaddle."

The final count of Union casualties: 750 killed, 2,492 wounded, more than 1,500 missing, and an incalculable loss of confidence.[11]

No Plans

The experience of the wounded and injured in the aftermath of the battle made the defeat worse. Unable to imagine the scale of the coming devastation, the Union's Medical Bureau provided few medical supplies, made no provision for field hospitals, and made no plans for evacuating casualties. The Confederate army did no better.

Eventually the Union army would have more than eleven thousand doctors on its payroll, but at the beginning of the war the Medical Bureau staff consisted of thirty surgeons and eighty-six assistant surgeons, who had learned their trade in the army's seventy-nine frontier outposts and the Mexican-American War. Some were too old to be fit for active service. Twenty-four of them resigned shortly after the fall of Sumter to join the Confederate army. Three more were dismissed for disloyalty. Those remaining were assigned to positions as medical directors. The experienced military doctors serving at the frontier posts were called back east over the summer of 1861, their places taken over by civilians for the duration of the war.

Some two hundred new medical officers joined the army between April and June. These volunteer physicians varied in their medical expertise. Few were surgeons, and none had experience in the realities of battlefield medicine. Some of them were not even doctors. Medical student William Williams Keen, who later became a professor of surgery at Jefferson Medical College in Philadelphia and was the first surgeon to successfully remove a brain tumor, reported that he was recruited by his mentor, John H. Brinton, an experienced brigade surgeon, to replace a man named Smith whom the state authorities had appointed as assistant surgeon for the Fifth Massachusetts. When Keen argued that he knew little as yet about medicine and nothing about military medicine, Brinton answered, "That is quite true. But on the the other hand, you know a great deal more than Smith."[12]

In addition to the question of battlefield experience, professional army doctors were also divided from the volunteer physicians by the matter of military protocol. According to one observer, there was no one available to teach new surgeons in the volunteer regiments either the technical aspects of battlefield medicine or the protocols of military service. Accustomed to working alone in their civilian practices, and with no sense of why these things might be important, volunteer surgeons were apt to disregard both as "a species of red-tapeism, to be discarded by men of energy."[13] Later in the war, surgeons, military and otherwise, would complain about the same attitude on the part of volunteer nurses, who came to the task with neither medical nor military backgrounds and a tendency to sidestep the rules of both when they deemed fit.

The elderly and inflexible bureaucrats unable to imagine large-scale warfare and the inexperienced volunteer force faced their first major battle together at Bull Run.

Medical Care at the First Battle of Bull Run

On July 21, William S. King, twenty-four-year veteran of the Medical Bureau and medical director of the Army of the Potomac, rode alongside General McDowell on the field at Bull Run. By his own account, "My impression at the commencement of the battle was, that there would be a brisk skirmish, and then the rebels would most probably fall back and take up a new position." Consequently, he did not coordinate assignments for the mass of volunteer physicians. He provided no guideline for treating battle wounds, something most civilian doctors had no experience with. And he arranged neither evacuation plans nor hospital arrangements for the wounded after the battle, assuming that each regiment's surgeon would be responsible for the men under his care. Several hours after the battle began, thinking "it would be a small task . . . to make a list of the killed and wounded," King set out, notebook in hand, to count the number of each.[14] On the ground around him, men lay torn and mangled: legs, arms, and bodies crushed and broken. Those who were able waved their arms and cried for help. One soldier had his face completely shot away. Some had been felled by sunstroke and exhaustion rather than enemy fire. The ground below them all was soaked with blood.

As his count of the dead approached one hundred, King realized how desperate the battle was. He directed his assistant David Magruder, who had remained behind at McDowell's field headquarters as King's liaison, to send out the ambulances as quickly as possible and then go to Sudley Church, which was nearby and out of the line of fire, to set up a field hospital for the wounded. King then rolled up his sleeves and worked alongside his field surgeons to tend the wounded, leaving Magruder to create hospitals out of sows' ears.

Magruder did his best to prepare the field hospital at Sudley Church. His men removed the church's pews, gathered hay from nearby fields to make bedding, covered the floor with blankets, and brought in buckets of water. By midafternoon, several regimental doctors, including William Keen, medical student turned assistant surgeon, arrived at the hospital, ready to treat the wounded men from their regiments as the ambulances unloaded them. Within two hours, the improvised hospital overflowed with the wounded and dying. Magruder then commandeered three nearby buildings. When they too were full, he ordered the wounded to be placed under the trees of an apple grove near the church. The doctors performed amputations in the open, visible to those with minor injuries and to those waiting for their turn with the scalpel and the bone saw. Keen quickly realized that the doctor he was assisting had never performed surgery and had little knowledge of the anatomy of the upper arm; Keen talked him through the operation, telling him where to cut and sew to keep the patient from bleeding to death. According to one eyewitness account of Sudley Church, a volunteer staff officer from Massachusetts, "Blood trickled from the ambulances like water from an ice cart, and directly in front of the church door was a large puddle of blood."[15]

Sudley Church was not the only makeshift hospital on the field. Regimental surgeons everywhere did their best to improvise shelter for the men in their care. The surgeon of the First Connecticut, showing more forethought than many of his fellows, commandeered a four-room house near the battlefield and ordered the regimental band to follow their comrades onto the field and retrieve the fallen. Another regiment took over a two-and-a-half-story stone house on the Warrenton Turnpike, so close to the battlefield that shells smashed into its walls as the surgeons worked.

Every improvised hospital was a scene of carnage. As a reporter from the *New York Daily Tribune* described the scene at one, "Men, dying and just dead, covered the floor, and filled the rear yard with frightful misery. Civilians and soldiers had turned surgeons, and were amputating and binding up the limbs of the wounded."[16] An eyewitness at another field hospital made no attempt to hide his horror: "The rooms were crowded, and all around on the green sward were men mortally wounded . . . They lay so thick around that I could hardly step between them, and every step was in blood . . . I gave them what little assistance I could, until becoming faint and sick, I was compelled to leave."[17]

Reading these accounts, it is hard to remember that the wounded soldiers who made it to Sudley Church and its counterparts were the lucky ones. More than a thousand wounded men were left on the battlefield. Some, bloodied and often shoeless, managed to walk the twenty-five miles to Washington in search of aid. More lay helpless where they fell, without water or shelter, their suffering made worse by a cold rain that began falling early on the morning of July 22 and continued for two days. It was several days before King organized ambulances, or at least a ragtag assortment of carts and wagons, to find the wounded and transport them to Washington. It was a difficult task, made harder by the fact that the Confederates commanded the field. Many men died before help arrived.

The Medical Bureau had introduced ambulances for the first time only two years before the war. Bull Run was their first serious trial run, and it revealed glaring problems not only in their distribution and use but also in the design itself. An army board had recommended four-wheeled ambulances, which had been tested with some success on expeditions in the plains. They were difficult to load and their springs were stiff but still luxurious compared to the standard army wagon. Unfortunately, the Quartermaster Corps ignored the board's recommendations and decided on a two-wheeled vehicle designed by Clement Alexander Finley, two years before his promotion to surgeon general. When the war began, the only field test the Finley design had undergone was use as a carriage for pleasure jaunts by officers and as light trucks by the Quartermaster Corps. Working under the untested assumption that the two-wheeled ambulances were superior for transporting seriously wounded men, the Quartermaster Corps issued four times as many of them as the four-wheeled design.

Their performance at Bull Run demonstrated that the design was fundamentally flawed. Nicknamed "the avalanche" by the sick and wounded who traveled in them, Finley ambulances consisted of two removable stretchers with a chassis that rested on four elliptical springs. Flimsily constructed of light-weight wood, they were prone to breakdowns. Worse, they proved to be excruciating for wounded men to ride in. Soldiers would scream in pain as they rode and beg to be let out.

Accommodations for the wounded once they reached Washington were as badly organized as the ambulance service that evacuated them. The six military hospitals created in and around Washington in the months before Bull Run were already overcrowded with dysentery patients when the battle began. Once again, the army improvised medical shelters for the care of the wounded, requisitioning churches and temples, the top floor of the US Patent Office, Saint Elizabeth's Insane Asylum, hundreds of private homes, and even the Capitol Building.

Samuel Gross, professor of surgery at Philadelphia's Jefferson Medical College, arrived to find the city demoralized. The shelters were overflowing, and soldiers lay in the streets in large number, many of them on the bare ground.[18] Charles S. Tripler, King's successor as medical director of the Army of the Potomac, claimed that the disorder was made worse by the fact that there was no system in place for assigning the wounded to hospitals. Regimental surgeons sent men from the field to the general hospitals with no way of knowing whether there were beds (or even floor space) available. It was not unusual for men to spend the night in the ambulances, which drove from hospital to hospital looking for a vacancy for their hapless cargo. The discharge process was just as haphazard. Men were released from the hospital with no way to get back to their regiment and nowhere to stay in the city.

Nursing the Wounded

Dix's nurses and a score of informal female volunteers stepped into the chaos and began their work.

Maria W. Abbey was one of a group of six women from Brooklyn who volunteered in response to a call for nurses delivered a week after the fall of Fort Sumter by Rev. Henry Ward Beecher, the most famous preacher in the United States at the time; he was the brother of Harriet Beecher Stowe, whose 1852 novel, *Uncle Tom's Cabin,* gave faces to the political and economic arguments about slavery. Abbey and her companions arrived in Washington on May 2 and were assigned to the Union Hotel Hospital. Even before Bull Run, she complained that there was no organization and that it was difficult to do anything systematically. After the battle, the hospital over-flowed with the wounded "and we had no rest then," she remembered.[19]

Eliza Howland, a New York socialite who would later serve with her sister, Georgeanna Woolsey, on a United States Sanitary Commission hospital transit ship, worked with surgeons and convalescent soldiers in a stifling ward improvised in an uncompleted storage room on the top floor of the Patent Office in Washington. The wounded and ill lay in groups of six on crude tables built from pieces of construction scaffolding. A system of pulleys carried barrels of water, baskets of vegetables, and sides of beef up the marble face of the building and through a top-floor window.

Former missionary Harriet Dada and her friend Susan Hall had been accepted as Dix nurses and were waiting in New York to be called to service. At noon on July 22, they received instructions to come to Washington with orders to report to Miss Dix. When they arrived the next day, Dix told them they were needed in Alexandria. Once at their hospital, a dark stone building that had formerly been a seminary, they found it packed with the wounded, some on beds and more on mattresses spread on the floor. Many were still in their uniforms, covered with their own blood and the dust from the burning summer battlefield. Unlike the Patent Office hospital, this one had no soldiers detailed as attendants for the first few weeks, so the two nurses did everything, with little sleep or food. The work was so hard that two weeks passed before Dada had time to write her family and tell them where she was. Despite the demands of their first assignment, Dada and Hall served together through the end of the war, transferred from hospital to hospital as needed.

Nancy Atwood was a widow with one child and worked as a seamstress in Bangor, Maine, when the war broke out. Since she was strong and healthy and had considerable experience as a domestic nurse, she thought it was her duty to volunteer, just as her brother felt it was his duty to join the Union army. She signed on as a nurse with the Sixth Maine Infantry Regiment in May 1861 and arrived at the front just in time to hear the roar of the cannons at Bull Run. With one other nurse, Mrs. Hartsun Crowell, also of Bangor, she nursed the wounded from the battle at a field hospital located on Robert E. Lee's farm on Arlington Heights. With the rains that began on July 22, their tents were blown away several times, and she often found herself tending to suffering men in the pelting rain, with no dry clothes available for either nurse or patients.

Women from throughout the Washington, DC, area also volunteered on an ad hoc basis. Some of them nursed, while others merely "visited," a term used to describe women who brought comforts but did not get their hands dirty. Clara Barton became the most well known of the Washington-based women who volunteered in the aftermath of the First Battle of Bull Run—famous even in her own time as "the soldier's friend."

Born in Massachusetts in 1821, Barton was working as a clerk at the United States Patent Office when the war began, one of only four women employed by the federal government before the war. After Bull Run, she visited the wounded in the improvised hospital on the top floor of the Patent Office every day, bringing them delicacies and helping where she could.

She soon became a one-woman relief agency. She developed a personal supply network of "dear sisters" who sent her packages of food, clothing, wine, and bandages to distribute to the troops, and she received so many boxes that she had to rent warehouses to store them. Over time she became convinced that she was needed on the battlefield, where she could help men as they fell.

When the Army of the Potomac was mobilized in the summer of 1862, Barton convinced Colonel Daniel H. Rucker, head of the Quartermaster Corps depot in Washington, to give her a wagon, a driver, and a pass signed by Surgeon General Hammond that gave her "permission to go upon the sick transports in any direction for the purpose of distributing comforts to the sick and wounded, and nursing them, always subject to the direction of the Surgeon in charge."[20]

Armed with her pass, she distributed supplies to the field hospital at Falmouth Station, near Fredericksburg, but she still felt she was not doing enough. When she heard that fighting had broken out at Cedar Mountain, she headed for the battle-field. Thereafter, in battle after battle, Barton ran soup kitch-ens, provided supplies, nursed the wounded, and tried to keep track of the men who died so she could tell their families what had happened to them. In between battles, she returned to Washington, where she collected the latest batch of supplies, wrote impassioned letters thanking the women who provided them, and fought with bureaucrats to be allowed to continue her work.

Barton's experiences caring for men after Bull Run ulti-mately led her to the battlefield, where she became a familiar figure of comfort to wounded men. So familiar was she that scores of the men she helped named their daughters "Clara Barton" in her honor. She was unique, both in her direct approach to helping soldiers and in her fame after the war. But she was by no means the only woman inspired to volunteer as a nurse by the disaster at Bull Run.

• • •

The horrors of the battle and its aftermath inspired popular outrage. A reporter from the *New York Times* summed up the feelings of many: "The worst sight of all was the ambulances, coming back empty, or with only tired soldiers in them. As the rain poured and the darkness drew on, our thoughts would go out to the hundreds of gallant fellows who were lying wounded and uncared for in the bushes, under the rocks and the forest trees, along the ravine of Bull's Run."[21] Others wanted answers and assurances that such a disaster would not occur again. The editor of the influential *American Medical Times* laid the blame for the medical disaster on Finley and demanded, in the name of the entire medical profession, to know why the wounded were not brought off the field in a systematic way.[22] Frederick Law Olmsted wrote a scathing denunciation of men and officers alike, with a particular emphasis on the failings of the Medical Bureau, in his report on the Union's performance at Bull Run for the United States Sanitary Commission.

But the medical failures at Bull Run also inspired change. The newly formed United States Sanitary Commission began to inspect existing hospitals and lobby for the construction of new ones. Using Olmsted's report as a weapon, they pushed Congress for the appointment of a new surgeon general and reform of the Medical Bureau's seniority system. Their first success was smaller, however. On August 3, 1861, Congress passed an act that added ten additional surgeons and twenty additional assistant surgeons to the regular army and created a corps of fifty medical cadets, made up of medical students who could dress wounds at general hospitals and drive ambulances or carry wounded men from the field.

That same bill authorized the surgeon general to hire female nurses at a salary of $12 a month, plus a soldier's ration. Dix's dream of an army nursing corps was now official.

Chapter 3

Volunteers

"I immediately wrote to all the people of influence
I knew, begging them to procure me some place
in the war as nurse, or whatever I could do."
—Mary Phinney von Olnhausen[1]

The news of the defeat at Bull Run and the shameful failure of care for the nation's wounded soldiers after the battle led a second wave of women to volunteer their services as nurses. Florence Nightingale's *Notes on Nursing* inspired some, while others were driven by the same desire to combine patriotism with action that led young men to enlist in the first rush of enthusiasm for the war. Some were called to nurse by religious zeal; others by the financial need caused by a husband's absence. Louisa May Alcott, for example, was eager to have a part in the war from the beginning. Soon after the fall of Fort Sumter, she wrote in her diary, "I long to be a man; but as I can't fight, I will content myself with working for those who can."[2] In the evenings she curled up with a medical book and studied the care of gunshot wounds; as soon as she turned thirty, she contacted Dix for a place as a nurse. Whatever their motivation, women who wanted to do more than collect supplies and sew shirts contacted anyone they thought might be able to help them get a position in a hospital: local clergymen and surgeons, hospital directors, local and national Sanitary

Commission officers, Miss Dix, Surgeon General Finley and other members of the Medical Bureau, and, in at least one case, President Lincoln.

While some received an immediate answer, most suffered the frustration of waiting for a reply that in many cases never came. Some received what appear to be form rejections, such as the one the secretary of the Michigan Soldier's Relief Association sent to applicants: "We are in daily receipt of similar applications . . . and we are obliged to say to you as we do to all others, that we will place all such applications on file, and procure positions for them as fast as possible . . . While we commend the patriotism of these ladies . . . we must remind them that there are many thousands of their sex scattered over the whole Union who are offering to make the same sacrifice."[3] Others received personal notes designed to discourage them. Amy S. Bradley, who served first as a regimental nurse and later under the auspices of the United States Sanitary Commission, contacted two surgeons regarding the possibility of nursing for the Third Maine regiment. One answered, "I am fearful that you would be deprived of many comforts and even necessaries of life and that you would be sorry that you had left those comforts for the rough life of the camp."[4] Bradley not only joined the regiment by the end of the year but went on to reform the convalescent camp outside of Alexandria, living under conditions that were more than rough.

Perhaps as many as half of those who served in the war chose to bypass Miss Dix and the official channels. Some, like Estelle Johnson and her sister, followed their husbands to war. According to Johnson, when her husband and brother-in-law enlisted, she and her sister objected, "telling the recruiting offi-

cer that if our husbands went we should go too, but not thinking that such a thing could be." To their surprise, they heard
back from the recruiting officer within a week: "The colonel
said that although nurses had not been called for he wanted us
to go." A month later, they were formally sworn in to the
Fourth Vermont Regiment, Company J, in the presence of the
colonel, the major, and the governor of Vermont.[5] Others like
Lucy Fenman and Modena McColl unofficially joined a regiment and "went from place to place wherever the 'boys' were
ordered."[6] Some simply presented themselves on the battlefield
or at a hospital and began to work. Many found their way to
the front to take care of husbands, sons, and brothers, and then
stayed on after their own relative's death to care for other wom-
en's men as a way to "soften [one's] grief by assisting in the
work."[7]

There were many paths for aspiring nurses to take. The
lives of Mary Phinney von Olnhausen and Anne Reading illus-
trate two of those that led to the Mansion House Hospital in
Alexandria, Virginia, in August 1862.

Mary Phinney von Olnhausen

Mary Phinney von Olnhausen was forty-three years old
when the Union troops fled the field at the Battle of Bull Run.
She was exactly the type of woman Dorothea Dix looked for as
a member of the new nursing corps: an educated middle-class
widow with reformist tendencies and a history of hard work.

Most of what is known about von Olnhausen comes from
an account compiled by her nephew James Phinney Munroe,
from her letters, and an incomplete autobiographical sketch.

Published in 1904, *Adventures of an Army Nurse in Two Wars* was part of the flood of Civil War memoirs, biographies, regimental histories, pamphlets, poems, and diaries that appeared once the war was far enough away to generate nostalgia but still recent enough for readers to feel an interest in the experience of everyday people who had served.

Born in Lexington, Massachusetts, in 1818 to a lawyer with a passion for farming, Mary was the fifth in a family of ten children. According to her nephew, she was not a particularly "girly" child: "In a generation whose women shuddered at a grasshopper, she used to tame spiders and to give pocket-refuge to toads and snakes."[8]

When her father died in 1849, the family farm was sold and Mary and the other unmarried daughters were forced to look for ways to support themselves. Thirty-one years old and probably resigned to never marrying, Mary took an unusual route for a middle-class woman who needed to earn a living. Rather than teaching or serving as a companion to an older, wealthier woman, she enrolled in the newly founded School for Design for Women in Boston, one of a group of such schools founded in the midcentury in Northern cities with a strong manufacturing presence. The curriculum of such schools was designed to train women in textile and wallpaper design, wood engraving, and other marketable artistic skills. The benefits of such training went two ways: women who needed to support themselves learned a marketable skill, and American industries, particularly the textile mills, were able to lessen their dependence on expensive imported French designs. Mary was considered one of the best designers in her class. After graduation she found steady employment as a textile designer in the New

Hampshire fabric mills, working first in Dover and later in Manchester.

In Manchester, Mary's life took an unexpected twist. She made friends among a community of German immigrants, some of the thousands of European refugees who fled their own countries following the political revolutions of 1848. For the most part, such refugees were moderate reformers who fit in well with what some described as the "benevolent empire" of voluntary reform associations that spread through New England and the Midwest in the first half of the nineteenth century— dedicated to causes that included temperance, Dorothea Dix's pet projects of penal and asylum reform, women's rights, education, and, above all, abolition. Among the Manchester community of "Forty-Eighters" was Gustav, Baron von Olnhausen. Most of the 1848 revolutionaries belonged to one of two groups: urban workers and artisans angered by the impact of industrialization on their ability to make a living, or middle-class liberals who wanted to play a greater role in government. Gustav, who preferred to call himself Gustav A. Olnhausen once he reached the United States, was unusual: a reformer who was also a member of Saxony's minor aristocracy. He studied at the University of Munich in 1827 and 1828, worked as a chemist in Prague in 1830, and studied at the University of Edinburgh in 1840. In Manchester, he used his considerable scientific training to secure employment as a dye chemist in the same mill where Mary worked as a designer.

According to Mary's nephew, "their engagement seems to have been a foregone conclusion before it became an actual fact."[9] They married in Boston in 1858, when Mary was forty and enjoyed a brief, happy marriage: "A little house filled with flowers, ferneries, aquaria, (for they were alike in their love of nature) and peopled with birds, lizards and even tamed toads, was the centre of their happiness; their chief pleasure, beyond that of their perfectly sympathetic life together, being found in their work, in holiday walks through the woods and in picnics and little impromptu parties with their many friends."[10] Two years later, Gustav became seriously ill and required surgery. The fact that the surgery took place at a general hospital in Boston, devoted to charity cases, makes it clear that their financial situation was precarious, something that would remain true for Mary throughout her adult life. The surgery was considered a success initially, but he died of complications on September 7, 1860. Mary, though still practically a newlywed, was a widow at forty-two.

Within two months of his death, in search of work and a distraction from her grief, Mary Phinney von Olnhausen left her home to help her younger brother George, who had claimed a homestead in the frontier state of Illinois with his invalid wife and four small children. The railroad had not yet made its way to the part of Illinois where the Phinney homestead was located, so Mary traveled the last miles in a wagon drawn by horses and oxen. It was a six-hour ride across the prairie, through a landscape of deep black mud lightly covered with snow.

When she reached the "station," she found it was nothing more than a barnlike building, with a single house to keep it company in an otherwise empty landscape of "everlasting mud."[11] No one was waiting for her, but the stationmaster assured her she was in the right place. She settled down to wait for her brother in a room as barren as the landscape around her: the windows were caked with dust, the lone chair was hard and uncomfortable, and the fire was nearly out. After a long and dreary wait, her brother finally arrived in a farm wagon with no springs and a rush-bottomed chair where the seat should be, drawn by "a sorry pair of mules"—very different than the carriage she had expected and emblematic of her new life on the prairie. As they drove off, the snow fell harder until it was impossible to see anything. The ride seemed as if it would never end, and Mary gave in to despair: "The great sorrow I had left behind came back with twofold force, and the desolation of that dismal prairie hidden by falling snow was more than I could bear."[12]

The Illinois scenes in Mary's autobiographical sketches will seem familiar to anyone who has read Laura Ingalls Wilder's *Little House on the Prairie,* set roughly ten years after Mary's own prairie experiences. She arrived to find a warm welcome, a cup of hot tea, and the prospect of useful employment. Her sister-in-law was too enfeebled by malaria to work. The well had been dry for weeks, so she had to melt snow to provide water for all their needs. Anything that needed to be done fell to Mary; it sometimes seemed to her like "one of those tasks set by cruel masters in fairy books."[13] In fact, work was exactly what she needed.

The spring brought beauty with it, turning the prairie into paradise in Mary's eyes, but paradise was always short-lived in her life. When an invasion of armyworms destroyed her brother's corn crop in one day, he declared it was useless to replant because it was too late in the season; not discouraged, Mary replanted the eighty acres with the help of a neighbor and an outdated corn planter. She proudly noted in her autobiographical notes that "he never had a better or a bigger crop."[14] When a neighbor's dogs attacked a recently bought pig while her brother was away from the house, Mary beat off the dogs with the help of the children and then struggled to kill and butcher the pig, which was injured beyond hope of saving.

While Mary and her brother fought to make a living from the unforgiving land, rumors of war made their way to the prairie. The Phinney farm was four miles away from the post office and the family often went many days without receiving a letter or a newspaper. Nonetheless, over the course of winter and spring, news of the pending war reached the farm, piece by appalling piece. South Carolina, Florida, Alabama, Georgia, Mississippi, and Louisiana seceded from the Union in quick succession and formed a provisional government. State militias took over federal forts and arsenals throughout the south. Tennessee and Texas seceded in their turn.

When news of the fall of Fort Sumter and the First Battle of Bull Run confirmed the rumors of war, Mary decided to volunteer as a nurse, or whatever else she could do to help the war effort. She wrote to anyone she knew who had any influence. Then, like women all over the North who wrote similar letters, she waited while the war went on without her. The Union's senior generals changed as often as dance partners in a reel: Lincoln replaced head of the Army of the Potomac General McDowell with General George McClellan shortly after Bull Run, promoted McClellan to general-in-chief in November, and demoted McClellan once more four months later. In March 1862, the Army of the Potomac took Yorktown and Williamsburg in the Union's first offense. A few days later at Shiloh, Grant forced the Confederate army to withdraw at the cost of tremendous Union casualties. In the Seven Days' Battles in late June, the Army of the Potomac retreated in its turn before Lee's forces, with enormous losses on both sides. At the Phinney homestead, distant from the front in Illinois, the war brought loss on a small scale as well: the family's crops were good, but they had no way to get them to market because the military controlled the railroads. They burned corn as fuel that winter, and Mary mourned the waste.

Finally, after a year, Mary refused to wait any longer. She headed back to Massachusetts, determined "to find some way to work for the soldiers."[15] Traveling east by train, she got a sense of the scale of the war for the first time as regiments boarded the already packed train at every city.

Back in Boston, she contacted Miss Dix, who promised to place her at once. In early August 1862, more than a year after the "terrible affair at Bull Run" had inspired her to volunteer, von Olnhausen received a summons to come to Washington—with only two days' notice. As was often the case with Miss Dix's nurses, after all the delays and waiting, Mary Phinney von Olnhausen was needed in a hurry. The Battle of Cedar Mountain was under way, and four hundred wounded men already lay in need of care at Culpeper, Virginia.

Anne Reading

Anne Reading was a professional nurse, to the limited extent that such a thing existed in the United States at the beginning of the Civil War. Unlike von Olnhausen, she didn't join the army's nursing corps from patriotic zeal but because she needed the work.

Anne was born on September 24, 1823, in Bethnal Green, then a working-class neighborhood in London known for slums, market gardens, and small-scale manufacturing, including silk weaving and boot making. (Later in the century the neighborhood would become infamous as one of the areas frequented by Jack the Ripper.) Reading was the eldest of eight children. Her father may have been a messenger, a job that would have placed him among the working poor. Most of what is known about her comes from her journal, edited by one of her descendants in 2006.

It appears that Anne worked as a nurse in several British hospitals prior to March 1855, when she sailed for Turkey as part of the third contingent to join Florence Nightingale's nursing corps. Despite Nightingale's early efforts, nursing was still considered a lower-class job in England, associated in the popular mind with dirt and drink. Nonetheless, there is no reason to believe Anne was anything less than respectable since Nightingale held high moral standards for her nursing corps.

Florence Nightingale had already earned a reputation as a nursing reformer when the Crimean War broke out in March 1854. Against the wishes of her wealthy and influential family, she trained at the innovative school attached to Lutheran Hospital in Kaiserswerth, Germany, where Pastor Theodor Fliedner established the first of the Protestant nursing orders known as deaconesses. On her return, she worked as the superintendent at a private charity hospital for ailing governesses, a population that shared the poverty but not the social stigma of the typical patient in a general hospital at the time. She was on the verge of taking a position as the head of nursing at King's College Hospital when England entered the war in the Crimea.

The Crimean War was the first to be fought in the press as well as on the battlefield. War correspondents reported not only on the movement of troops, but also on the conditions under which soldiers fought. William Howard Russell, the first and most famous of the new breed of reporters, revealed the conditions of the sick and wounded in the British camps to an outraged British public and called for a solution: "Are there no devoted women among us, able and willing to go forth to minister to the sick and suffering soldiers of the East in the hospitals of Scutari? Are none of the daughters of England, at this extreme hour of need, ready for such a work of mercy?"[16] In response, Secretary of War Sidney Herbert gave Nightingale a commission to form a nursing corps and the lofty and very specific title of "Superintendent of the Female Nursing Establishment of the English General Hospitals in Turkey." The title would seldom be used. Her nurses knew Nightingale as the lady-in-chief, and the soldiers called her "the Lady with the Lamp," as she was the only woman allowed in the wards at night.

On October 21, 1854, Nightingale and a group of women of varied nursing experience—ten Roman Catholic nuns, fourteen Anglican sisters, and fourteen lay nurses from various hospitals—sailed for Turkey. They arrived at the Barrack Hospital in Scutari, in Turkey outside of Constantinople, on November 4. They found no furniture, no blankets, and no medical supplies. The latrines were clogged and naked men lay on the floor in their own excrement. Before Nightingale's corps could nurse, they had to clean. Nightingale's first task was to acquire hundreds of scrubbing brushes and set convalescent soldiers to clean the wards from floor to ceiling.

Anne set out from London on March 24, 1855, one of a group of twenty-seven nurses that was part of a third round of nurses sent from England to the British convalescent hospitals at Kulalee, also near Constantinople. Only a month before, an official "Report upon the state of the hospitals of the British Army in the Crimea and Scutari" described the duties of Nightingale's nurses in detail, including dressing wounds, assisting doctors with the care of wounds, ensuring patients received the diet, drink, and medical comforts ordered by the doctor, and, most important of all from Nightingale's perspective, seeing that both the wards and the patients were clean.[17]

Nurses received a list of gear they needed to provide for themselves, including a dark cotton gown, two flannel petticoats, and as much underclothing as their boxes would hold, as well as a list of uniform items the government would provide over the course of their first year of nursing. The list ended with the clear admonition that "no nurse is to expect any gift of clothing beyond this."[18] Nonetheless, just before Anne and her companions started on their journey, Lady Canning, one of the titled women who supported the hospital where Nightingale worked before the war, arrived at the station accompanied by a servant in livery who carried two large parcels containing "shawls of superior size and quality."[19] It was a welcome start to a long and often cold voyage.

Unlike the nurses she would work beside in the American Civil War, whose letters, diaries, and memoirs often focused on gruesome details of wounds and illness, Anne described very little of the medical details of her work in the Crimea under Nightingale, perhaps because she was already familiar with the grim realities of surgical nursing. Instead she focused on the beauty of Constantinople and the details of her daily life. She shared an apartment with four other nurses a short distance from the hospital. Mornings and evenings were very cold, but the midday heat was so intense that it was impossible to be outdoors. The workday had a clear routine, similar to that of the nursing orders Nightingale had taken as her model:

> We rose at 7 o'clock, made our beds, then went out for prayers. After prayers we had breakfast and then went into the wards to attend to the patients until 1 o'clock. We had dinner and then back to the wards from 3 o'clock until 5:30. We then went for a walk until 6:30 when we had tea. After tea we were permitted to occupy our time as we pleased. We had prayers, then supper and retired for the night about 10 pm. On Sunday morning we go to the hospital at the usual time and at a quarter to eleven the bell rings for service. It is held in a very large ward and is a very pleasant sight in this far off land.[20]

This orderly daily schedule was radically different from what Anne would experience at Mansion House Hospital.

Anne's status as one of Nightingale's nurses would prove invaluable over the course of her nursing career, but she served less than three months in the Crimea. In early June, she fell ill while visiting Constantinople. A chill and a violent headache developed into what was then called "Crimean fever," now believed to have been brucellosis, a highly infectious bacterial disease carried by animals. Back at Kulalee, she went to work at the hospital the next day because they expected a large number of sick and wounded men to arrive from the Crimea. It was her last day at work as a Nightingale nurse. The next morning she was too sick to go to the hospital. Fevered, she passed in and out of consciousness for several days, cared for constantly by one of the other nurses. Her doctor finally reached the conclusion she would never recover her health if she remained in Turkey. She left Kulalee on June 25, 1855, on a transport ship filled with sick and wounded English soldiers who had been discharged from combat duty for medical reasons.

After a long period of convalescence, Anne spent the next five years working as a surgical nurse in London, first at University Hospital and later at St. Mary's Hospital. In 1860, "looking for a more extended sphere of practise,"[21] she decided to sail to the United States, where her younger sister Jenny worked in Yonkers. She arrived in New York City in October and soon found lodging with a German widow and her adult children. While she looked for nursing work, she helped the daughter make cloaks and mantles on a piecework basis, one of the often grueling cottage industries that allowed women to make a scanty living working at home.

Anne had been in New York for a full month when she saw an ad for a nursing job. She went immediately to ask about the position, but the gentleman who was hiring looked over her credentials and told her she needed a better job than he could offer her. He referred her to a friend who was connected with St. Luke's, a private hospital run by the Anglican Church. At first it seemed like another dead end. Most of the nurses there were Anglican deaconesses, who worked without compensation. At first Miss Ayers, the lady superintendent, told Anne they not only had no nursing vacancies, but they had a waiting list of job applicants. Upon looking at Anne's testimonials, however, Miss Ayers suggested a compromise: Anne could work for them for three months for board, lodging, and washing. If they could not offer her a paid job at the end of that time, they would help her find another position.

Reading asked for several days to think it over. The next morning she took the train to Yonkers so she could consult with her sister. The offer was not ideal, but work of any kind was scarce in New York, where the economy had not yet recovered from the crash of 1857. Reading decided to take the job.

She began work at St. Luke's on December 17, three days before South Carolina seceded from the Union. In her journal she describes a "neat and comfortable" hospital that was a far cry from the public hospitals of the day, with white bedroom furniture and white counterpanes, a few books in each room, coconut matting in the hallways to mute the sounds of footsteps, and the still-rare luxury of indoor water closets and hot-air heating. Her journal over the next few months reports holiday celebrations, visits to friends in the country, and the pleasure of watching snow fall on Central Park from the comfort of a heated room. "Here every day brings its duties, its privileges and its enjoyments," she wrote with apparent contentment. "We do not have much of what the world calls pleasure but we do enjoy peace and quietness, food and rainment [*sic*] and a comfortable home, such as thousands in America, aye and in England, too, would be glad to possess."[22] She shows a clear satisfaction with her work during her first months at St. Luke's, as well as a sense of superiority about the relative skills of English and American surgeons, in one case noting, "It is here considered to be a very clever operation though in the London hospitals it would be thought of little importance."[23]

The outbreak of war disturbed Anne's fragile sense of financial security. The Northern economy had never quite recovered from the panic of 1857, and the secession of the Southern states brought renewed panic and an economic downturn. Bankers feared the Southern states would repudiate their debts, and merchants feared Southern purchasers might stop buying Northern goods. By May, Anne was all too aware that financial difficulties had trickled down from Wall Street to the man on the street. The firm in Yonkers where her sister had worked was closed. People who had depended on day labor to support themselves now wandered the streets of New York, starving, destitute, and miserable. Where her American counterparts wrote in their letters and diaries of the men they knew enlisting from patriotic zeal, Anne saw it as a financial necessity for many: "There is now nothing left for a man to do but enlist for a soldier for in that way alone he can contribute towards the support of his family."[24] By July, Anne began to tour other hospitals and mental asylums, in what looks like the early stages of a job hunt: assessing both the quality of their facilities and their pay rates in comparison to those at St. Luke's.

When the opportunity came, Anne proved herself to be more skilled at networking than many of the women who sought to join the new army nursing corps. On Monday, April 7, 1862, Mrs. Fabbric, an influential woman who was one of St. Luke's regular charity visitors, came into Anne's ward. In the course of discussing the war and hospitals, Anne took a calculated risk and told the visitor she wanted a position nursing the sick and wounded in the army. After that, things moved quickly. On Wednesday, Mrs. Fabbric brought Anne an invitation to meet the following morning with a local committee that hired nurses. The next day, after some effort to bargain over the salary, she accepted a position as an army nurse at the standard rate of $12 a month.

Anne gave notice to St. Luke's on April 11. On April 13, she received instructions to go to Mrs. Dix in Washington; from there she would be sent wherever she was most needed. She was told to limit her luggage to a small traveling trunk and a carpetbag containing whatever she required for immediate use. Since she had no permanent home in the United States, she arranged to leave the rest of her belongings at St. Luke's.

Preparations made and goodbyes said, she noted in her journal, "I am now anxiously awaiting orders."[25]

Trains, Ships, and Baggage Cars

Once appointed, nurses faced a new challenge: traveling to their assignments.

In the early months of the war, new nurses paid their own expenses and made their own arrangements as best they could, often hampered by inexperience and Victorian ideas about propriety. More than one woman found her way smoothed by chance encounters with men who escorted them to the next stage in their journey.

By 1862, the government was required to provide travel expenses for nurses working for Dorothea Dix, but getting the proper documents was often a challenge. In *Hospital Sketches,* Louisa May Alcott subjects her fictional counterpart, Tribulation Periwinkle, to an only slightly exaggerated version of her own efforts to obtain the free rail pass from Boston to Washington to which her appointment entitled her. Over the course of two days she was referred from one official to another, including at one point the governor of Massachusetts, and sent from one side of the city to the other. Even her "General," an anonymous version of Miss Dix, told her, "Don't be discouraged; and if you don't succeed, come to me and we will see what to do next" but gives her no practical assistance. She had reached the point where she felt that "if I had been in search of the Koh-i-noor diamond I would have been as likely to find it"; she was about to give up and buy a ticket, when she ran into her brother-in-law, who helped her run through the bureaucratic maze needed to get her official pass, just in time for dinner with her sister and a sentimental farewell at the train station.[26]

Alcott turns real bureaucratic snarls into comedy, but she was not the only one to experience such problems. Anne Reading had similar difficulties acquiring her transportation pass at the end of her service. She waited for several hours at the Sanitary Commission office while the clerk carried her papers to the surgeon general. He returned with them unsigned; Surgeon General Hammond had examined her papers and refused to sign them because they didn't specify whether she was a volunteer or a paid nurse, and only paid nurses were to receive free rail passage. Desperate, she went to Dix for help, catching her just as Dix was on the brink of leaving on one of her endless hospital visits. Dix wrote out a certificate stating that Reading was a paid nurse. Reading then hurried back to the Sanitary Commission office, half frozen by the intense cold of the windy March day. The clerk, who seems to have been more obliging than those encountered by Trib Periwinkle, took the papers once again to the surgeon general, who gave the order for her free passage to New York. The clerk brought the papers back to her with his apologies for the delay and the offer of a bottle of sherry to keep her company during the long night of travel. Reading accepted them both with gratitude.

Even when tickets were in order, travel over what now seems like a short distance could involve a complicated series of transfers. A trip from Boston to Washington could take several days and required taking a train to New London, Connecticut, a steamship from there to New Jersey, then three more trains with transfers between stations in Philadelphia and Baltimore. Sometimes even a complicated series of transfers would have seemed like a luxury. Nurses who worked in field hospitals, in particular, became adept at taking whatever form of transportation presented itself, from ambulance to baggage wagon. Emily Cone, who served in the Cumberland Hospital in Nashville, reported traveling "alone" in a boxcar with three hundred men. Lucy Campbell Kaiser, who worked in various locations in northern Missouri, often traveled by horseback over long distances and, on more than one occasion, talked her way onto a troop transport river steamer.

• • •

The number of women who volunteered tapered off after 1862, but women continued to apply for positions well into 1864. In some cases, a male family member was wounded and needed nursing. Some finally turned thirty. In some cases, a family situation changed. And sometimes, as in the case of Mary Gardner Holland, a woman simply felt she could wait no longer.

"The first gun fired on Sumter fired every drop of my blood," Holland wrote in 1895. "Had it been possible I should have made my appearance at the first battle of Bull Run." But her elderly mother depended on her. Bending to family duty, she worked during the day to support herself and her mother and spent her evenings volunteering for the Sanitary Commission, as thousands of other Northern women did throughout the war. Finally she told her mother that "there were married women, with families of half-grown girls, who could not go to the front, but could do what I was doing." It was time for her to do more.

Like the women who first applied for nursing appointments immediately after Bull Run, Holland tried every method she could think of to get an official appointment at the front. In 1864, after exhausting all other options, she came across a copy of Dix's Circular No. 8, which inspired her to apply for a position through Miss Dix. She had one problem with the listed requirements: giving up her skirt hoops. "I felt as if I could not walk without a hoop." But determined to nurse, she decided, "Well, if I can't walk without it, I will crawl; for I must go and I will do the best I can."

Soon after that, she read in the paper that wounded troops were flooding into Washington so quickly that more help was needed at once. She wrote immediately to Miss Dix: "I am in possession of one of your circulars, and will comply with all your requirements. I am plain-looking enough to suit you, and old enough. I have no near relatives in the war, no lover there. I never had a husband, and am not looking for one. Will you take me?" She heard back from Dix in a few days: "Report at once to my house, corner of 14th Street and New York Avenue, Washington."

Having entered the service late, Holland worked as a nurse in the Washington area for only fourteen months at the end of the war. During the day she was in charge of the linen room. The job was hard. But no matter how tired she was, she spent her evenings and sometimes the entire night doing what she called "real nursing": taking care of the wounded soldiers.[27]

Whether they volunteered within the first weeks of the war or the final months, from a sense of duty or a need for work, Civil War nurses were always clear what the priority was—the soldiers.

Chapter 4

Nurses on the Hospital Transport Ships

"Imagine a great river or sound steamer filled on every deck—every berth and every square inch of room covered with wounded men; even the stairs and gangways and guards filled with those who are less badly wounded; and then imagine fifty well men, on every kind of errand, rushing to and fro over them, every touch bringing agony to the poor fellows, while stretcher after stretcher came along, hoping to find an empty place; and then imagine what it was to keep calm ourselves, and make sure that every man on both boats was properly refreshed and fed."
—Katharine Prescott Wormeley[1]

Anne Reading's plans were changed while she was en route to her first assignment from Miss Dix, thanks to the efforts of two doctors who had worked with her at St. Luke's Hospital.

Reading was scheduled to take the train on May 5, 1861, to Baltimore, where she was to receive her travel passes and assignment from Miss Dix. Two days before her departure, the two doctors, Dr. Watts and Dr. Peters, received their own summons for service on the *Ocean Queen*, one of the newly established hospital transport ships run by the United States Sanitary Commission. The doctors were authorized to bring several nurses with them, male or female, and they tried to convince Reading to accompany them. She refused, pointing out that she had been hired by Dix through the Women's Central Association of Relief (WCAR) as part of the army nursing corps and that they were working for the Sanitary Commission. Since Dix and the Sanitary Commission worked separately, she could not simply move from one job to another. (The relationship between Dix, WCAR, and the Sanitary Commission was complicated. The WCAR screened potential nurses for Dix for a time, but she was never part of the Sanitary Commission and found herself increasingly at odds with the commission's leaders as the war continued.) Reading pronounced herself satisfied with her job arrangements, but the doctors insisted they would try to get her transferred to their ship once they reached Baltimore

The doctors pulled strings, but they didn't achieve quite the results they desired. When Reading arrived in Baltimore on May 6, she met with Miss Dix, who gave her a transportation pass to Fort Monroe, located at Hampton Roads, Virginia, near the mouth of the Chesapeake Bay, and the site of a major Union hospital where Reading expected to work. Pass in hand, she joined a group of twenty women headed to the same destination. Once at Fort Monroe, Reading's traveling companions chose to rest while they waited for further orders; Reading chose to visit the military hospital instead, a former hotel now under the army's control.

Reading's busman's holiday to the military hospital was probably the last quiet moment she would enjoy for some months. When she returned to her traveling companions, she found they had all received orders to proceed to Yorktown, which the Confederate army had abandoned on May 4. The Union troops, having taken possession of the city, were in pursuit of the retreating rebel army, leaving behind the sick and wounded. Nurses and surgeons were needed immediately.

In Yorktown, Reading discovered that unbeknownst to her she had been transferred from Dix's nursing corps to the Sanitary Commission's hospital transport ships, where the need for nurses was critical. The *Ocean Queen*, with Dr. Watts and Dr. Peters, was at Yorktown when Reading and her companions arrived the next afternoon. The nurses assigned to the ship, including Amy Morris Bradley, had begun to load sick and wounded soldiers, about a thousand in all, many of them ill with typhoid fever. When Reading arrived at the ship, Dr. Watts hurried over to tell her how glad he was that she was there and how desperately she was needed on the *Ocean Queen*. His satisfaction lasted only until Frederick Law Olmsted, the Sanitary Commission's treasurer and the organizing force behind the hospital transport fleet, came on board and claimed Reading. The *Ocean Queen* would be sailing back to New York soon with its passengers; Reading could not be spared.[2]

The next day Reading set out on her first assignment as a member of the hospital transport service, traveling to West Point on the steamer *Wilson Small* to pick up a group of wounded soldiers. She would spend the next four months moving from one steamship to another, caring for the casualties produced in General George McClellan's disastrous Peninsular Campaign.

The Formation and Mission of the United States Sanitary Commission

The United States Sanitary Commission had its roots in the ladies' aid societies that women across the Northern states formed for the support of the Union's soldiers after the fall of Fort Sumter in April 1861.

Perhaps as many as ten thousand local aid societies were formed in the first year of the war alone. Modeled on the mission aid societies common at the time, their purpose was to make and collect food, clothing, and medical supplies for the Union's soldiers. They turned homes, schools, and churches into small-scale factories and shipping warehouses.

Over the course of the war, the aid societies would provide millions of dollars of much needed supplies and much appreciated luxuries for the troops, but their initial efforts were sometimes as chaotic as the new army itself. With no understanding of how the still-developing military distribution system worked, their boxes were often literally sidetracked at the rail yards to make way for troops and army stores—leaving cakes to mold and jars of jelly to ferment and explode. Some groups produced goods that betrayed a fundamental ignorance about soldiers' needs. The most dramatic example of this was the early enthusiasm for making "havelocks," white cloth cap covers with long tails that covered the back of the neck and shoulders. Made popular by British general Sir Henry Havelock in India four years earlier, the caps were intended to protect men who fought in hot climates from suffering sunstroke. From the perspective of ladies in Maine, Virginia in the summer was as tropical as Madras. In fact, soldiers complained the havelocks made them even hotter because they blocked the air from circulating around their heads and faces. Since havelocks weren't standard uniform issue, many soldiers abandoned them as useless. More ingenious, or thriftier, men kept them to use as gun patches, dishcloths, and coffee strainers.

Disturbed by the waste of time, energy, and material symbolized by mistakes like the ill-fated havelocks and the rush of overzealous and undertrained nursing volunteers, Dr. Elizabeth Blackwell, the first licensed female doctor, and Rev. Henry Bellows, a popular Unitarian minister, arrived independently at the idea of uniting the hitherto independent ladies' aid societies into a central organization. On April 25, 1861—just six days after Dorothea Dix's meeting at the White House—Blackwell called an informal meeting at the New York Infirmary for Women of women with experience in reform work to discuss the possibility of forming a Women's Central Association of Relief. A notice of the meeting accidentally found its way into the *New York Times*; instead of a small meeting of known organizers, "the parlours of the infirmary were crowded with ladies, to the surprise of the little group of managers."[3] At the meeting, Blackwell outlined three objectives for the proposed WCAR: managing the efforts of existing ladies' aid associations and encouraging the creation of new local associations; coordinating with the army's Medical Bureau about the needs of the rapidly growing army so members' efforts weren't wasted; and creating a system for selecting and training volunteer nurses. Two men, Rev. Bellows and Dr. Elisha Harris, superintendent of Hospitals at Staten Island, also attended the meeting. Both would play critical roles in the creation of the United States Sanitary Commission, an organization that would go well beyond the scope of the ladies' aid societies from which it sprang.

Encouraged by the enthusiasm of the initial meeting, Dr. Blackwell called an open meeting four days later at the much larger Cooper Institute, to be presided over by Rev. Bellows. The hall was packed: New York papers estimated the attendance at between two and three thousand. Repeated waves of applause interrupted Bellows's speech, in which he praised the outpouring of aid for the troops and then called for New York's aid societies to gather under what he described as "an appropriate head" designed to "give explicit answers to the ten thousand questions everywhere arising."[4] Dr. Blackwell and her associates followed Bellows's speech with a presentation of the WCAR plan and the election of a board of managers for the new umbrella relief organization, made up of twelve men and twelve women. The board then elected Dr. Valentine Mott, a founding faculty member of the university medical college of New York, as president and Bellows as vice president—a shrewd recognition on Blackwell's part that, while the women of the WCAR were more than capable of managing the grassroots support efforts, the organization was unlikely to succeed in its efforts to build a relationship with the Medical Bureau without a male spokesman.

On May 15, Rev. Bellows and three doctors associated with the WCAR boarded the first train to travel from New York to Washington since the Baltimore riots on April 19. Their goal was to learn firsthand what the relief associations could accomplish and how they could work with the Medical Bureau. Bellows would later say that "the first idea of a Sanitary Commission, which certainly had not entered my head when we left New York, was started between us in the cars twixt Philadelphia and Baltimore—in a long and earnest conversation."[5] Over the course of the thirteen-hour train ride they discussed the question of how to safeguard the health of soldiers on and off the battle-field. They hoped to avoid repeating the British experience in the Crimean War, where inadequate supplies and medical care killed more British soldiers than were lost on the battlefield. Once in Washington, the committee toured military camps and hospitals with the help of Dorothea Dix, giving Bellows his first look at the inadequate arrangements made to house and care for the troops, wounded and sound alike, who arrived in the capital every day. Bellows wrote home to his wife that "the amount of sickness and suffering among the troops forbids my neglecting anything I can possibly do to bring the matter home to the Government."[6]

Over the course of several days, as Bellows met with Acting Surgeon General Colonel Robert C. Wood, generals, cabinet members, and President Lincoln himself, his goals changed from formal recognition of the WCAR's three-part plan to the creation of a civilian sanitary commission that would focus on the broader questions of army health that the army itself was prone to forget; this was a change that not only bypassed the efforts of the WCAR, but that Bellows presented as a way to control the extent to which the efforts of ladies' aid societies and volunteer nurses disrupted the army's systems. In a letter to Secretary of War Simon Cameron, dated May 18, Bellows and his fellow committee members offered themselves as mem-bers of a sanitary commission who would serve as advisors to the government with a mandate to inspect military camps and hospitals and the power to enforce sanitary regulations for the benefit of the soldiers. The proposal made no mention of the WCAR, which had paid to send the committee to Washington in the first place, and reduced the question of female nurses to a side issue. On June 9, Cameron approved the creation of "a Commission of Inquiry and Advice in respect of the Sanitary Interests of the United States Forces," soon to be known as the United States Sanitary Commission (USSC). President Lincoln signed the order four days later with a noticeable lack of enthusiasm, remarking that he feared the commission would be "a fifth wheel to the coach,"[7] an awkward addition to the Union's improvised and rickety war machine. Certainly the army's Medical Bureau viewed the creation of a civilian body with a mandate to ask questions and make improvements in matters of the army's health with suspicion, if not outright hostility. But whether the army liked it or not, the United States Sanitary Commission was now official and ready to begin work.

Rev. Bellows was named president of the commission, but its secretary, Frederick Law Olmsted, was responsible for the group's real achievements. Best known as the landscape architect responsible for designing New York's Central Park, Olmsted had already demonstrated a talent for organization. Under his leadership, the Sanitary Commission became a flexible and powerful agency for the care of suffering soldiers. The executive board of the commission was all male, but women continued to dominate the organization at the regional and grassroots level. Twelve regional branches of the commission—located in New York, Boston, Buffalo, Chicago, Cincinnati, Cleveland, Columbus, Detroit, Louisville, New Albany, Philadelphia, and Pittsburgh—coordinated and directed the activities of the thousands of local societies that chose to come under its umbrella. Not all aid societies chose to join forces with the Sanitary Commission. Some local societies, such as those that allied themselves with Clara Barton, remained independent. In addition, two other large-scale relief organizations competed with the USSC for volunteers and resources: the St. Louis–based Western Sanitary Commission, which served regiments in the western campaigns, and the YMCA's United States Christian Commission, which focused on caring for soldiers' souls as well as their bodies. Nonetheless, historians conservatively estimate some 7,000 local ladies' aid societies allied themselves with the United States Sanitary Commission during the Civil War; the commission itself was more generous in its estimate. In 1865, the *USSC Bulletin* claimed 32,000 affiliated aid societies.[8]

The Sanitary Commission was ready to step into action in July 1861, when the debacle of Bull Run proved the Medical Bureau was unprepared to protect the health of its soldiers. Olmsted, frail and permanently crippled in a carriage accident, personally inspected twenty military camps near Washington. Other male volunteers inspected and reported back to the commission on the condition of the military's improvised hospitals. The commission built new hospitals using an innovative pavilion design intended to promote air circulation in the wards. Regional branches funneled supplies from local organizations to military hospitals and convalescent camps.

All of these tasks were well within the scope of Bellows's original proposal to Secretary Cameron. In March 1862, General George McClellan's Peninsular Campaign presented the Sanitary Commission with a new challenge.

The Peninsular Campaign Begins

In the spring of 1862, General George McClellan, commander of the Army of the Potomac, was under increasing political pressure to take the offensive. President Lincoln had issued General War Order No. 1 on January 27, directing all United States forces to advance against the Confederate army on February 22—George Washington's birthday, a date chosen for its symbolic significance. McClellan ignored the order. Now both Lincoln and his new secretary of war, Edward Stanton, were proposing an overland advance straight south from Washington against the Confederate capital at Richmond, Virginia.

McClellan pushed through a more ambitious plan that would allow him to bypass the Confederate army massed at Bull Run. Beginning in mid-March, using a fleet of some four hundred steamboats, he moved more than 100,000 men—along with more than twelve hundred wagons and ambulances, three hundred pieces of artillery, fifteen thousand horses, and countless tons of supplies—south to Fort Monroe, in what would be the largest American amphibious operation prior to the Allied invasion of Normandy in 1944. On April 4, the Army of the Potomac began its advance toward Richmond up the swampy lowlands of the narrow Virginia Peninsula between the York and James rivers.

When McClellan's forces reached Yorktown, the site of George Washington's decisive victory over Lord Cornwallis ninety-one years previously, the general mistakenly believed that the Confederate army vastly outnumbered his troops, thanks to poor information from his staff. His intelligence section was staffed by civilian agents provided by the Pinkerton Detective Agency. Pinkerton agents were skilled at capturing counterfeiters and bank robbers, but they were not accustomed to estimating troop strengths from conflicting and erroneous reports, many of them gathered from escaping slaves. The agents consistently overestimated the size of the Confederate forces at two or three times their actual strength. At Yorktown, their reports of the size of the Confederate forces ranged from 40,000 to 100,000 troops; General John G. Magruder originally commanded fewer than 15,000 men at Yorktown. Magruder reinforced Pinkerton's overassessment of Confederate troop numbers with an elaborate ruse. He ordered logs painted black and placed in temporary fortifications, known as redoubts, to give the appearance of many artillery pieces. (When they were discovered after the Confederate retreat, the press mockingly called them "Quaker guns.") Magruder then marched his men back and forth between the redoubts. Not much of an illusion, but enough to fool a general who was already convinced that a large Confederate army held the city.

Lincoln urged McClellan to attack. McClellan, increasingly convinced that he faced overwhelming odds, instead chose to besiege Yorktown, giving Confederate general Joseph E. Johnston, one of the victorious commanders at Bull Run, time to reinforce Yorktown with additional men. In early May, McClellan finally attacked. The Confederate forces slipped away in the night on May 4, leaving behind empty trenches and a few landmines—a new and devastating war technology. Finally on the move, McClellan pursued them to Williamsburg, where they fought a savage holding action before the city fell on May 5. On May 15, McClellan set up his headquarters on the muddy little Virginia river known as the Pamunkey. The Union army pushed its way up the river, creating supply bases at strategic spots as they moved forward: Eltham's Landing, Cumberland Landing, and finally White House Landing, the point where the York River Railroad crossed the Pamunkey.

The Army of the Potomac was ready to advance on the Confederate capital.

The Hospital Transport Service

While McClellan and his quartermaster worked out the details of an amphibious assault on the Virginia Peninsula, the Medical Bureau and the Sanitary Commission considered the consequences of such a strategy on the already overburdened resources of the army's medical system. In addition to high battle casualties, field hospitals could expect large numbers of ill soldiers thanks to the malarial swamps. The inhospitable terrain of the Virginia peninsula, with its swampy forests and miry roads, would make it difficult to transport wounded and sick men from the battlefield with horse-drawn wagons. The obvious answer was a water-based evacuation system, but the army's prior effort at hospital transport ships had been a failure. Instead of trying again, the army contracted with the United States Sanitary Commission to operate a semi-independent hospital transport system, using steamships to evacuate wounded and sick soldiers through the James and Pamunkey rivers and then take them up the coast to Northern hospitals. The army quartermaster would provide a fleet of ships to serve as hospital transports; the Sanitary Commission would staff and supply them. Olmsted was put in charge of the program and traveled with the ships over the course of the campaign. On occasion he would allow himself to become involved in the care of soldiers as well as logistics: Georgeanna Woolsey noted in her diary that Olmsted would sometimes slip into a cabin when the ward was quiet and sit on the floor by a dying German "with his arm round his pillow—as nearly round his neck as possible—talking tenderly to him [in German] and slipping away again quietly."[9]

The commission received its first steamboat, the *Daniel Webster*, on April 25, and volunteers spent the next five days scrubbing it clean, installing bunks, and outfitting it for medical use. Over the coming weeks, the commission converted another fourteen ships into floating hospital transports; they included three steamers capable of making the ocean passage from Fort Monroe to New York, and the appropriately named *Wilson Small*, a shallow-draft boat that could navigate creeks and shallow tributaries and would be used to bring both wounded and nurses downriver to the larger transport vessels. Each ship was staffed by at least one volunteer surgeon, one assistant surgeon, a "lady superintendent," a ward master, and two nurses for each ward, some of whom, like Anne Reading, were paid nurses rather than volunteers. The line between volunteer and nonvolunteer was always blurry, and occasionally the source of difficult relationships among paid nurses, unpaid nurses, and surgeons. Amy Morris Bradley, for instance, asked by a surgeon whether she was a paid nurse, ranted in her diary, "To think that I, *poor Amy Bradley* would come out here to work for *money* and that the paltry sum of twelve dollars per month and Rations! . . . Thank God I had a higher motive than a high living & a big salary."[10] Medical students worked as volunteer dressers, which meant serving as a physician's assistant, with special attention to dressing wounds.

The inclusion of female nurses on the ships represented a major change in Sanitary Commission policy. Even though providing a corps of trained women nurses was one of the original missions of the WCAR, the all-male executive board of the Sanitary Commission—faced with continued army resistance to the idea of women in military hospitals and increasingly at odds with Dorothea Dix over questions of jurisdiction—abandoned the idea of training and hiring nurses as early as November 1861. Olmsted, however, had assumed from the beginning that nurses would be part of the hospital transport service. The commission's goal, as outlined by Olmsted, was to ensure "that every man had a good place to sleep in, and something hot to eat daily, and that the sickest had every essential that could have been given them in their own homes."[11] He envisioned the transport ships as being less like hospitals and more like a home away from home, where an injured soldier could rest and recover in relative ease, complete with women to prepare beds for incoming casualties, staff kitchens to prepare special diets for the ill, and comfort the wounded—replicating the middle-class domestic experience of nursing a family member in an institutional setting.

Olmsted also envisioned the ships as a secure place for middle-class and elite women to serve away from the rough atmosphere of overcrowded military hospitals. For every woman who volunteered as a nurse, another was held back by the disapproval of family, friends, and society's assumptions about proper behavior for a lady. Some feared ruined reputations as a result of the moral laxity of military hospitals. A friend warned Harriet Whetton that "so much is said about the nurses who have gone. Some of the men say that they are closeted for hours with the surgeons in pantries and all kinds of disorders go on."[12] Other naysayers argued women would lose their femininity through exposure to the coarse realities of hospital nursing, vividly described by an anonymous doctor in a letter to the influential *American Medical Times:*

> Imagine a delicate refined woman assisting a rough soldier to the close-stool, or supplying him with a bedpan, or adjusting the knots on a T-bandage employed in retaining a catheter in position, or a dozen offices of a like character which one would hesitate long before asking a female nurse to perform, but which are frequently and continually necessary in a military hospital.[13]

Some feared they would be subject to sexual advances from the soldiers they were there to nurse, an event that seems unlikely given the condition of most of the soldiers described in the letters and memoirs of the nurses themselves. For women who wanted to volunteer but had not been able to stand up against those who discouraged them, the hospital transport ships, under the control of the Sanitary Commission rather than the army's Medical Bureau, seemed to offer an opportunity to serve away from the dangers of both the battlefield and army hospitals.

Anne Reading was an anomaly among the women who staffed the hospital ships. Olmsted attracted an unusual number of self-described ladies to the transport service, many of them volunteers Dix had previously turned away. He actively recruited New York socialites Eliza Woolsey Howland and her sister

Georgeanna Woolsey as lady superintendents before he had even completed his negotiations with the government for ships. Both women had successfully completed Dr. Blackwell's short-lived nurse training program at the New York Infirmary for Women and Children. They reported for duty with less than a day's notice to serve as lady superintendents when the Sanitary Commission took possession of its first ship, the *Daniel Webster*, on April 25; they brought with them a trunk filled with towels and old sheets, soap, cologne, oil silk, sponges, a small camp cooking stove, and a spirit lamp. Their first task as lady superintendents was sewing a flag marking the *Daniel Webster* as a hospital transport, which they did surrounded by the ship's carpenters and contraband slaves who were making final repairs to the ship. Only after their flag was hoisted did they buckle down to the real work of getting the filthy river steamer into condition to receive patients, a job that took several days of unladylike labor.

"Transport Women" in Action

The hospital transport service plunged into action on May 4, when the Confederate army evacuated Yorktown. Olmsted scrambled to field a team to take care of the sick and wounded left behind. Amy Morris Bradley, who had previously spent eight months as a volunteer field nurse with the Third Maine regiment, arrived at Fort Monroe on May 6. Olmsted met her there and ferried her on the *Wilson Small* upriver to Yorktown, where she transferred to the *Ocean Queen*. Anne Reading and her twenty-some traveling companions arrived at Yorktown the next day. Six of them were assigned to the *Ocean Queen*. Others, including Reading, were put to work on the river steamers.

Yorktown was Reading's first close view of war in the field, something she was never exposed to in the Crimea. The Confederate forces had evacuated the city in the night with so little notice that men left pork stew and half-baked biscuits on their campfires. The hills were dotted with abandoned baggage and Magruder's redoubts, with their Quaker guns. The Union troops were preparing to go upriver in full pursuit and the pier "was crowded with men, horses, casks, swords, guns, contrabands, and everything else that was warlike."[14]

The hospital transport service was preparing to go upriver as well. The next day Reading was part of a team that traveled in the *Wilson Small* to West Point, where they picked up twenty-one severely wounded men and brought them back downriver to the *Elm City*, which would deliver a total of four hundred soldiers to a hospital in Washington. As soon as they had transferred their patients to the *Elm City*, another steamer pulled up alongside them. Reading and the other nurses had just sat down to tea when Olmsted came on board and said, "Ladies, here is the *Knickerbocker* with one hundred and fifty men, sick and wounded on board. They have had nothing to eat since the day before yesterday." The nurses abandoned their own meal without hesitation, and in minutes they were on board the *Knickerbocker*, tending to hungry and wounded soldiers. Those strong enough to eat got tea with bread and butter. Those too faint were given brandy and water or beef tea as the case required. Once they were fed, the nurses washed them and dressed their wounds; three days later they took on another 150 men and began the process again.[15] They then conveyed the men to Washington, attending to their comfort as best they could in the hold or on the deck of the crowded *Wilson Small*.

The routine never ended. Nurses brought a batch of soldiers on board, cared for them, in some cases became attached to them—an emotion that appears to have been generally more maternal than romantic—then turned them over to nurses on the next stage of their voyage, and steamed back upriver to begin the cycle again.

While they were on the transport ships, the nurses were both in the center of the war and distant from it. The flow of damaged bodies was seemingly unending, but news about the course of the war arrived at a less dependable rate. Seldom interrupted by references to the larger action of the war, there is a numbing monotony to their accounts of traveling back and forth on the Pamunkey River between Fort Monroe and the Harrison and White House landings. Katherine Wormeley estimated that her team recovered, treated, and transported almost four thousand men in one three-day period at the height of the campaign.[16]

The occasional adventure broke up the ship's tedium. In one incident Reading and her companions left the ship and took a small tug upstream to search for a group of men rumored to be lying farther upriver with no one to help them. On another occasion, Reading was thrilled to be introduced to General McClellan, who was told she had been a nurse in the Crimean War. She received a hearty handshake from "Little Mac," and thanks "that an Englishwoman would render them a service in such a time of need."[17] But such moments were rare. The most common excitement occurred when the army confiscated ships without warning to use as troop transports; nurses grew accustomed to scrambling from one ship to another with only a few minutes to prepare. For the most part, the action of the war remained at a distance while the nurses dealt with its heartbreaking effects.

At the end of June, the Seven Days' Battles reversed the momentum of the campaign. Despite McClellan's cautious nature, his troops had advanced steadily toward Richmond. Now Lee pushed back. McClellan's forces outnumbered Lee's by almost two to one, but the Confederate general forced McClellan first to abandon the supply line at White House Landing and then to retreat with the Confederate army in pursuit. Suddenly the hospital transportation service was plunged into the middle of the war. Gunboats lined the shores of the river. The fleet worked around the clock to ferry the sick and wounded from the Harrison and White House landings to Yorktown or Fort Monroe, with a protective convoy. In addition to removing wounded soldiers, the transport ships also removed as many stores as possible from the supply depots. Each steamer towed store ships behind them: Reading's ship towed twelve supply-laden schooners away from White House Landing. But they did not have enough time to take everything. As Reading's ship left, soldiers were burning the supplies they left behind so there would be nothing for the Confederates to take possession of. As Reading noted in her journal, "Thus we left that once beautiful place, the White House at the head of the Pamunkey River, blackened and charred, a blazing head of ruins."[18]

On July 27, Reading took part in her first exchange of wounded prisoners. Her ship received orders to hoist a white truce flag alongside its hospital flag and travel in a guarded convoy to City Point; there they would take on wounded soldiers who had been taken prisoner in the retreat from White

House Landing, and were now being exchanged for Confederate prisoners. The convoy of ships arrived shortly after the Confederate train reached the station at City Point. Reading was saddened by the sight of the remains of the formerly pretty town and noted that those living in the peace and comfort of England could have no idea of the misery endured by those living in the midst of the war. She found it strange to see "our men being led or carried by the rebel guard from the [train] cars to the steamer with as much care and tenderness as if they were brothers."[19]

It was difficult to believe these same men had been engaged in deadly combat with each other only days before.

Life on the Ships

The Sanitary Commission promised its nurses, and perhaps more importantly their families, that service on the transport ships would be a sheltered experience. In reality, the nurses on the transport ships were closer to the battlefield than their counterparts in the military hospitals and saw some of the worst scenes of suffering of the war. Even Bradley, who had already seen more battle injuries than any other nurse in the hospital transport service, before becoming the atypical lady superintendent of the *Knickerbocker*, found herself unprepared for the condition of the wounded brought by train to White House Landing after the Battle of Fair Oaks (known as the Battle of Seven Pines in the South) on May 31. She was overwhelmed by emotion as she watched the mutilated soldiers carried on board on stretchers and carefully placed on the cots she had prepared for them. For nearly an hour she struggled to control her feelings, weeping and protesting, "Must I see human beings thus mangled? O, My God, why is it? Why is it?" She finally pulled herself together after the surgeon admonished her: "Miss Bradley, you must not do so, but prepare to assist these poor fellows." Ashamed of herself for losing her focus, she choked back her tears and told herself, "Action is the watchword of the hour!"[20] Many women returned home after their first look at the condition of the men aboard the ships. Those who remained worked harder than they had ever worked before.

Reading was not the only nurse on the ships to come from a working-class family. Bradley was the daughter of a Massachusetts cobbler. But most of the nurses who came to the boats through the Sanitary Commission were from more privileged backgrounds. Several were members of prominent New York families. One was married to the son of a shipping magnate, another was the widow of a naval officer, and two were wives of Sanitary Commission officers—a testament to the commission's belief in Olmsted's rhetoric of the hospital ships as an extension of the middle-class home. (As the Peninsular Campaign went on, George Templeton Strong's pride in his wife's service wore thin. By mid-June he was, by his own description "entreating, conjuring and commanding her to . . . come straight home,"[21] where he was engaged in his own form of war service as the Sanitary Commission's treasurer.) Bradley termed them "the Aristocrats" and grumbled that Olmsted gave them preferential treatment in assignments. Such women were more accustomed to supervising servants than scrubbing floors themselves.

On the boats, they often worked for two or three days with little sleep and meals snatched when the demands of duty allowed. They hauled buckets of water for cooking, cleaning, and laundry and cooked endless gallons of gruel and beef tea over spirit lamps. The smaller steamers patrolled up and down the peninsular rivers, taking on men and providing an occasional opportunity to go ashore—only one of several reasons why river steamers were a plum assignment compared to the larger ships that carried men from the river steamers to hospitals further north. Sometimes a shore visit allowed for sightseeing; the Custis farm near White House Landing, where George Washington spent the early years of his marriage was a pilgrimage shrine for Union nurses and soldiers. More often, transport women disembarked to forage supplies from a military encampment. For instance, on one occasion when Georgeanna Woolsey needed to prepare dinner for hundreds of wounded soldiers, she commandeered a stove from an officer's tent and took it back to the boat in "a triumphant procession [through town], waving . . . bits of stove pipe and iron pot-covers."[22] As Katherine Wormeley told a friend, the nurses did a little bit of everything: far more than was included in the official description of the job.[23]

One volunteer, Eliza Harris, described conditions aboard the *Spaulding* after the Battle of Fair Oaks: "There were eight hundred on board. Passageways, state-rooms, floors from the dark and fetid hold to the hurricane deck, were all more than filled; some on mattresses, some on blankets, others on straw."[24] After a long day of amputations, seventeen arms, hands, feet, and legs lay piled in an area below deck. At night, after washing out her skirts to get rid of "the mingled blood of Federal and Confederate soldiers which covered many portions of the floor," she lay down "with the sick, wounded and dying all around, and slept from sheer exhaustion, the last sounds falling upon [her] ears being groans from the operating room."[25]

Clothing was another big change in their lives. Not bound by Dix's restrictions, many of the nurses arrived wearing the ribbons and ruffles typical of women of their class, but they soon abandoned the filthy dresses in favor of a skirt and a man's flannel shirt, worn with the collar open, the sleeves rolled up, and the shirttail out. They dubbed the shirts "Agnews," the name of the doctor from whom they stole the first shirt.

Like their counterparts in military hospitals on land, the nurses on the transport ships found themselves at odds with doctors and military personnel at a very basic level. The nurses looked at each patient as an individual who deserved at least a moment of individual care. Woolsey stopped to learn each soldier's name, write it on a piece of paper, and pin it to his clothing so he would not go unidentified. She and her comrades argued that it only took a moment to give a man a drink and an orange to eat, which was time well spent if it saved him from exhaustion while he waited for a meal.[26] But the men they worked with saw those moments as interfering with the process of transferring soldiers from the landing to the ship and performing the basic triage that had often not happened on the battlefield. These arguments over the nature of care between nurses and doctors continued well past the short life of the Sanitary Commission's hospital transport service.

The End of the Transport Service

In the weeks after May 4, the Sanitary Commission hospital boats transported thousands of sick and wounded men from the Virginia Peninsula to military hospitals in New York, Philadelphia, Washington, Annapolis, and Baltimore. But in mid-July, Confederate gunboats began firing on the Sanitary

Commission's ships, removing the last illusion that the transport ships were safe. Olmsted refused to accept new female volunteers and began to demobilize the existing forces. Some women chose to go home. Others, like Amy Bradley, Harriet Douglas Whetten, and Annie Etheridge continued to work on transport boats under the army's command. By the end of the month, the commission had turned all responsibility for transporting casualties back to the Union army.

On July 31, Anne Reading and her colleagues on the *Spaulding* received orders to transfer the rest of the men on board to the *Saint Mark*, an army-run transport ship. The next morning, Dr. Jenkins, the chief army surgeon from the *Saint Mark,* came on board the *Spaulding* and asked Reading what she intended to do next. She told him she wanted to head back to Baltimore and take a position in Miss Dix's nursing corps, as she had intended to do before the Sanitary Commission snatched her up. He gave her a letter of recommendation, then asked if she would work on the *Saint Mark* for a time since they had no female nurses on board—clear proof that some army doctors had begun to see the worth of female nurses. For the next two weeks, Reading worked aboard the ship, nursing wounded men as they moved from the peninsula to the Northern hospitals. At one point, the *Saint Mark* had three hundred casualties on board, many badly wounded and none of them in good condition. Most had been held in the prison camps in Richmond for five or six weeks. They were dressed in rags and half starved, "like skeletons having barely enough skin to cover their bones," a condition Reading attributed to Confederate malice rather than to Confederate poverty. Some of them were so weak they could scarcely drink the water and wine the nurses gave them through their tears of joy for their release from captivity. When the *Saint Mark* finally docked at Philadelphia on August 13, one of the men who had been in prison in Richmond offered Reading a ring he had made out of a piece of bone and begged her to accept it as a token of gratitude for the kindness she had shown him.[27]

The next day, Reading presented Dr. Jenkins's letter of recommendation to the army's medical director in Philadelphia and asked for work. He told her no female nurses could be engaged "without the sanction of Miss Dorothea Dix."[28]

Having made her request for government work, Reading headed to New York for a well-deserved rest. She arrived late in the evening two days later and went straight to the rooms of her friend Sophie. She rested for a full day, then went to St. Luke's, where she picked up her letters from England and visited with friends. It took her only a few hours to notice the impact of the war on the economy of the city. After a run on the banks in December, New York bankers suspended specie payments to their customers. Eight months later, coins had disappeared from circulation, and postage stamps filled their role as the popular currency. Merchants used them to make change, and carriage drivers demanded them as payment. The need to get work as soon as possible must have seemed even more pressing.

Late the next night, on August 19, Reading received a telegraph from Miss Dix telling her to come immediately to Washington. The hospital transport service was finished, but the war was not.

Chapter 5

Arriving at Mansion House Hospital

"We stopped before a great pile of buildings, with
a flag flying before it, sentinels at the door, and a very
trying quantity of men lounging about. My heart beat
rather faster than usual, and it suddenly struck me that
I was very far from home; but I descended with dignity,
wondering whether I should be stopped for want of a
countersign, and forced to pass the night in the street.
Marching boldly up the steps, I found that no form
was necessary, for the men fell back, the guard touched
their caps, a boy opened the door, and, as it closed
behind me, I felt that I was fairly started, and
Nurse Periwinkle's Mission was begun."
—Louisa May Alcott, *Hospital Sketches*[1]

A visitor to Alexandria, Virginia, in July 1860 once
observed, "We do not believe there is any place in
the whole bounds of the Union where the people
enjoy more of the real comforts of life than in Alexandria."[2]
The city where George Washington attended Sunday services in a small brick church was not only a thriving seaport
but also a ground transportation hub. The Alexandria Canal
funneled coal from the Appalachian coalfields through
the port, and three rail lines connected the city to the
agricultural riches of both the Shenandoah Valley and the
developing American West. Regular steamboat service

traveled north to Baltimore and New York City and south to Richmond and Fredericksburg, while frequent ferries shuttled passengers across the river to Washington and Georgetown and back. Improvements in transportation led to the creation of foundries and factories, a rare thing in the antebellum south; the 1860 census listed ninety-six small factories and commercial workshops in the city. Alexandria's economy was booming, and so were its expectations for the future.

James Green's Mansion House Hotel was a symbol of the city's new affluence. Green was an English-born entrepreneur who arrived in Alexandria sometime after 1800. A carpenter by trade, he established a furniture factory in the 1830s and went on to become the wealthiest man in his adopted city. In the 1840s, he converted a three-story brick building that had once housed the Bank of Alexandria into a luxury hotel. Built in the Italianate style and topped with an octagonal cupola, Green's Mansion House soon earned a reputation as one of the finest hotels between Washington and New Orleans. A review in the *Alexandria Gazette,* dated May 24, 1849, described the Mansion House as a "spacious and newly furnished Establishment."[3] Its amenities included a scenic view of the surrounding landscape, a restaurant that offered select wines and liquors, oysters and other delicacies, and a billiard table for the amusement of hotel guests. Visiting merchants, salesmen, and tourists crowded its hallways, and members of local society hosted dinners, balls, and other social events in its public rooms. Business was so good that Green began construction on a new four-story wing in 1855.

The fall of Fort Sumter, however, would bring an end to Alexandria's boom times, and to those of Green's Mansion House Hotel.

Alexandria Occupied

Alexandria held the distinction of being occupied by the Union army longer than any other Confederate city during the war. In the months after Abraham Lincoln's election in December 1860, Alexandria, like much of Virginia, maintained an ambivalent position on the question of secession. That changed with the fall of Fort Sumter and Lincoln's call for 75,000 volunteers to put down the Southern insurrection. On April 17, a convention of delegates in Richmond voted in favor of Virginia's secession. In Alexandria, the volunteer militias, whose commanders had previously forbidden any public display of support for the Confederacy, celebrated the fall of Sumter with a seven-gun salute. One of Green's competitors, James W. Jackson, owner of the Marshall House Hotel, raised a huge Confederate flag, paid for by public contributions, on the pole above his roof and swore it would come down only over his dead body. Smaller Confederate flags fluttered in windows and off porches. Alexandria was "secesh" and proud of it.

As war drew near, the quality of daily life decreased. The Union blockade of Southern ports, known as the Anaconda Plan, slowed traffic in the normally busy seaport. Wharves stood deserted. Food prices soared. Travel and communication with places outside the city became more difficult as the army confiscated horses and carts and the federal government seized local mail boats. Schools and businesses closed, leaving behind vacant buildings that would later be commandeered for use as soldiers' billets and hospitals. Those residents who could, fled the city. Anne Frobel, whose family stayed throughout the war and whose diary is one of the primary historical sources for life in wartime Alexandria, described the scene near one of the city's railway depots: "a dense crowd thronged the streets, carriages filled with people, wagons, carts, drays, wheelbarrows all packed mountain high with baggage of every sort, men, women and children streaming along to the cars, most of the women crying, almost every face we saw we recognized, and all looking as forlorn and wretched as if going to an execution."[4] On May 16, only days before federal troops would invade the city, a Northern visitor lamented, "A more people-forsaken and desolate city I have never seen than Alexandria. The houses are low, dirty, and closed; the streets are narrow, filthy, and rough, and the people in the sackcloth of sullen humiliation . . . The withering blight of secession had stamped its seal upon all around."[5] It was hardly the same city the earlier visitor had described only ten months before.

Across the Potomac, the Union's political and military leaders watched Alexandria with concern and made plans for rapid movement. With Virginia's secession the city posed a strategic threat to the capital.

On May 23, Virginians ratified the Ordinance of Secession in a popular vote. Less than twenty-four hours later, the Union army captured the city. Eight Union regiments moved into place over the course of the night, unaccompanied by either fife or drum so as not to rouse the sleeping city. One column marched across the Long Bridge that had connected Washington to Virginia since 1809; another came across the towpath over the aqueduct, one mile to the north of the bridge. Colonel Elmer Ellsworth and the Eleventh New York Volunteer Infantry, known as the Fire Zouaves for their distinctive uniforms modeled on those of French infantry units in North Africa, crossed by boat and entered the city through the wharves. Moving quickly, Union soldiers occupied the city's three railroad depots and the telegraph office. Just before dawn, the federal ship *Pawnee* steamed into the harbor, with its eight Dahlgren guns trained on the city, and ordered the city's militia units to surrender or vacate. Most of them were already gone. At some point in the morning, Colonel Ellsworth, accompanied by some of his Zouaves, attempted to remove the Confederate flag from the roof of the Marshall House Hotel; Jackson shot him dead only to be killed immediately by a Zouave. The flag, indeed, was removed from his roof over his dead body. Their respective compatriots saw both men as martyrs—the first of the war. Alexandria would remain under Union occupation for the remainder of the war. The same strategic location that had made the city a threat now made it valuable to the Union. The "people-forsaken and desolate" city was transformed into a major operational hub for the Army of the Potomac. Mary von Olnhausen reported that the street outside Mansion House Hospital was never quiet: she could hear marching soldiers, the groans of the sick and wounded, and the rumble of heavy cannon at all hours of the day or night.[6] (One of the patients reported a more pleasant version of the constant noise of an occupied city: "I hear from my room, from the time I first wake in the morning till I go to sleep at night the clank, clank, clank, of the soldiers (artillery & cavalry) swords as they rattle on the sidewalk as they are passing up & down. That sound is almost

as regular as the ticking of a clock, from morning till night."[7])
The quartermaster's storehouses now crowded the previously
deserted wharves. Train depots that had thronged with residents fleeing Alexandria now teemed with troops and supplies
on the move. Camps for the growing army sprang up on the
surrounding hillsides, and shantytowns filled with escaped
slaves, known at the time as "contrabands," who had found
their way to the relative safety of the Union-occupied city.

Occupied Alexandria also needed to make provisions for
another growing population: the sick and wounded who poured
into the city, a thousand or more at a time, from the battlefields
at Bull Run, the Peninsular Campaign, Cedar Mountain, Fredericksburg, and Shiloh, carried by boats and trains, in horse-
drawn ambulances, and, after Bull Run, on their own exhausted
legs. Dr. John H. Brinton reported at one point in late August
1862, during his brief tenure as the medical director of transportation in Alexandria, that he was on his feet for three days
and two nights assigning the wounded to hospitals as they
arrived.[8] On August 30 alone, after the Second Battle of Bull
Run, four hundred vehicles of various sorts, nearly two thousand horses and mules, and more than one thousand drivers
and attendants were needed to recover the wounded from the
battlefield. Just as the growing army needed camps and barracks, the growing army of the wounded needed hospitals.

Mansion House Occupied

Alexandria was the site of the first general hospital the
Medical Bureau opened after the First Battle of Bull Run: Hallowell's School, which was converted into the Old Hallowell

Hospital. The building was used as a school from 1832 to 1860, when the principal closed it in order to give out-of-town students a chance to get home safely before the war broke out. Besides, he admitted, he found it "almost impossible to direct the minds of students to profitable study"[9] with the distraction of war on the horizon. The four-story building was dark, damp, and dirty, with narrow stairways. Its only toilet facilities were outhouses located more than forty yards away—inconvenient but probably more sanitary than establishments like the Union Hotel, where the location of the water closets contributed to the spread of waste-born diseases. It had room for not quite one hundred beds. It soon became clear that more facilities would be needed.

By the end of the war, Alexandria had thirty-three military hospitals of different sizes and designed for different purposes, not including the infamous Camp Convalescent located outside the city, known by those condemned to stay there as Camp Misery. One of those hospitals was the Mansion House Hospital, formerly Green's Mansion House Hotel.

For several months after Alexandria was seized, Union officers were billeted at the Mansion House Hotel and at Green's home, the adjacent Carlyle House, the "mansion" for which Mansion House was named. In his diary, Green's son complained about the noise and the manners of their new "guests." Those who were billeted at the Green home kept the family awake, dancing and singing overhead, while those at the Mansion House were making a mess that would require months of cleaning and repair. The Greens would soon wish noisy Union officers were all they had to complain about.

In November 1861, James Green received a letter notifying him that the government was confiscating the hotel for use as a hospital. They gave him two days to vacate, but even with the help of his employees from the furniture factory it took more than a week to move everything. The government offered Green a large rent for the mandatory use of the hotel, but when the first month's payment came due, he learned that rent payments depended on his taking an oath of allegiance to the United States government. He refused, leaving the rent uncollected.

Mansion House Hospital was the largest of the army's fourteen general hospitals in Alexandria, with 516 beds and a library with an organ on the first floor, where those soldiers who were ambulatory could read and gather for church services. Joseph Spafford, a soldier from the Fourth Vermont Regiment who was diagnosed with pleurisy and sent to Mansion House from his regiment in April 1862, wrote a remarkably enthusiastic account of the hospital's accommodations, telling his family that "they keep everything as slick & nice as at any Hotel." He even raved about the rations: "We have bread & butter, oysters, chicken, roast beef, boiled beef, and in fact as good as we could ask if it were a Hotel & we were stoping here."[10] This is a glowing description of military hospital food that does not match that given in other sources for the period. Possibly he did not want his mother to worry.

Mary von Olnhausen's first impression of the hospital, several months later, was that it was loud, confused, and crowded. The surgical ward showed its origins as a hotel with many small rooms opening off of a broad hallway, a design that was not efficient for its new purpose. So many cots were crammed into each room that it was barely possible to pass between them, even without the forbidden hoops under her skirts.[11] Spafford, looking at the hospital with the eyes of a man who had recently arrived from the mud and gore of the field in a horse-drawn ambulance, was more positive: "This Hos [*sic*] is a splendid building, I think the best in the city."[12]

Mary Phinney von Olnhausen Arrives at Mansion House

Mary Phinney von Olnhausen arrived in Washington in August 1862, shortly after what she described as "that awful Cedar Mountain battle."[13]

On August 9, a corps of Union soldiers led by General Nathaniel P. Banks stumbled upon Stonewall Jackson's infantry at the base of Cedar Mountain, near Culpeper Court House, Virginia, also known prior to the battle as Slaughter's Mountain. One Union army surgeon remarked that it was "truly named for the slaughter was tremendous on both sides."[14] Outnumbered three to one by Jackson, Banks lost more than a third of his men: 314 killed, 1,445 wounded, and 622 missing.[15] As was so often the case in the Civil War, the horror continued after the battle was over.

Thomas A. McParlin, medical director of the federal Army of Virginia at the time and later medical director of the Army of the Potomac, established dressing stations near the battlefield and an evacuation hospital at Culpeper Court House, where military trains could take on the wounded and carry them the fifty miles to Alexandria. By the next day it was clear to him that the surgeons on the ground, overwhelmed by the numbers of wounded, had lost track of the primary goal: sending the wounded to Alexandria. Instead they focused on the amputations they believed were needed to save men's lives; one doctor alone performed twenty-two thigh amputations and an uncounted number of arm amputations in a twenty-four-hour period.

There was no one to attend to soldiers with relatively minor wounds. Supplies and tempers ran short. Even though trains were available, every building that could be turned into a shelter—churches, the Masonic hall, private homes, and even a tobacco barn—were filled with hundreds of wounded men. Hundreds more lay in the hot August sun awaiting evacuation, many of them dehydrated and groaning for water. McParlin sent the orders a second time, reminding doctors that the wounded were to be sent on by train as soon after they arrived as possible. Hours later, he discovered that nothing had changed; he went to Culpeper Court House himself and saw to it personally that the first train of railroad cars was loaded with men and on its way.[16] After nine days of hell, the last trainload of wounded from Culpeper Court House reached Washington on August 18.

When von Olnhausen first arrived in Washington she expected to go to Culpeper Court House. Miss Dix had just received a telegram that there were four hundred soldiers lying there with their wounds undressed and no one to care for them. "She goes herself and takes me," she wrote to her friends at home in Lexington. "So already the work has begun."[17] Instead, some change of plan led Dix to place von Olnhausen at Mansion House Hospital in Alexandria, possibly in response to an appeal from Medical Director McParlin for volunteers—

specifically "surgeons and nurses (male)"[18]—to come to Alexandria to help with the wounded. The call for "nurses (male)" would have been an irresistible challenge to Dix.

As she often did, Dix accompanied the new nurse to her assignment, perhaps in this case because she wanted to warn von Olnhausen that the surgeon in charge of Mansion House was determined to keep Dix nurses out of his hospital. Von Olnhausen was to ignore whatever trouble he gave her and not complain about how she was treated no matter what happened. It was not a reassuring start to a new job.

Once at Mansion House, Dix left von Olnhausen in the hospital office and went in search of the chief surgeon, Dr. Alfred Summers. While she waited, von Olnhausen watched the wounded from Cedar Ridge arrive. All of them were in the condition in which they had been taken off the battlefield. Some of them had lain outside in the summer heat for three or four days "almost without clothing, their wounds never dressed, so dirty and so wretched."[19] Those who could walk were helped on foot into the hospital. The worst were carried in on stretchers. Those who died in the hospital were carried out almost as quickly. Von Olnhausen worried that it was more than she could bear and feared that Miss Dix would never return. It seemed to von Olnhausen like she had waited forever.

Finally the nursing superintendent arrived with Dr. Summers, who looked von Olnhausen over with what seemed to her to be a savage eye. He told her he had no room for her. Dix had not yet succeeded in her efforts to place her nurses at Mansion House, and the doctor intended to keep them out. Dix was aware that Summers intended to make the hospital so uncomfortable for von Olnhausen that the new nurse wouldn't stay long, but she was determined that von Olnhausen tough it out. When von Olnhausen told Dix she could not stay if she didn't have a place to sleep, Dix brushed aside the forty-year-old volunteer's concerns and told her, "My child . . . you will stay where I have placed you."[20]

With no room of her own, von Olnhausen slept at the bedside of her patients or in a corner of one of the rooms for several weeks. Occasionally one of the other nurses would "extend the hospitality of the floor" in her room to von Olnhausen, who would have a straw bed dragged in and get a few hours of rest. "It was no use to complain," she wrote in her half-finished memoir. "The surgeon simply stormed at me and said there was no room." When Miss Dix arrived at the hospital on one of her whirlwind visits, she would tell von Olnhausen, "You can bear it awhile my child; I have placed you here and you must stay."[21]

It was often difficult to arrange housing for female nurses, a problem doctors used as a means of keeping female nurses out of the hospitals. Where some limited space was available, such as in former hotels and boarding schools, nurses slept in hospital closets or packed together in a single room. In some hospitals, nurses hung a curtain across a corner to create a space for themselves. In the most extreme cases, nurses were quartered in private homes as much as three miles away from the hospitals where they worked.

Even after a nurse had been assigned space in a hospital, circumstances were always subject to change. The arrival of a new nurse could mean a private room had to be shared. When patients' family members arrived, often having traveled a long distance and with little means to support themselves in a strange city, nurses grumbled yet shared their quarters. Von Olnhausen, having finally been assigned a room of her own, tells of a period when a revolving cast of incoming nurses and family members visiting patients left her with five women to find sleeping quarters for. She managed to find empty beds for two of them in her ward, "but we were still four,—all widows, all old, and all but me exceedingly pious, and ministers' widows at that." Sleeping was hard enough, with "only bedding for two, and the room not large." Crowded rooms created the added problem of lack of privacy: with her unwanted visitors sitting in her room all day Sunday, then Monday, then Tuesday, it was impossible to write letters or even keep the room tidy. She couldn't dress or wash in peace and the ward was so cold she could not sit there with any comfort. Between lack of privacy and running errands for her hapless visitors, she was completely worn out by the time she had the room to herself once more.

Von Olnhausen was just starting to feel settled when all her arrangements were turned upside down by the arrival of a new nurse at the hospital, one who claimed to have served in the Crimea. Von Olnhausen was not sure she believed the new nurse's tales of the Crimea, but admitted there was no doubt she was English and an experienced nurse.

Anne Reading Arrives at Mansion House

Anne Reading's introduction to Mansion House Hospital was considerably different from von Olnhausen's. Reading arrived in Washington from New York City on the afternoon of August 20, after traveling all night and morning. She went straight to Miss Dix's home, where she learned that the ever peripatetic Dix was in Baltimore.

Dix's servants sent Reading to the Union Hospital in Georgetown, which served as a way station for nurses while they waited for their assignments. Reading was not as vehement as Alcott and others in her condemnation of the hospital, possibly because she had just spent four months on the hospital transport ships, but she certainly wasn't impressed. The hospital steward showed her into a room "with nothing in it but three miserable looking little beds" and two strangers with whom she would share the room. Having been promised breakfast, she went downstairs "expecting a comfortable repast." Instead the steward gave her coffee, "such miserable stuff, little more than colored water . . . That, and a piece of dry bread composed my breakfast. I might certainly have had butter if I chose but the smell of it almost made me sick so I did not venture to taste it."[22]

Miss Dix greeted her the next morning with enthusiasm: she had so many places that needed a good nurse that she hardly knew where to send Reading. Since the nursing supervisor had a morning full of tasks to complete, she settled Reading in a comfortable chair with the morning papers, a pile of books, and a plate of "sweet cracknels"—a brief respite between the squalor of Union Hospital and the challenges of a new assignment.

In the afternoon, Reading, still unsure of her final destination, traveled to Alexandria with Dix and a woman who had come to Washington specifically to visit the different hospitals in the region. After inspecting several of Alexandria's hospitals, they came to the Mansion House. Reading noted in her journal that "almost everyone employed there had some grievance to complain of. The nurses said they were overworked and the Doctors did not behave well to them. As for the surgeon in charge, he was a perfect brute and much more to the same effect. Miss Dix smiled, and said to me 'This is the very place you should come to, for you do not mind these horrid doctors and these poor things are so afraid of them that it makes them miserable.'" Reading thought it sounded like an unpleasant situation, but she needed the work and was determined to make the best of things, so she kept her peace.

Reading's first encounter with Dr. Summers was similar to von Olnhausen's. Dix accosted him on the street and said, "Good morning, Doctor. I have found a most excellent nurse for you." He spun around and snarled what seems to have been his stock answer to the arrival of a new Dix nurse: "Madam, I have not room for another nurse." According to Reading, he changed his position when Dix told him who Reading was and where she had worked before. The Nightingale reference worked its magic once more.

The evening Reading arrived, Dr. Summers assigned her to a small ward with some severe cases. The next morning, while dressing her patients' wounds, she amazed the doctor with her technique, the English method of bandaging being different than that practiced in the United States. He soon brought several other doctors into her ward to observe her skills.

The next day Dr. Summers sent for Reading. She found him in conversation with several others doctors and tried to excuse herself, but he waved her back. "Madam, I am going to give you charge of the large medical ward." He then announced to the other doctors, "Gentlemen, this is the best nurse I ever met with. She can dress wounds equal to any surgeon and not one of our people can compare with her in putting on a bandage."[23]

Von Olnhausen had previously been in charge of the ward that Summers transferred to Reading. She did not take the change well.

Von Olnhausen's account of Summers's transfer of the ward is remarkably close to Reading's; if anything, Summers is even more complimentary of Reading in von Olnhausen's version of events, not only proclaiming that Reading was the most splendid nurse in the country, but that she was the kind of woman he intended to fill the hospital with. To make matters worse, von Olnhausen had to share her room with Reading for several weeks, until Reading's sister Jenny, also an experienced hospital nurse, joined her in mid-September.

"I almost preferred no bed, as at first," she wrote to her family in what she described as a "growling letter." "But I would not say one word it seems so selfish to complain here."[24] She then proceeded to complain at length. By her account, the ward was without a female nurse for a long time before she took charge of it. She worked hard to get it clean and orderly, and to get rid of the ward master, who was "a horrid wicked man" who "treated the patients too cruelly."[25] Now, moved to a smaller, less difficult ward, she found she just wasn't as interested in the new patients. Her heart was still in the old ward. She acknowledged Reading's superiority in bandaging but condemned Reading in terms based on the conventional assessment of professional nurses at the time, saying, "Like all old hospital nurses, [she] is no nurse otherwise."[26] Von Olnhausen's care of her patients was as all encompassing as a mother with a seriously ill child. She cooked special dishes for them, watched over them at night when they needed her, and only left her ward to eat or sleep. By contrast, Reading went over her patients' wounds several times a day but did not spend all her time in the wards, keeping a routine that sounds very similar to that of the Nightingale hospital in the Crimea, in which nurses attended patients in the wards at regular times unless the press of newly arrived wounded required nurses to work round the clock. It is possible that Reading, if asked, might in turn have declared her new co-worker "no nurse."

Von Olnhausen ends her account with a description of Reading's first moments in her new ward, an incident that, for obvious reasons, does not appear in Reading's journal. Just as von Olnhausen was leaving her old ward, she heard a horrible noise in the entry. Looking out, she saw Reading being dragged along by two officers, dead drunk and swearing like a trooper. "So that's the way she took possession of her new ward!" she told her correspondents. "I think my exit was better than her entrance."[27]

Hostile Doctors and Inexperienced Nurses

Dr. Summers was not the only physician to oppose the introduction of female nurses, especially ones chosen by Dorothea Dix, into army hospitals. In fact, meeting a hostile doctor was almost a rite of passage for nurses as they arrived at a new hospital.

Georgeanna Woolsey, writing later about the early days of the war, described their shared experience: "No one knows who did not watch the thing from the beginning, how much opposition, how much ill-will, how much unfeeling want of thought, these women nurses endured. Hardly a surgeon whom I can think of received or treated them with even common courtesy.

Government had decided that women should be employed, and the Army surgeons—unable, therefore, to close the hospitals against them—determined to make their lives so unbearable that they should be forced in self-defence to leave. It seemed a matter of cool calculation."[28]

Many doctors objected to women in military hospitals on the grounds of feminine delicacy, both mental and physical. An anonymous doctor summed up this position in a letter to the influential *American Medical Times*. "S. G." shared his concerns regarding the ability of women to do anything more than give the "delicate, soothing attentions which are always so grateful to the sick, and which . . . none know so well how to give, as do noble, sensible, tender-hearted women." He argued that male surgical cases required "strong arms and attentions which any reasonable man is loath to exact from female nurses," making female nurses not only an annoyance in the ward but a "useless annoyance."[29] Many shared S. G.'s sentiments; it was commonly believed that working in a hospital would coarsen even the most refined woman. As one surgeon in Alexandria told Harriet Dada, "A lady ceases to be a lady when she becomes a nurse."[30]

The opposite side of the fear that working in a hospital would erode female delicacy were concerns about the effect of women on the morals of the patients. One doctor beseeched Surgeon General William Hammond to issue an order prohibiting nurses from "throwing themselves into the Arms of Sick & Wounded soldiers and Lasciviously Exciting their Animal passions."[31] (Presumably these nurses had ceased to be ladies.) Another told the surgeon general he thought women in the hospital's laundry and kitchen was a good thing. Not only were both the hospital and the men cleaner, but the moral effect of a woman's presence rendered the patients "more amenable to control." But when those same women became nurses "laying aside the natural delicacy of the sex, the proper respect for them is lost or forgotten and they become worse than useless."[32] In all hospitals, any question that a woman's virtue had been compromised was grounds for dismissal, even when proven false.

Some doctors resisted working with volunteer female nurses on the seemingly reasonable grounds of their lack of training: the same factor that made a difference in Summers's reception of von Olnhausen and Reading. Looked at more closely, the question of lack of training becomes less clear. Soldiers who were assigned to nurse during their convalescence had no more training than the women they worked alongside, and could not even claim the domestic experience of nursing family members. Moreover, a large number of the doctors who volunteered for Lincoln's ninety-day service were as ill trained for battlefield medicine as the nurses they objected to. John Brinton, who had studied in the clinic- and laboratory-based medical programs in Paris and Vienna, derided the quality of most of the medical volunteers he worked with during the war, saying that the doctors and nurses alike were seldom of any use. With no training, they did not know how to take care of the soldiers. In some cases, they barely knew how to take care of themselves in the context of war. He was particularly dismissive of the volunteer nurses, whether they came through Miss Dix or the Sanitary Commission: "helpless, irritable and unhappy; each one thinking herself of much importance, and acting under the direct orders of the Secretary of War, and very often indeed they had seen him before starting." In his opinion, the doctors, for whom he at least expressed some sympathy, were often not much better.[33] Doctors who objected to female nurses on the grounds of lack of training often agreed with Brinton that "good women nurses were a godsend; those who would really nurse and work," by which he meant women who would do what they were told, not advocate for individual patients, and make no trouble.[34]

By Brinton's irritable standards, few of the volunteer nurses made the grade as "good women nurses." Nonetheless, in the end, most of the women who took a nursing position in one of the army's hospitals wore down individual doctors' objections to their presence as they learned how to do the job. The longer a nurse was on the job, the more likely she was to conquer the prejudice of the doctors she worked with.

Even Dr. Summers came to value von Olnhausen. In a letter dated January 1863, she proudly reported: "You will be glad to know the change in Dr. S's treatment of me. I guess he finds it creditable to him to have some ladies around."

One night when they were expecting a batch of wounded, he came to her door and politely asked her to go through her ward with him. Von Olnhausen showed him around with considerable pride: clean beds and fresh clothing waited for the incoming men, the fires were bright and warm, and sponges, cold water, and medical supplies lay ready for use.

Summers complimented her on the condition of the ward, and told her none of the other wards were in such good condition. She beamed. Then he turned to her and asked if he could come to her room for a few minutes as he had something to say to her. It was a startling request. At the time even middle-aged widows who bathed unknown men in the course of their workday did not entertain men to whom they were not related in their rooms. Nonetheless, she agreed.

Once in the privacy of her room, Summers apologized for the fact that he had sometimes been rude to her. He said she thought he did not like her and then boomed in a voice "about three times louder than a bull," "But madam, you are mistaken; I am more than satisfied; I would have you leave on no account; you have done and are doing more to elevate the tone of this hospital than anyone in it, and anything you ask for your ward or for yourself I will grant . . . with you . . . , madam, this house shall be the first hospital in the country."[35]

Signs of progress and professionalism appeared as the war went on, one doctor and one nurse at a time.

Chapter 6

Learning by Experience

"Custom inures the most sensitive person to
that which is at first most repellent, and in the late
war we saw the most delicate women, who could not at
home endure the sight of blood, become so used to
scenes of carnage, that they walked the hospitals and
the margins of battlefield, amid the poor remnants
of torn humanity, with as perfect self-possession
as if they were strolling in a flower garden."
—Mark Twain and Charles Dudley Warner,
The Gilded Age[1]

"It will be necessary to imbibe a little more of the
heroic before I can be of much help during an
operation . . . All laughed at me even to the patient;
but it isn't expected that a Yankee school-ma'am can
be transformed into a dissecting surgeon in a
minute, guess it will take about a fortnight."
—Elvira Powers, *Hospital Pencillings*[2]

Few of the new nurses had training in either medical pro-
cedures or practice. Volunteers with no experience other
than nursing a relative through a bout of measles, pneumonia, typhoid, or dysentery—all serious illnesses requiring
dedication, courage, and, in some cases, a lack of queasiness—
were plunged into the chaos of crowded hospitals and a stream
of broken bodies that rose and fell according to the fortunes of

war. Brains oozing from head wounds. Jaws half shot off. Gut wounds. Perforated lungs. Gangrenous limbs. When the wounded arrived—fifty, four hundred, or a thousand at a time—no one had the time or inclination to take a newly fledged nurse aside to show her how to dress a wound or explain the system. Many volunteers began nursing without even the most basic introduction to the work they were there to do.

On Mary Phinney von Olnhausen's first night at Mansion House Hospital, the wounded from Cedar Mountain flowed through the door, ragged, mud-caked, and bloody. Their bandages looked like they had not been changed since someone first dressed their wounds. And their faces were drawn with exhaustion and pain. Von Olnhausen had no chance to find her way around the hospital or learn her duties. Instead an orderly showed her into the surgical ward and someone told her *what* to do, but not how to do it. As a young woman she had been the unofficial nurse and surgeon for every scrape and wound suffered by her venturesome neighbors. It was not adequate preparation for dealing with the effects of cannon shells, bayonets, and the new deadly bullets known as minnie balls on the human body. Faced with carnage on a scale she had not been able to imagine, she wanted to throw herself down and give up. It seemed like a hopeless task. How could she do anything to help them? The only thing she could do for them now was learn: she followed the doctors and watched as they examined and dressed soldiers' wounds. "So I began my work," she wrote in her unfinished memoir, "I might say night and day."[3]

Von Olnhausen's experience was not unusual.

Hannah Ropes, later Alcott's supervisor, arrived at the Union Hotel Hospital in Washington the morning of July 4,

1862, just as the wounded from the final days of the Seven Days' Battles began to reach the city. She ate a slice of boiled beef and a loaf of bread and caught a few moments' sleep before the hospital sergeant woke her up to tell her the wounded were on the way and the hospital staff needed to get ready. Most of the nurses were away for the evening, so Ropes and a young doctor hurried to make beds and prepare supplies for 150 men, including clean shirts, drawers, and stockings. Only six patients arrived that night. The staff went to bed, expecting to be called out again at any moment. Morning came, and still no wounded arrived.

It was afternoon before Ropes heard "a quick step over our private stairs in a wing of the "castle" and a voice: "All of the nurses report at the office of the surgeon." When she and the other nurses ran down the main hall stairs they saw "from the broad open entrance into the hall, to the base of the staircase, there bent, clung, and stood, in dumb silence, fifty soldiers, grim, dirty, muddy and wounded." She does not seem to have been as overcome by the prospect as von Olnhausen, perhaps because the men reminded her of her son "in fifty duplicates." Ropes's first job was to stand by the doctor while he took the name of each soldier and assigned him a bed. (Georgeanna Woolsey would have approved. She argued constantly with surgeons on the hospital transport ships that it was important to learn the name of each wounded man as he arrived.) Like Mansion House, the building was poorly designed for its new purpose. Men had to be led or lifted up the great staircase to the ballroom and banquet hall on the second floor that served as wards. Once there, the nurses divided them up and washed them. It took four hours.[4]

Alcott arrived at Union Hotel hospital that December. Unlike von Olnhausen's experience at Mansion House, she had the luxury of three days to learn her way around the wards before the wounded from Fredericksburg arrived. It wasn't long enough. Her nursing career began with the death of a patient. Then another nurse left unexpectedly, and she was plunged into responsibility for a forty-bed ward, housing one man with pneumonia, one with diphtheria, two with typhoid, and "a dozen dilapidated patriots, hopping, lying and lounging about." She spent her time washing faces, serving rations, giving medicine, and sitting on a very hard chair while her patients stared at the new nurse, who tried to hide her discomfort under "as matronly an aspect as a spinster could assume." It was not quite what she had expected. There was no romance in bathing fevered brows. In fact, she was a little bored. So when she heard wounded were "in-coming," she felt a thrill of excitement, for just a moment. Then she "peeped into the dusky street lined with what I at first had innocently called market carts, now unloading their sad freight at our door . . . and I indulged in a most unpatriotic wish that I was safe at home again, with a quiet day before me."[5]

It was job training of the roughest, least structured kind.

Dr. Elizabeth Blackwell's Nurse Training Program

At the beginning of the Civil War, the primary source of trained nurses in the United States were the nuns who staffed twenty-eight Catholic hospitals throughout the country, several hundred of whom served in army hospitals over the course of the war. There were no nursing schools in the United States, although at least two programs existed in Europe: the school in

Kaiserwerth, Germany, where Florence Nightingale trained, and Nightingale's own school at St. Thomas Hospital in London, which opened in June 1860.

Ironically, it was easier for an American woman to become a doctor than a trained nurse in the years immediately before the Civil War. Although most medical schools remained closed to women, the first certified female doctors founded women's medical schools in Boston, Philadelphia, and New York in the 1850s and 1860s. By 1861, there were more than two hundred women in the United States with a medical degree. It was not an easy career path. Even after earning a degree, most graduates of women's medical colleges were denied access to the wards of big-city general hospitals—which remained the best place to obtain clinical experience—and most found it difficult to attract patients to a private practice unless they worked with their fathers or husbands. Barred from working in existing institutions, female doctors created separate women's medical institutions like dispensaries and hospitals, aimed at the same population of urban poor served by the larger general hospitals. The first of these was the New York Infirmary for Women and Children, founded in 1857 by physicians Elizabeth and Emily Blackwell and Marie Zakrzewska.

Born in England in 1821, a year after Florence Nightingale, to a family of reformers, Elizabeth Blackwell was the first woman in the world to become a doctor with a degree from a certified medical school. Her family moved to the United States while she was child, where they eventually settled in Cincinnati, Ohio. As far as contemporary opinion was concerned, Blackwell's ambition to become a doctor was even more shocking than Nightingale's desire to become a nurse. Unlike Nightingale, her family supported her aspirations, but she met with far more resistance from the world at large. Twenty years after Blackwell received her degree, many people still shared the opinion of Professor Thomas Laycock of the University of Edinburgh, who "could not imagine *any decent woman* wishing to study medicine;—as for any *lady,* that was out of the question."[6] In addition to a general perception that medicine was no job for a respectable woman, many male doctors discouraged women from entering the profession because they were afraid they would lose female patients to female doctors, especially for intimate problems. In fact, Blackwell's desire to go into medicine was inspired by a friend dying of what was probably uterine cancer and who wished she could have been examined by a female doctor rather than undergoing the embarrassment of being examined by a male.

Blackwell was lucky enough to find an experienced physician willing to teach her despite her gender—the same career path taken by most of her male counterparts, who typically apprenticed with established doctors for several years before opening their own practice or attending medical school. After two years of study as an apprentice, she moved to Philadelphia, then the center of medical study in the United States, and began applying to medical schools. She had plenty of individual mentors, but they made no difference. Twenty-nine medical schools refused to admit her. She became so frustrated that one of her advisors, Dr. Joseph Pancoast, suggested she attend his classes in Philadelphia disguised as a man, a solution she rejected because it would only give her the knowledge and not the degree. Finally, Geneva Medical College in upstate New York accepted her as a student.

Her acceptance at Geneva was a fluke. While in Philadelphia, she had impressed a famous physician, Dr. Joseph Warrington, who recommended her as a student to Geneva. The school's administrators didn't want to accept her but they also didn't want to upset Dr. Warrington. They decided to let the students vote on whether to let her in, sure they would reject her. By all accounts, the students believed the application was a joke perpetrated by a rival medical school. To the administrators' surprise, and perhaps horror, the students unanimously voted to admit Blackwell. In January 1849, after a year of study, she graduated first in her class, at the age of twenty-eight.

Her degree did not immediately open doors for other women. In fact, after the newly established American Medical Association censured Geneva Medical College for issuing her degree, the school's president announced that Blackwell's acceptance had been an experiment, not a precedent. The college subsequently refused to accept any more female students, including Blackwell's sister Emily.

In the fall of 1849, Blackwell went to Paris, motivated by the same quest for clinical experience that drove many of her male contemporaries abroad. In Paris, she once again faced a male medical establishment hostile to the idea of female doctors and was unable to obtain permission to attend clinical instruction. And once again, well-intentioned men suggested she attend clinical demonstrations dressed as a man.

Instead she decided, with great reluctance, to accept the advice of Pierre Louis, a French physician now known for his contributions to what would become epidemiology and the modern clinical trial. At his suggestion, she entered La Maternité, then the world's leading maternity hospital and training school for midwives, where she could gain more practical experience in obstetrics in a short time than she could get anywhere else. For four months she lived in a dormitory with twenty Frenchwomen, most of them ten years younger than she was and, by her standards, uneducated in anything other than their chosen profession. In many ways the program was more difficult than most American medical schools at the time. It was certainly more focused. In addition to a full course of lectures, students spent several days each week *en service*—working in the maternity wards and clinics. They were not allowed newspapers or any books unrelated to medicine. It was a world entirely separate from that experienced by male medical students in Paris. Near the end of her studies at La Maternité, Blackwell contracted a serious infection that cost her the sight in one eye and ended her hopes for a career as a surgeon.

After Paris, Blackwell spent several months as a clinical student at St. Bartholomew's Hospital in London. She returned to New York in the summer of 1851, where she realized her struggle to be a doctor had just begun. In some ways getting a medical education had been the easy part. Her private practice was slow to develop, and she was not allowed to work in the city's hospitals, not even the women's wards. She faced more than institutional roadblocks. Because many people believed "female doctor" was a euphemism for abortionist, landlords did not want to rent her office space, and she received anonymous hate mail. Finally she started her own dispensary on New York's East Side, which later developed into the New York Infirmary for Women and Children. The infirmary had three goals: to provide medical treatment to women and children by women physicians, to give clinical instruction to female medical students, and to train nurses.

Blackwell saw the Civil War as a challenge to those involved with medicine and sanitation. She was particularly concerned about the lack of trained nurses for the Union army. Under her leadership, one of the first acts of the Women's Central Association of Relief was to offer a course on basic nursing techniques at the New York Infirmary for Women. Blackwell and the WCAR committee chose a group of ninety-one women from a large number of applicants, including Georgeanna Woolsey and Harriet Dada. Woolsey was not sure she would pass the interview. Her family thought she was too young, too pretty, and too full of nonsense to be a nurse. Before going to her interview, she took the flowers out of her bonnet and the flounce off her dress so she would look like less of a "fly-away." Finally, she passed, the examining board having inadvertently left the space blank where her age should have been.

Blackwell gave her students nine lectures on subjects that included wound care and hygiene, but the heart of the program was a month working in the wards at Bellevue Hospital, where they learned practical nursing. Woolsey described the program as "a month's seasoning in painful sights and sounds." On May 14, 1861, she presented herself at the hospital for instruction, armed with a blue ticket that identified her as one of the WCAR's students. She and twenty other women were led through the hospital in procession and assigned wards. Left in the middle of a long ward filled with beds of sick men, she panicked for a moment. Then she and her partner took off their bonnets and went to work.

Her first day in the ward, she was shocked when the young house doctor barked at her, "Nurse, basin!" She handed him the basin promptly. Just as promptly, she fainted when she saw a wound probed for the first time. But over the course of the month she and her associates learned as much as they could in a short time. Their days began at six in the morning and lasted late into the afternoon. They heard bedside lectures from the house doctors as they made their rounds, wrote down every-thing they saw, and made elaborate sketches of all kinds of bandages and the ways of applying them. Woolsey bandaged everyone she met for practice, until she could make her "reverses" without a wrinkle. At the end of the month, she felt she and her fellow students were competent to deal with "any very small emergency, or very simple fracture."[7]

By the end of Blackwell's course, her students may have been better trained in what to expect than many of the doctors who joined the army. Even with this level of training, Dix did not accept all of the women who completed Blackwell's course, but most of them found a place to serve with or without her approval.

Blackwell's original ninety-one women were the only ones she trained as nurses for the Civil War. Shortly after the first class "graduated," the United States Sanitary Commission was approved. Bellows and the other male leaders of the Sanitary Commission abandoned the WCAR's goal of recruiting and training nurses in favor of what they saw as bigger issues than the care of individuals.

Binding Wounds

Most volunteer nurses did not arrive on the job "competent to any very small emergency, or very simple fracture." Their skill levels were closer to those of Mary Phinney von Olnhausen, who recognized that she was horribly ignorant and could do no more than try to make the men comfortable.

The most obvious skill nurses needed to learn, and the one they took the most pride in mastering, was how to dress and bandage a wound. Even as late as February 1865, when von Olnhausen could account herself an experienced nurse, she fluttered with pleasure when the army medical director who supervised the region where she was then stationed sent word that "his nine surgeons, after examining those wounds, said they had never seen wounds so well dressed and such bad wounds soon getting well; and, for himself, that I was the best wound-dresser in the country."[8]

Depending on the nature of the injury, dressing a wound could be more than a simple matter of replacing a soiled bandage with a clean one, as Elvira Powers realized soon after her arrival at Jefferson General Hospital in Indiana, when she was asked to hold a soldier's gangrenous arm while a more experienced nurse changed the dressing. The wound had previously been packed with bromine-saturated oakum—a fibrous material made by unpicking tarred rope that some doctors of the time considered preferable to cotton lint as a dressing thanks to its superior absorption and the supposed decay-inhibiting qualities of the tar. Now it was time to remove it. The red and swollen elbow of the soldier's arm rested in Powers's hand while the senior nurse used a pair of pincers to pick off first the pus-soaked oakum and then burnt pieces of flesh from the edge of the raw wound. Powers remained steady until the man began to cry for mercy and his elbow quivered in her palm. Knowing from past experience that they might have another patient to care for in a moment if she stayed, she dropped the arm into the hand of another nurse "and mentally calling upon the heroism of all the braves [she] had ever heard" reeled to the tent opening. After a moment in the fresh air, the danger of fainting passed. "All laughed at me," Powers reported ruefully, even the patient.[9]

For a wound to heal, dead and infected matter had to be removed, a process that could be undertaken with surgical tools, topical disinfectants like bromine, iodine, or common vinegar, or as Powers discovered, bandages that would pull infected tissue away when changed. In some cases dressings needed to be changed many times a day. Hannah Ropes, writing to her daughter Alice several weeks after arriving at Union House Hospital, told her, "I have now learned how to take care of a shoulder wound. They are slow to cure and must have many dressings a day. Indeed, I had no idea it was such a slow and painful process—the uncertainty about what is in the wound, the waiting for the indications suppuration alone furnishes."[10]

Exploding cannon balls shattered soldiers' arms and legs. Falling horses crushed them. They received an occasional bayonet stab or saber slash. But musket balls caused the vast majority of wounds at roughly 94 percent. The soft lead bullets known as minnie balls, in particular, caused far worse damage than a modern steel-jacket cartridge would. With a hollow cylindrical base and a rounded conical nose, minnie balls flattened when they met human flesh, tearing through muscle and bone. When hit, bones would splinter and shatter into hundreds of spicules: sharp, bony shreds that the force of the bullet drove through muscle and skin. These bullets usually lodged in the body and almost always left an infected wound that would seldom heal and often lead to amputation.

It was a rare nurse who could bring herself to help at amputations. Mary Newcomb, who amputated a soldier's finger when no doctor was available and claimed, "I believe I could have taken off an arm or leg without flinching" was an exception.[11] Amanda Akins Stearn's experience was more typical. She viewed her first amputation on June 18, 1864, after she had been in service in Washington's Armory Square Hospital for fourteen months. A soldier under her care needed to have his arm amputated and she "suddenly came to the determination to witness it," if she could find the nerve and someone to accompany her. She and two other nurses, Sisters Grigg and Israel, attended the operation. Israel felt faint and had to leave the room for a time, but soon returned. Stearns managed to stay until they tied off the arteries. At that point her legs began to shake and a wave of nausea came over her. She decided it was prudent to leave. She retreated to the ward, where she sat for a while with some camphor, one of the ingredients used to make smelling salts. Eventually the ward master walked her back to her quarters. According to Stearns, Sister Grigg was made of sterner stuff and "never wavered to the end."[12]

Tending the Whole Man

Bandaging wounds, "putting up" splints, and assisting at amputations were the most dramatic part of nurses' work. But, in fact, most of the soldiers who ended up in the Union army hospitals were struck down by an enemy more insidious than a minnie ball from a Confederate musket. Infectious diseases, including pneumonia, cholera, malaria, dysentery, and typhoid, accounted for 64 percent of the deaths among enlisted men in the Union army. (The rate was lower among officers, who enjoyed better-quality food and less crowded living conditions, but were also twice as likely as enlisted men to be killed in action.) Providing fluids, nourishing food, clean bed linens and clothing, and physical and emotional comfort was often as important as any medical treatment.

Many of the tasks women undertook in the hospitals were domestic chores writ large: feeding patients, making beds, overseeing and sometimes doing laundry. Writing two years after the war, Jane Hoge, one of the leaders of the Chicago branch of the United States Sanitary Commission, claimed that women's domestic skills were essential to running a hospital: "The right of women to the sphere which includes housekeeping, cooking and nursing has never been in dispute. The proper administration of these three departments makes the internal arrangements of a hospital complete."[13] Hoge wrote about the domestic aspect of nursing from the perspective of a woman who did not empty bedpans on a regular basis during the war. Women who put in their time on the hospital floor took a less elevated position on the daily chores of nursing.

Each of the domestic tasks brought its own challenges. Feeding patients, for instance, was seldom as simple as delivering trays to the bedside. Nurses coaxed along patients who had trouble digesting or were particularly weak with glasses of eggnog, milk punch, beef tea, and an occasional sip of brandy and water. The more disabled patients required physical help to eat or drink. Even carrying trays from kitchen to ward could be a challenge at some of the hospitals that had been converted from other uses, like Mansion House. Von Olnhausen groused about having to go up and down four long flights of stairs ten or fifteen times a day because she didn't have the facilities to even warm a drop of water in her ward. "If it were not for this," she wrote, "I would like my ward better than any other in the house; but it takes the wind."[14]

Who cooked what for the patients was a political issue for hospital staffs as much as a nursing chore. Field nurses and those on the transport ships often had to cook simply because there was no one else there to do it. Georgeanna Woolsey reported she once cooked and served 926 rations of farina, tea, coffee, and "good rich soup, turkey, chicken and beef," made from home-canned goods sent by the women of the Sanitary Commission, in a single day.[15] In the general hospitals, much of the cooking was assigned to untrained convalescent soldiers, which may explain the quality problems that von Olnhausen complained of to the inspector general in September 1862. The day before he arrived, she told him indignantly, the bean soup and beef tea, both staples of the hospital kitchen, were so salty no one could swallow a second spoonful. The beans were so hard they would have made anyone who managed to eat them violently ill.[16] Lucy Campbell Kaiser, the only woman stationed at Jefferson Barracks Hospital in February 1862, not only served as nurse and superintendent, but took it upon herself to instruct the "half-sick" soldier who acted as cook,[17] perhaps as a matter of self-defense. Outraged nurses would sometimes take over the kitchen when military cooks failed to produce meals appropriate for men who were too sick to eat, often triggering a confrontation over the control of kitchen equipment.

Illnesses, particularly those that affected the gastrointestinal system, made it hard for patients to tolerate the so-called full, or common, diet served to active soldiers and invalids alike, which was often heavy, greasy, and coarse. One medical officer attached to a regiment described it as "death from the frying pan."[18] In 1864, Annie Turner Wittenmyer, state sanitary agent for Iowa, convinced the army to hire experienced women to superintend "special diet" kitchens in the general hospitals, a change that raised both the quality of convalescent food and the status of cooking as a hospital job.

Born in 1827, Wittenmyer was the energetic young widow of a well-to-do merchant in Keokuk, Iowa. Well before the war began she was already actively engaged in benevolent activities in her hometown. She had a particular interest in free education for underprivileged children, a concept she expanded to include having her students washed and clothed. The outbreak of war gave her the opportunity to expand her scope.

As the corresponding secretary of the Keokuk Ladies' Soldiers' Aid Society, Wittenmyer was not only active in collecting supplies for the military camps and hospitals surrounding Keokuk, which was the hub of Iowa's military activity. She was also a key figure in the effort to coordinate Iowa's relief work through the Keokuk society and distribute their supplies to Iowa regiments. She regularly traveled to wherever Iowa regiments were based, bringing with her bandages, medicine, clothing, and food and collecting information about what the troops needed most, first as a representative of the aid society and later as the official state sanitary agent.

The need for special-diet kitchens was brought home to her on one of these trips. On a visit to a hospital in Sedalia, Missouri, in the winter of 1862, she found one of her brothers among the patients, a sixteen-year-old boy whom she had thought was a hundred miles or more away. One of the hospital attendants was serving breakfast in the ward. Her brother waved the breakfast away with a look of disgust.

"If you can't eat this, you'll have to do without; there is nothing else," the attendant told him and moved on to the next patient. Wittenmyer examined the meal: a dingy wooden tray that held a tin cup of strong black coffee and a leaden tin platter on which a piece of fried fat bacon swam in its own grease next to a slice of bread. She couldn't blame her brother, who was ill with typhoid and dysentery, for refusing the meal.[19]

She nursed her brother back to health and began to think about a system for providing wounded and ill soldiers with nourishing food that would tempt failing appetites. It was early in 1864 before she was able to give her full attention to the project. Having wound up her duties as the Iowa State sanitary agent, she convinced the United States Christian Commission to fund the creation of special-diet kitchens in military hospitals, with herself as the supervising agent.

The concept of the special-diet kitchen, like so many of the nursing innovations in the Civil War, was first introduced by Florence Nightingale in the Crimea. The idea was that the surgeon would prescribe the appropriate diet for each patient who required what was known as a low, or special, diet. Menus were divided into full or common diet, half diet, and low or special diet to meet the needs of convalescent, sick, or very sick patients. It was a labor-intensive project: the special kitchen at Benton Barracks Hospital in Missouri produced 62,000 special-diet dishes in the month of August 1864 alone.[20] As was often the case with improvements proposed by women, surgeons resisted the change at first, but soon saw the positive results of the new system. By the end of the war, the army had established more than a hundred special kitchens, in which "delicacies" such as toast, chicken, soup, milk, tomatoes, jellies, tea, gruel, and vegetables supplemented or replaced the standard hospital menu.

The innovation of special-diet kitchens improved the quality of patients' food, but did not end conflict between nurses and cooks in all cases. Amanda Akin Stearns's memoir includes a detailed and running feud with "those 'fiends' who preside in that kitchen"[21] at Armory Square Hospital in Washington.

The same gastrointestinal illnesses that inspired the creation of the special kitchens also drove the most time-consuming of hospital tasks: cleaning. While memoirs and letters often speak of mud and blood, for the most part they maintain a polite silence on the other common element of military life in the Civil War—diarrhea. An average of 78 percent of the Union army suffered from diarrhea, nicknamed the "Tennessee quick-step" by the troops, over the course of the year. Even with the best efforts at camp hygiene and sanitation, the practical effect of that statistic was cholera, typhoid, and more diarrhea.

Nurses, supported by convalescent attendants, occasional chambermaids, and an army of laundresses, fought to keep hospitals clean in the face of a seemingly endless flood of filth. It was a monumental task, even by standards of cleanliness that required the patient's undergarments to be changed just once a week and saw nothing wrong with reusing lightly soiled bandages. Ward floors were dry-scoured clean with sand. Bedpans were emptied whenever they were used. (This seems obvious to a modern reader, but evidently some nurses and attendants needed to be trained to do this.) Keeping a supply of clean shirts, clean underwear, clean sheets, and clean bandages required a heroic effort—especially when a given patient might require nurses to "put *three* clean dressings and a shirt on him daily," all which would need to be thrown away because they were so stained with blood and pus. The newly constructed general hospital at Portsmouth Grove, Rhode Island, reportedly boasted a steam washing machine that could mash and mangle four thousand pieces of laundry a day,[22] an innovation that improvised hospitals like Mansion House could only envy. A report on the condition of hospital transport ships, presumably written by a male sanitary inspector, concluded: "Whitewash and women on a hospital ship are both excellent disinfectants."[23]

For many nurses, and their patients, one of the most uncomfortable tasks was bathing wounded soldiers, a process that often led to blushing on both sides of the sponge. Ropes, writing to her daughter Alice in August 1862, told her bluntly that "wounded men are exposed from head to foot before the nurses and they object to anybody but an "old mother."[24] Alcott, an old maid by the standards of the time if not an "old mother," made light of what for many unmarried women was a truly shocking experience. She was prepared to deal with her first rush of wounded soldiers until her supervisor gave her a basin, sponge, towels, a block of soap, and instructions to tell them to strip off their socks, coats, and shirts, wash them as fast as she could, and put clean shirts on them. Alcott was stunned: "If she had requested me to shave them all, or dance a hornpipe on the stove funnel, I should have been less staggered; but to scrub some dozen lords of creation at a moment's notice . . ." Having already reminded herself she was there to work, not weep, she then "drowned her scruples in her washbowl" and prepared to scrub.[25]

Caring for a soldier's physical needs was often the first step toward caring for his emotional and spiritual needs as well. Many nurses spent evenings in the wards, where they read to soldiers, soothed them to sleep, or listened to their stories. Von Olnhausen told one of her correspondents: "You would be amused to hear me entertaining them in the evening. I go the whole rounds, taking my little campstool, or kneeling by their beds. They all treat me with such confidence. I know all their histories and sorrows; they talk just like I was their mother."[26] Always a night owl, Alcott took the late-night shift once she felt she understood her work. She traveled among her patients, visiting one with "a dressing tray full of rollers, plasters, and pins; another, with books, flowers, games and gossip; a third with teapots, lullabies, consolation and, sometimes, a shroud"[27]— needed when a patient did not survive the night. Ropes would often hold a troubled man's hand until he relaxed enough to sleep. These quiet evening moments seemed to sooth the nurses as well as the nursed, as if they needed to time to recognize each man or boy as an individual rather than a medical case. To remember that the patient was a person, not the chest wound in ward B.

Caring for the person and not just the wound often included helping patients write letters; von Olnhausen claimed that if she had known writing letters for patients would be part of her duties she never would have enlisted.[28] Some suffered from broken, wounded, or missing arms that made it impossible to hold a pen, some were too feeble to sit up, and some were illiterate, but they all had things to say. With the help of the nurses they wrote to their wives, parents, pastors, old friends, brothers, sisters, and sweethearts. Sometimes they dictated a letter and added a line in their own hand at the end. Sometimes they struggled to find the words and left the nurse to fill in the blanks for them. They asked for warm socks and apples. They thanked ladies' aid societies for the comforts they had received and begged family members to come visit. All too often they wrote to say goodbye.

Nurses of all denominations believed it was important to sit with a dying man. Sometimes they helped him write a will or a farewell message. They bathed his forehead, held his hand, and gave him sips of water. They assured him that the pain would soon be over. When a man wanted prayer, they prayed with him or participated in the last rites alongside the hospital chaplain. Often after a man died, nurses had the hard job of telling family members who arrived too late that their son, brother, or husband was dead.

The concept of a "good death" was important in mid-nineteenth-century America. Dying words mattered. In some cases they provided an ending to the story of a life, lived well or ill. In other cases, they offered lessons or insights to those who attended the deathbed. Family members gathered around a dying relative not only to give and receive comfort, but also to act as witnesses to the state in which a man died. Nurses often played that role for the men under their care, witnessing their last words on behalf of their families. In one case, von Olnhausen witnessed a soldier's last words and then invented something better for his grieving parents to hear. "He was the wickedest boy I have ever seen die," she wrote. She tried hard to make him say a word of farewell for his parents, but he refused. Almost his last breath was an oath. When his parents arrived several days later, his mother longed so much for one word from him that von Olnhausen couldn't bear it: "I had to invent a bit just to make her a little comfort."[29]

Wicked or heroic, Union or "secesh," "I never leave a man to sleep or to eat when I think he will soon die," von Olnhausen wrote. "It seems at least as if a woman ought to close these poor fellow's eyes; no mother or wife or sister about them. I feel I must be all to them then, and the last words of many dying men have been thanks for what I have done. It is so splendid to be able to do anything for them; I do not lose my interest or enthusiasm one bit. Everybody said, when I first came, 'Oh, you'll get over this after a while and be hard just like us,' but I never can. If possible I feel more than then."[30]

Chapter 7

Becoming Indispensable

"The one fault that they find is 'that
I have too much sympathy for the sick'!"
—Amy Morris Bradley[1]

"I have been a 'female nurse' since a year ago last
October and only regret that I did not go in the beginning when a mistaken humility was all that withheld me
. . . I went with many misgivings—but now I know what
women are worth in the hospitals. It is no light thing to
hear a man say he owes you his life and then to know that
mother, wife, sister or child bless you in their prayers."
—Ella Wolcott[2]

"I am hearing too many blessings now-a-days
from sick and dying men to be in doubt any
longer whether or not I am doing good."
—Elvira Powers[3]

W hen they first began the job, many Civil War
nurses—new to hospital work, uncertain of their
skills, and often faced with opposition to their
decision to nurse both in the hospital and at home—doubted
whether their work was valuable. But over time, as they saw the
impact they had on the lives of individual soldiers, they came
to believe they were indispensable to the men they served.

As a group, nurses were committed to caring for soldiers as individuals. They complained that doctors often viewed wounded soldiers as "cases" rather than people, a position Katharine Wormeley described in a letter to her mother, written on May 30, 1862, from the hospital transport ship *Knickerbocker:* "Squads of civilian doctors are here, waiting about for 'surgical cases.' There must be dozens of them doing nothing, and their boats doing nothing,—waiting for a battle. They would not look at a sick man; bless you, he's not their game! It is '*cases*' they want."[4]

This fundamental conflict reflected the basic difference in the nature of the work done by the two groups. Military doctors were overburdened by the sheer numbers of wounded soldiers after a battle and could seldom devote more than a few minutes to individual cases. On the battlefield, the surgeons' first job was "the paralyzing task of sorting the dead from the dying, and the dying from those whose lives might be saved."[5] Amputations in particular depended on speed: tissues had to be cut, bones sawed, and blood vessels tied off in a matter of minutes to minimize a patient's suffering and maximize his chances of survival. After Gettysburg, by one account, it took three hundred surgeons, many of them civilian volunteers who arrived after the battle, five days to perform the necessary amputations.[6] There was no time to think about individuals.

Even when a new rush of wounded arrived, nurses' work occurred on a slower and more intimate schedule; they spent time comforting patients as well as tending to their physical ailments. Nurses attached to a specific regiment often had existing relationships with the men they took care of. The first soldier Amy Morris Bradley nursed in the Third Maine Volunteers was a former student of hers. "And now I have got to fill his mother's place by his bedside," she told the surgeon, who was also an old friend. In the military's general hospitals, which took patients from all regiments, nurses developed new relationships with their patients. They often spoke of the men in their wards as their "boys"; reciprocally, wounded men frequently referred to nurses as "mother," which the younger nurses found difficult until they realized it was an expression of respect. Louisa May Alcott, tending a dying man, was surprised to realize that "to him, as to so many, I was the poor substitute for mother, wife or sister,"[7] a realization that changed how she treated the soldiers under her care thereafter.

Because of this sense of connection, nurses would fight to keep a man alive even after a surgeon pronounced his case hopeless, and celebrate when they won because, as Harriet Foote Hawley put it, "I can't let them die—If they do a piece of my life goes too."[8] Anne Reading detailed a case in which her sister Jenny saved a patient's arm with careful nursing after the surgeon decided amputation was required, dressing it three times a day instead of once, burning off the slough, a layer of dead fibrous tissue that separates from a previously clean wound, with nitric acid, and scraping the exposed bone. To her delight, the soldier not only returned to active service thanks to her efforts, but he was promoted while still in the hospital; "and Jenny had the satisfaction of sewing his first shoulder straps on his uniform,"[9] another task performed by a nurse in the absence of mother, wife, or sister.

Nurses began to define themselves as advocates for patients, a role that both built on and stepped beyond hospital nurses' traditional duties of dressing wounds, giving medicine, feeding patients, sitting with the seriously ill, and scrubbing wards. As advocates, nurses quarreled with doctors and hospital stewards over details of diet, control over boxes from the ladies' aid societies, and the very nature of patient treatment. Most saw themselves as promoters of more humane care. Some exposed corruption, greed, and neglect at the risk of losing their positions. At least a few reached the conclusion that they could run the hospital better than those in charge. Katharine Wormeley, after several months with the hospital transport ship program, summed up the feeling of many women who were frustrated by the failures of the system: "I should like to have charge of a hospital now. I could make it march, if only I had hold of some of the administrative *power*."[10]

Breaking through Red Tape

The army's general hospitals stood at the intersection of two overlapping and sometimes contradictory organizational structures: the medical hierarchy of the hospital itself and the larger hierarchy of the army. The volunteer nurses of the Civil War did not fit neatly into either structure.

In the civilian general hospitals of the 1850s, which were few in number and located only in the largest cities, medical and administrative functions were divided. A panel of visiting physicians and a house staff of doctors provided medical care, assisted by rotating cadres of medical students, while a warden, who reported to the board of directors rather than to the physicians, ran everything else, including hiring and firing non-medical staff and providing and distributing food and supplies for the wards. A resident matron, who served as the housekeeper for the hospital, reported to the warden and was the immediate supervisor of the female staff, including nurses, cooks, cleaners, and laundresses. Day-to-day care of patients was left to female nurses and male orderlies, none of whom had anything resembling specialized training.

When the army established its own general hospitals at the beginning of the war, they combined the structure of a civilian general hospital with that of an army post. The chief surgeon held an officer's rank and functioned as a military commander within the hospital, with authority over both his staff and his patients. He was supported by a ward physician for every seventy-five to one hundred patients and, later in the war, by a handful of medical students working as wound dressers and assistants. Other than the chief surgeon, the most powerful member of the staff was the hospital steward, who filled the same role as the warden in a civilian hospital. The steward was responsible for the condition of the wards, the hospital's commissary, and the apothecary—a combination that gave him considerable control over the comfort of patients and staff and provided enormous opportunities for black market dealing and other forms of corruption. Stewards exercised their authority in the hospital through ward masters, often convalescent soldiers, who were in charge of the nursing and cleaning in each ward. Male nurses and cooks, who were also usually convalescents, stood below the ward masters in the hospital's organization.

Within the larger structure of the military, a general hospital's chief surgeon reported to the regional medical director. (In the case of Alexandria, the medical director was based in Washington.) Medical directors in turn reported to the surgeon general. Although the chain of command was clear, the relative autonomy of military hospitals created tensions with higher-ranking military officers, who often tried to exercise authority over a general hospital in their vicinity. This problem was common enough that the War Department sent out occasional reminders that the heads of military hospitals reported to the surgeon general; and that they were in charge of both the medical and military operation of their institutions.

If military hospitals were an anomaly within the military hierarchy, volunteer female nurses were an anomaly within the hierarchy of the hospital: it was as difficult to find their place within the hospital's structure as it was to find them a place to sleep within the hospital's walls. Although nursing as a function held a clearly defined place in the military hospital, female nurses' status as civilians placed them outside the established chain of command, at least in their own minds. In theory, nurses came under the authority of the ward master. But many female nurses were recruited with the expectation that they would hold a position with the moral authority of a traditional hospital matron; they saw their role as supervising not only the male attendants in their ward but the ward master as well. Moreover, those nurses who did not receive a salary for their work often did not consider themselves bound by the hospital's rules or chain of command. When a ward master "came tripping up" to tell Mary Newcomb that by staying in the ward late to tend to a patient she was violating the chief surgeon's order that lights had to be extinguished at nine o'clock, she exploded: "You tell that surgeon whoever he is, I will burn just as many lights as I please. I am no hired nurse. I volunteered my service free and there shall be no red tape, but I will break it when humanity demands it."[11]

Dorothea Lynde Dix, n.d.
Library of Congress

Mary Phinney von Olnhausen, n.d.
*James Phinney Munroe, **Adventures**
of an Army Nurse in Two Wars.*
(Little, Brown, and Company, 1904)

Louisa May Alcott, ca. 1860
*Used by permission of Louisa
May Alcott's Orchard House*

Clara Barton, ca. 1863
National Archives

Elizabeth Blackwell, ca. 1855
*Blackwell Family Papers, Schlesinger Library,
Radcliffe Institute, Harvard University*

Amy Morris Bradley, n.d.
*MOLLUS-Mass Civil War
Collection, USAHEC*

Eliza Woolsey Howland, n.d.
*MOLLUS-Mass Civil War
Collection, USAHEC*

Hannah C. Ropes, ca. 1861
*MOLLUS-Mass Civil War
Collection, USAHEC*

Georgeanna Woolsey Bacon, n.d.
*MOLLUS-Mass Civil War
Collection, USAHEC*

Katharine P. Wormeley, n.d.
*MOLLUS-Mass Civil War
Collection, USAHEC*

Great meeting of the ladies of New York at the Cooper Institute on April 29, 1861, to organize a society to be called "Women's Central Association of Relief," to make clothes and lint bandages, and to furnish nurses for the soldiers of the Northern Army.
New York World-Telegram and the Sun Newspaper Photograph Collection, Library of Congress

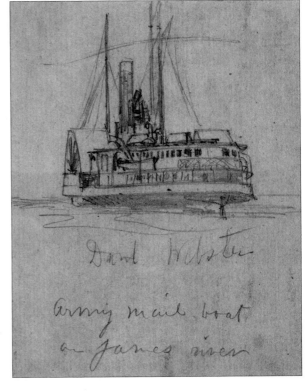

The hospital transport ship *Daniel Webster* moved wounded and sick soldiers from the rivers of the Virginia Peninsula to hospitals in Washington, Philadelphia, and New York.
Library of Congress

The Union Army commandeered Mansion House Hotel for use as a hospital in 1861.
Library of Congress

Bird's-eye view of Alexandria, Virginia showing the location of Mansion House Hospital and other hospitals, ca. 1863.
Library of Congress

Union Hotel Hospital was notorious for its crowded conditions and poor sanitation. Photo likely dated 1862.
National Photo Company Collection, Library of Congress

Conditions at Camp Convalescent, located outside of Alexandria, Virginia, were so bad that the men stationed there called it "Camp Misery."
Library of Congress

A year into the war, field hospitals were still not equipped to handle the large numbers of casualties suffered in each battle.
Library of Congress

Nurse Abby Gibbons from New York City sitting with wounded soldiers outside a hospital at Fredericksburg, Virginia. Fredericksburg became a "city of hospitals" after the Battle of the Wilderness, May 1864.
Library of Congress

Ambulance drill at the headquarters of the Army of the Potomac. These two-wheeled ambulances were so uncomfortable that troops called them "avalanches."
Library of Congress

Embalming surgeon at work on soldier's body.
Library of Congress

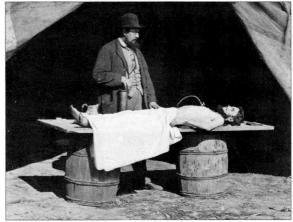

Nurses and officers of the US Sanitary Commission in Fredericksburg, Virginia.
Library of Congress

In the later years of the war, the Union army built well-organized field hospitals, like this one at Brandy Station, Virginia, close to expected battlegrounds. *Library of Congress*

The U. S. Army adopted ambulances only two years before the war began. They had no experience using them on the battlefield prior to the First Battle of Bull Run. *Library of Congress*

Transports on the Potomac River, Jones Point, Virginia. *Courtesy of the U.S. National Library of Medicine*

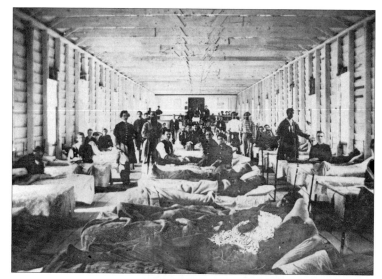

Interior ward in the convalescent camp near Alexandria, Virginia, after Amy Morris Bradley's reforms, July 1864. *Library of Congress*

Wounded soldiers under trees, Marye's Heights, Fredericksburg, after the battle of Spotsylvania in 1864. *Library of Congress*

US Christian Commission at Gettysburg General Hospital, August 1863. *Library of Congress*

Union hand stretchers at work at Marye's Heights in May 1864. Over fifty thousand hand stretchers of various patterns were issued by the Union government during the war.
*Francis Trevelyan Miller, **The Photographic History of the Civil War Vol. 7** (The Review of Reviews Company, 1911)*

Even cutting-edge Civil War hospitals, like Harewood General Hospital, were crude by modern standards.
Library of Congress

Nurses spoon-fed soldiers who were unable to feed themselves.
MOLLUS-Mass Civil War Collection, USAHEC

The willingness to ignore bureaucracy in the name of humanity was a regular theme in Civil War nurses' interactions with authority. Sometimes nurses broke through army red tape without meaning to, especially when the issue was small and the rule was rigid. Mary Phinney von Olnhausen found herself "always running against some of their rules." Even when she was in the right she was tempted to say "darn the rules"; between the army and the hospital there were so many regulations she found it hard to keep track of them, and they sometimes seemed designed to keep the work from getting done. [12]

By contrast, women on the transport ships actively encouraged each other to break the rules, including what Katharine Wormeley described as a "prevailing disease" of "kleptomania" among the nurses, who boarded steamers headed back to Washington or Philadelphia and carried off anything they felt could be of use to their patients—pails, essence of beef, sugar, lemons, whiskey, nutmeg graters, corkscrews—on the grounds that "*they* are going back where they can get more; while to us who remain here such articles are as precious as if they were made of gold."[13] Amanda Akin Stearns, who nursed at Armory Square Hospital in Washington, did not hesitate to order special-diet meals for thirty new patients or give medicine without a prescription when the occasion seemed urgent and no doctor was available, claiming she had "been in the army long enough not to ask questions."[14]

The same disregard for hospital, military, and, occasionally, social rules led nurses to ignore the chain of command altogether when they saw something they felt was not right. In the name of defending their patients, they called on whatever authority was available, up to and including the secretary of war.

Food Fights

Hospital food was often the first issue on which nurses spoke up against the established order, perhaps because they were also affected by the quality of the food, and perhaps because they saw cooking as their area of expertise. For the most part women in nineteenth-century America knew more about cooking than the convalescent soldiers pressed into duty in hospital kitchens.

Nurses' diaries and memoirs are full of complaints about the quality and monotony of the food that appeared at their table. A month after she arrived at Mansion House Hospital, Mary Phinney von Olnhausen described the lack of variation in the menu:

> Our bill-of-fare has been unvaried from the time we came till now (I mean at the nurses' table); almost always sour bread, and always the worst possible butter, and coffee that can be imagined (I am speaking of breakfast), with sometimes a bit of tough, overdone steak, often no milk, and sometimes no butter. At dinner invariably worse beef, very much done, sometimes potatoes and sometimes not, and once in a while sweet potatoes, which, you know, I hate (but I always claim my share, as I can take it to some poor fellow in my ward), together with, about once a week, a small piece of pie. Twice we have had a change of baked salt pork instead of beef. For supper there are always the same sour bread and butter and *such* tea; and that is all.[15]

Elvira Powers, writing in 1864, soon after the institution of special-diet kitchens, noted that "the usual rations, such as tough army beef, baker's bread and stale butter, with muddy coffee, served in brown mugs, has been the diet for so long a time that it has ceased to be very palatable." She went on to suggest that "Northern people, who think that all Government employees fatten on commissary stores, ought to see the table which is set at this hospital. It is exceedingly plain; and it sometimes requires more moral courage than all are very long capable of exercising to inhale the odor" of the delicate foods produced by the special-diet kitchens "or daily to deal out jellys, blanc-mange and canned fruit without ever tasting."[16] Louisa May Alcott too complained the three meals each day were "pretty much of a muchness" and argued that "variety being the spice of life, a small pinch of the article would have been appreciated by the hungry, hard-working sisterhood."[17] The absence of edible butter was a particular sore spot; Powers jokingly requested someone "make a raid and capture a dairy—milkmaid and all."[18]

Food that was unappealing to nurses could be literally deadly for patients, particularly those suffering from gastrointestinal diseases such as cholera, dysentery, or typhoid. A typical midday full-diet meal, served to active duty soldiers, convalescents, and nurses, would be pork and beans and bread pudding, or the monotonous round of army beef, bread, and stale butter described by von Olnhausen and Powers. Sick patients on half-diet would be served mutton soup with meat, boiled potatoes, and bread. (Desperate for a little variety, von Olnhausen once begged the cook to give her a little mutton soup. He grumbled, saying that the soup was only for the patients, not the nurses; then he gave her a bowl. When she tasted it she thought it wasn't even good enough to serve to the well, let alone to the sick, with their capricious appetites and delicate digestions.[19]) Those so sick that they required the low or special diet would dine on cooked wheat cereal and bread, if they could bring themselves to eat at all. Fruit and vegetables were rarely on the menu except in those hospitals that maintained kitchen gardens during the growing season.

Nurses begged the cooks for special meals for the very sick, muscled their way into the kitchen to do extra cooking, and purchased the ingredients for more delicate menus for their patients from their own pockets. Von Olnhausen, in another self-described "growling letter," complained:

> Every day I buy eggs and milk, in fact almost every nice thing for the sick ones. I know I have the right to them here; but I've learned enough to know that all who make complaints to headquarters are not only unpopular there but are pitched into by all the house; so I just speak to nobody, get what I can, and buy the rest. Sometimes I can *make eyes* at the ice-box man and he'll give me a bit of chicken and mutton; but he isn't always to be melted any more than his ice, though he is the only one who really seems to work for the soldiers.[20]

She was not the only one to use her own money to buy luxuries for the sick. Elvira Powers, for instance, bought dried peaches for a fifteen-year-old soldier suffering from typhoid; fruit in particular seemed to appeal to sick men who had little appetite. The urge to purchase needed supplies went beyond food for the sick. The wealthy Woolsey family told their daughters to "buy whatever you see is needed or the surgeons and nurses want. Don't wait for red tape. If it is mattresses, cots, pillows, spirit lamps, food, sheeting, flannel, etc. To wrap wounded men in, or what not. You can have plenty of money, and it could not be better spent than in fitting up a hospital even if that is government work."[21]

In March 1863, von Olnhausen decided she'd had enough. Dr. C. was in charge of the commissary, so she went after him on behalf of her patients. She cornered him in his office and told him that the sickest patients would starve if the nurses didn't buy food for them. As was often the case when nurses went on the attack, Dr. C. became defensive. He said that he knew his nurse did not buy food for the men and called her into the office to prove it. His nurse said that she did buy food for her patients. He called in the other nurses; they all gave the same answer.

Eventually every nurse and doctor in the hospital was involved in the argument, which lasted most of the day. Dr. C. insisted that the men received everything that was called for in the new diet-table issued by the army. Some of the doctors agreed with him; others hotly denied it. At last they all went down to the basement, where the kitchens were located, to read the official list. It became clear that the patients were not getting even the quantity that was called for. (The quality was a different question altogether.) As a result of von Olnhausen's intervention, things were a little better, but she held no hope that the improvements would last: "Soon . . . it will be back to the old standard, for the wretch H [the hospital steward] or somebody will miss the money and get it back if possible."[22]

Sometimes even the most basic foods were scarce, particularly in regions close to the battlefronts. In November 1861, Lucy Campbell Kaiser, stationed in a contested area of Missouri, found that a soldier had reported her for not giving him enough to eat. She admitted, "I suppose it was true. The fact was I could not get enough food: butter out, sugar out, no crackers, poor bread, tough beef, no vegetables, no candles; in fact, the commissary was bare, and the officers in town on a drunk."[23] Cornelia Hancock, writing to her family from Gettysburg, reported, "Our stores have given out. There is nothing to cook with, hence I have nothing to do, and, therefore, have time to write. Such days will come here that we have to see our wounded men fed with dry bread and poor coffee; and I can tell you it is hard to witness some cursing for food, some praying for it . . . I would give anything to have a barrel of butter and some dried rusk."[24]

Nurses had no doubt that their patients would be much worse off if it weren't for the efforts of the women at home. Cornelia Hancock, who was quick to ask friends and family from Philadelphia's wealthy Quaker community for donations of shirts, drawers, cologne, rags, and sheets, emphasized with every plea that "Uncle Sam is very rich, but very slow"[25] and that whatever comforts the men received beyond the basic necessities came to them from the ladies' aid groups.[26] Almost from the first days of the war, nurses engaged in letter-writing campaigns, alternately begging friends and family for both necessities and luxuries for "their boys" and thanking them for goods received.

In addition to the formal ladies' aid societies, some groups of women allied themselves to specific nurses and kept them supplied. Clara Barton established her own network of suppliers; by the time she applied for a pass to travel to the battlefront in August 1862, she had accumulated three warehouses of food and hospital supplies. She kept those warehouses replenished over the course of the war by writing inspiring letters to her ladies and harrowing accounts of the suffering of "our boys" on the battlefield for the newspapers. Von Olnhausen did the same thing on a smaller scale, maintaining a relationship with the women of Lexington, Massachusetts. Her first thank-you letter to them is dated September 21, 1862, less than a month after she arrived at Mansion House:

> I have been so happy to get your two letters telling me about you all and especially about that box; —you can have no possible idea of the good it will do. I know what all the Sanitary committees in the North have done and how much they think the poor soldiers are comforted; but I can assure you that in the way of delicacies they get mighty little—none in fact,—and, so far, not even good, nourishing food.[27]

Weeks later she complimented the good ladies of Lexington on the superior quality of their bandages, telling them she could dress an arm or leg forty times as well with the bandages they made as with any others. She then requested even more: "And we are likely to want all we have if the report is true of the big battle [most likely the Battle of Perryville]."[28] Over the course of the war, she continued to wheedle, thank, and praise in equal measure. The ladies of Lexington continued to produce: "Till the very end of the war every month brought comforts from them. A soldier never went from my ward, either to his regiment or to his home, without some proper clothing and often a little money to help him on the journey. For this I take no credit; it was only through those dear friends I was able to do it."[29]

Even Anne Reading, who had no home base in the United States she could call on, did not hesitate to "beg for the boys" whenever someone she knew visited the hospital. Miss Gillson, a New York socialite who had worked with Reading on the hospital ships, was especially generous, providing "56 shirts, 120 towels, 120 pocket handkerchiefs, 6 bottles of current wine, 6 bottles of lemon syrup, and large quantities of jellies" in response to Reading's appeals.[30]

Control over the boxes and barrels sent from the ladies' aid societies became another point of contention among nurses and surgeons and hospital stewards. Surgeons, attempting to maintain control over prescribed meals for sick men, objected to the unsupervised distribution of food in the wards, though it is hard to imagine what a visitor might give them that would be worse than the common diet. Nurses believed that boxes turned over to the commissary often failed to reach the men for whom they were intended. In July 1862, soon after she arrived at Union Hotel Hospital, Hannah Ropes took control of the key to the storeroom that contained the medicinal wines, quarts of canned fruits sent by ladies' aid societies for the soldiers, and other prized supplies. There was an "almost universal complaint that delicacies sent to the patients [were] eaten by the nurses and surgeons." She was determined that wouldn't be true at Union Hotel Hospital on her watch.[31]

Von Olnhausen gained similar control over luxuries at Mansion House Hospital after a struggle with Dr. Summers in the fall of 1862. In the weeks since her arrival, her friends in Lexington had regularly sent her comforts for the patients under her care. She stored them in her room and shared them with the sick and wounded in other wards as well as her own.

One day, Summers called her into his office and said he understood she was in the habit of receiving supplies for the men. He insisted that in the future all such boxes were to be sent to the dispensary and distributed from there. Never one to mince words, von Olnhausen told him that the boxes she received were all from her personal friends in Lexington, not official supplies from the Sanitary Commission. She would throw what she had out on the pavement before she gave any of it "to his drunken dispensary clerks to be eaten and drank and used by them."

The doctor then told her there were several barrels of apples lying at the wharf addressed to her. This was no doubt what inspired his interest: the hospital had very little fruit, and everyone craved it. He claimed the apples were needed for the hospital and insisted she order them sent to him at once.

Von Olnhausen refused and told him she would send them back unless she could do with them what she chose. She then stormed out of the office and flew back to her room, sure the matter was not over.

Round two was quick in coming. Von Olnhausen was summoned to the office again; an order had come from the docks that the barrels of apples were still waiting to be delivered and must be sent for at once. Summers asked if she had changed her mind. She told him no and negotiated for a storeroom where they could be safely locked away, along with her boxes from the ladies of Lexington. The doctor agreed, but wanted her to take charge of their distribution for the hospital as a whole. She refused. She was there to nurse soldiers, not to be a dispensary clerk. She was too busy to both manage the stores and take care of her ward.

Summers was furious and ready to walk away from the deal, but von Olnhausen offered a substitute storekeeper as a compromise. A few days earlier Miss Dix had brought a widow, Mrs. B., to the hospital to oversee the special diet, and von Olnhausen felt she could trust her. By nightfall the apples were stored in a locked room, with the key in Mrs. B.'s charge. In a rare act of diplomacy, von Olnhausen sent a barrel to every ward, as well as one to the cooks and one to the doctor. She thought the problem was solved. The storeroom was now a "fixed fact" and she had the comfort of knowing that the whole house had enjoyed the fruit meant for the soldiers.[32]

The storeroom turned out to be only a partial solution. Eight months later, Mansion House Hospital was once again in an uproar about food. "Those miserable toads" in the dispensary had taken twenty-five pounds of sugar, twelve bottles of pickles, twelve bottles of cordial, and other delicacies from a Sanitary Commission package for their own use, leaving only twelve cans of milk for the patients. Von Olnhausen was indignant: "Isn't it a shame? Just look how the people at home are cheated and duped! I wonder anybody there ever trusts anyone concerned in the war."[33]

Nurses found themselves fighting their own version of the war, in which the dispensary, commissary, and kitchen marked the front lines.

Attacking Corruption

Mary Phinney von Olnhausen fought a constant battle against pilfering in the commissariat at Mansion House Hospital, a problem that made her declare "I can sooner forgive the Rebels who kill them" than the men who cheated her soldiers.[34] Nurses at other locations exposed surgeons and quartermasters who served soldiers substandard food and sold official provisions for their own profit. In many cases, the nurses found themselves subject to retaliation from the men they exposed, thanks in part to their own failure to understand the system and their relative lack of power within it. Mrs. S. A. M. Blackford, who presented the Illinois governor with complaints about inadequate food given to soldiers under her care, was dismissed for her failure to honor the proper chain of command. Her unsuccessful efforts at reinstatement included a letter to President Lincoln, repeating the offence that had gotten her fired in the first place by once again making an appeal to civilian authorities to redress military wrongs. She pled that while she had no doubt been "ignorant of military rules," all she wanted was "to get our sick and wounded enough to eat."[35] Not all the women who set out to expose corruption were so naive about how to work the system. Annie Turner Wittenmyer, proponent of the special-diet kitchens, and Hannah Ropes, of Union Hotel Hospital, for instance, had the political savvy and connections to effect change without compromising their positions.

Annie Turner Wittenmyer learned that special-diet kitchens solved the problem of feeding the most fragile patients but increased the temptation for corruption by providing more and higher-quality supplies to hospital kitchens. When the woman in charge of the special-diet kitchen at the army hospital in Madison, Indiana, complained to Wittenmyer about the quality of the food, especially the coffee, Wittenmyer sent one of her best assistants, Miss Lou E. Vance, to the hospital to investigate. Miss Vance soon discovered that the hospital's kitchen staff, on orders from the chief surgeon, were drying used coffee grounds and adulterating them with logwood dye, a century-old technique for passing off exhausted grounds as the real thing. The kitchen then reused the adulterated grounds and the surgeon sold a portion of the unused coffee beans on the black market.

Armed with affidavits from the kitchen attendants, Wittenmyer traveled to Louisville, Kentucky, the headquarters for the medical director of the region, where she demanded a private interview with Assistant Surgeon General Robert C. Wood. Wittenmyer laid out the case against the chief surgeon. Wood, who apparently had learned little in his encounters with Miss Dix several years previously, protested that the man was one of his best surgeons. Wittenmyer pushed back, saying the surgeon ought to be "hung higher than Haman," a reference to a biblical punishment that was as much about public humiliation as pain. She insisted the case be referred to the highest authority available without reference to military protocol, in this case the governor of Indiana; Wood insisted the case remain within the military system. Unlike the hapless Mrs. Blackford, Wittenmyer was not employed by the army, so was not subject to dismissal by Wood, and she had too much political power to be ignored. They compromised: Wittenmyer agreed to have the charges against the surgeon heard by a military commission, and Wood agreed to allow Wittenmyer to choose the members of the commission. In the end, the charges were never heard at all. As soon as the commission arrived in Madison, the surgeon telegraphed his resignation to Washington and fled, unpunished.

Hannah Ropes was even more successful in her efforts to bring a corrupt steward to account, a spectacular example of nurses' willingness to ignore the constraints of bureaucracy when in search of results.

Born in Maine in 1809, Ropes was an ardent social crusader from a prominent family of lawyers and public servants. Unlike many of Dix's nurses, she was neither an old maid nor a widow. Her husband abandoned her sometime around 1847, leaving Hannah to raise their two children alone. In 1855, Ropes moved to Lawrence, Kansas, where her son had filed a land claim. There, as an active member of the abolitionist movement, she soon learned that abolition wasn't a theoretical issue in "Bleeding Kansas" in the mid-1850s. Pro- and anti-slavery forces literally battled for control over the contested territory. Murder in the streets was a fact of life. Ropes was so fearful that her home could be attacked at any moment that she kept loaded pistols and a bowie knife on her table at night and three loaded rifles in the room.[36] In mid-1856, she moved back east to Massachusetts with her daughter Alice, leaving her son behind to maintain his land claim. Once safely in Massachusetts, she published a controversial tract opposing the legal expansion of slavery into the western states. The pamphlet, "Six Months in Kansas: By a Lady," proved successful and launched her career as an anti-slavery activist. By the late 1850s, she was well known not only to the abolitionist community in Massachusetts but also to the politically powerful as well, including

Henry Wilson, the state's senior US senator and subsequent chairman of the influential Senate Military Affairs Committee.

Like other women with an interest in abolition, Ropes was eager to do her part when the nation went to war. Nightingale's *Notes on Nursing* had already sparked her interest in nursing before the fall of Sumter, and when she learned Dix had called for applicants for an army nursing corps, Ropes got her affairs in order and headed to Washington. Unable to carry a musket in the name of freedom, she was ready to care for those who did. In fact, her first patient was not a wounded soldier. Senator Wilson collapsed in the entry of his house a few hours before Ropes arrived in town in June 1862, and his family asked her to take care of him as he recovered. Ropes spent her first two weeks in Washington at his bedside, with "Officers and Senators at the door in squads every day to see him."[37] It was an introduction to the highest level of Washington politics that most volunteer nurses did not receive.

Ropes began her nursing assignment at the Union Hotel Hospital on July 4, and Dix appointed her matron in charge of nurses at the hospital that fall. Soon thereafter, the hospital steward, who by his own admission was there "to make all the money he could out of the hospital,"[38] suggested Ropes join him in reselling hospital clothing, soap, and food. Ropes complained to the hospital's chief surgeon, Dr. A. M. Clark, who neither reprimanded nor dismissed the steward. She then took her accusations directly to Surgeon General William Hammond. Hammond, insisting all communications come through the proper chain of command, refused to act on Ropes's charges and referred the letter back to Clark, whom Ropes described in her diary as "ignorant of hospital routine, ignorant of life outside of the practice in a country town in an interior state, a weak man with good intentions, but puffed up with the gilding on his shoulder straps."[39] Clark, irate that Ropes had gone around him, demanded she prove the charges. Ropes declined: the evidence was clear for anyone to see in the kitchen, the larder, and the pinched faces in the wards.[40]

At the end of October 1862, the steward gave Ropes new cause for indignation when he struck a young soldier with a chisel and then imprisoned him in the hospital's guardhouse. The steward was taken aback when the boy's father arrived from Philadelphia the next day, in response to a telegram from Ropes, and demanded his son. Later that day, another man appeared and, without identifying himself, asked why the steward had jailed the boy. The steward swore at him and told him it was none of his business. The man walked past him into the ward, asked another patient for the names of the steward and the head surgeon, and wrote them down. When he shoved the note in his pocket, "his shabby coat fell open, revealing a *General's strap!*" General Nathaniel P. Banks, at the time in charge of the defense of the capital, then asked to speak to his old friend Hannah Ropes. She couldn't help gloating in a letter to Alice, "The cup of chagrin to the steward seemed full!"[41] It would shortly overflow.

The next day the steward chose to torment a different man, this one with no inconvenient relatives to pull strings on his behalf. He put a young German soldier named Julius, "who had no father, no mother and no friends in this country," into "the hole," a portion of the cellar partitioned off to hold soldiers for disciplinary purposes. As soon as one of the other nurses came to tell her, Ropes pulled on her bonnet and went in search of help. Instead of appealing to Dr. Clark, she went first to General Banks's headquarters. When she discovered Banks was in New York, she decided to pay a personal call to Hammond, who seems to have been unaware of her political connections. She sat in a stiff wooden chair outside Hammond's office and watched as he walked by without "the courtesy of a look or a nod, or even the old time civility of raising the hand to his hat." She asked for an immediate meeting, but Hammond's assistant put her off. Enraged, Ropes wrote in her diary: "Two rebuffs seemed about enough for a woman of half a century to accept without compromising her own dignity."[42]

Instead of waiting to see Hammond, Ropes took the problem straight to Secretary of War Edwin Stanton, where her reception was very different. Within ten minutes, she was at his desk and telling him her story. Stanton, whose dislike of Hammond was well known, was more than ready to investigate Ropes's charges. He called for the provost marshal, the officer with responsibility for investigating charges against army personnel. Before Ropes "got hold of the importance of the order," Stanton ordered the provost marshal to accompany her to the hospital and arrest the steward. Over the next four days, Ropes's complaints against the steward received as much attention as she could have wished: "Straps and buttons have been hurrying through the halls, wise looking men in long boots have stood about; and legal people have been into my rooms to take testimony." Even Thomas Perley, the medical inspector general, at whose home Ropes often attended Sunday dinner, made a perfunctory appearance. Dr. Clark was also arrested and held over the weekend. Anticipating possible reprisals against her, Stanton issued an order that the chief surgeon could not remove

Ropes from her place in the hospital, a precaution that proved necessary after Clark's release.[43]

Ropes's diary entry the next day began, "Today the whole house began to brighten."[44]

Amy Morris Bradley Reforms Camp Misery

In December of 1862, Amy Morris Bradley took on the role of patient advocate for the more than fifteen hundred men interned at Camp Convalescent, known to its inhabitants as Camp Misery.

Established in August 1862 just outside Arlington, about a mile from Mansion House Hospital, the camp was intended to solve the problem of soldiers not yet well enough to rejoin their regiments but too well to continue to take up a hospital bed. Under the control of the Army of the Potomac rather than the Medical Bureau, the camp rapidly degenerated into what Clara Barton described as "a sort of pen into which all who could limp, all deserters and stragglers, were driven promiscuously."[45] Located at the foot of a long slope that drained into the camp, it was damp even in dry weather. Rain turned it into a quagmire. The men were housed in torn and dirty tents without floors or fires and given standard army rations of salt pork, beans, and hardtack, which they were obliged to cook themselves over wood for which they scavenged as best they could. Little or no medical attention was provided to track the course of their convalescence. The strongest recovered without aid and went back to their units. The weakest began to die off as the temperatures dropped, with several freezing to death. Those who remained succumbed to the combination of exposure and filth and fell ill once more. Sanitary Commission agents began "kidnapping" the worst cases and taking them back to the hospitals.

Mary Phinney von Olnhausen came to hate Camp Misery as much as those interned there did. She swore that the convalescents who arrived at Mansion House Hospital from the camp needed more attention than men wounded in battle. She raged against the conditions in a letter dated November 9, 1862:

> I wish you could look into my ward tonight and see these miserable sick men who have come in from the convalescent camp during the last week. Such wrecks I never saw, all worn out with fever and diarrhea or some other chronic complaint . . . Several thousand have been there, just lying on the ground in tents, many without blankets, none with more than one, the worst possible food to eat, and growing sicker and dying every day . . . One night last week, about nine o'clock, five of these men were sent to me, and I had but three empty beds. Five such objects I never saw,—three with typhoid, one German with shaking palsy, and one with paralysis. They told me they had been pronounced fit for duty and sent out there, where they had been for three weeks or more, every day growing sicker. The night before it had rained steadily and they just lay in pools of mud. What can our government be doing to let such a place exist? Two of them have already died and one of the others, I fear, will.[46]

Change would come soon, thanks to a tiny, delicate-looking dynamo named Amy Morris Bradley.

Born in 1823 in East Vassalboro, Maine, Bradley was well accustomed to taking on challenges by the time the war began in 1861. Like many single women of the period, she became a schoolteacher, beginning at East Vassalboro, where she taught at the same school she had attended. She was eager to learn more, see more, do more, and earn more. With an eye on teaching in Boston, she saved enough money to pay for one term at a private school in the nearby town of Vassalboro, the last formal schooling she would receive. For the next few years, she made the most of whatever opportunities came her way, teaching wherever a family connection provided an opening, including a brief stint with her brother in Charleston, South Carolina,where she was ill at ease with the luxurious lifestyle enjoyed by her brother's in-laws and outraged by slavery and the political rhetoric that filled the papers. She returned home for a time to take care of her ailing father. When her father recovered, a sister-in-law who was weak and depressed after childbirth demanded her services. Bradley found herself being sucked into the position of unpaid family caregiver and peace-maker that was often the fate of spinster daughters of the time. When an opportunity to work in Costa Rica as the governess to two young girls arose in 1853, she grabbed it and fled.

The job in Costa Rica was a disappointment. The girls spoke less English than she had been led to expect, and her accommodations were shabby, even by the standards of a cobbler's daughter from rural Maine. And nothing from her prior experience had prepared her for the fact that the family would treat their governess as a servant rather than a member of the household. Unable to stand it, she borrowed money to repay her employer for her steamship passage, broke her contract, and set herself up as a seamstress. When the American consul came through town, he invited her to travel with his family to San José, where there were more opportunities for an enterprising American woman to make a living. Once in San José, she set herself the task of learning Spanish; within six months she read and wrote well enough to give up dressmaking and work as a tutor. She soon set up the first English-language school in Costa Rica, which was so successful that even the governor of San José enrolled his children there.

She sold the school and returned to the United States in 1857. Family members pressured her for loans and expected her to fall back into the caregiver role. Instead she chose to settle in Boston, where she enrolled in a bookkeeping class, taught Spanish, and enjoyed the cultural and social opportunities of the city. In time, she found steady employment as an English to Spanish translator for the New England Glass Company.

When the war came, she was determined to serve as a nurse. She met the qualifications for Dix's nursing corps: she once described herself as "homely as a stump."[47] But instead of applying via Dix, she began a persistent campaign to serve with the Third Maine Volunteers, many of whom were old friends and former students, including the regiment's surgeons, Dr. George E. Brickett and Dr. Gideon S. Palmer. Both Brickett and Palmer expressed concerns about the hardness of the life, especially since Bradley had suffered from serious respiratory illnesses her entire life, but ultimately welcomed her into the regiment. Palmer wrote for her to come as soon as possible: "I can assure you that you can do much good here and we should all be very much pleased to see you. I should for one, and what I say, you know I mean . . . let us know by letter at what hour you will reach Washington and we will send an ambulance—the best mode of conveyance we have—for you."[48]

Bradley served with the regiment for eight months. (During that period she visited Mansion House Hospital three times and decided that nursing in a general hospital would be too taxing for her: too many stairs, too many patients, and too much authority to defer to.) After that, she served on the hospital transport ships until they were shut down in August 1862. In September, she accepted the position of supervisor at the US Sanitary Commission Home in Washington, which served as a way station for soldiers in transit who were under financial or physical duress. Her main job was to supervise the staff who cleaned and cooked, care for the men, and help them navigate through the government red tape needed to receive their back pay, return to their regiments, or go home. She also had the authority to visit camps and hospitals as an official Sanitary Commission relief worker. It seemed like a job made to order for Bradley.

On September 23, Bradley made her first visit on behalf of the Sanitary Commission to Camp Misery, where she found a level of suffering she had never seen before. Thereafter she visited on a regular basis to distribute warm clothing, food, and blankets and began an ardent campaign, in conjunction with Sanitary Commission inspector Mary Livermore, to improve conditions at the camp. After several months of determined lobbying by Bradley and Livermore, who even managed a personal interview with President

Lincoln on the subject, the authorities agreed to move the camp to higher ground. They also approved Bradley's appointment as "Special Relief Agent of the US Sanitary Commission at the Convalescent Camp in Alexandria."

On December 16, 1862, Bradley left the comfort of the Sanitary Commission Home for hardship duty at the convalescent camp. The Sanitary Commission provided her with a horse and ambulance for her personal use and a pass that allowed her to travel back and forth between Alexandria and Washington via the Aqueduct Bridge. She went to the camp armed with two letters from Rev. Frederick Knapp of the Sanitary Commission, with whom she had served on the hospital transport ships and at the Commission Home. One was addressed to the commander of the camp, Colonel J. S. Belknap of the Eighty-fifth New York Volunteers, in which Knapp stated: "Miss Amy M. Bradley returns to your camp as the authorized agent of the Sanitary Commission to endeavor to cooperate with those already engaged in carrying out your plans for rendering comfortable the condition of the sick." The second was to the chief surgeon of the camp, to whom Knapp introduced Bradley as "an efficient and experienced nurse" who had "come at the suggestion of Col Belknap to render aid to the Union army." Before night her tent was up, her stove was lit, and she was ready to work.

Bradley took up her duties at the camp as soon as it moved to its new location on higher ground. She had assumed she would be able to build on existing administrative systems, but instead found that no systems existed at all. No barracks had been erected at the new site, and the men were in tents, sleeping on the half-frozen ground. Many had only a single suit of ragged, fever-soiled clothes and one army blanket. The Sanitary Commission sent wagonloads of supplies, but its agents distributed stores of clothing without regard for who needed what. With no laundry in the camp, items were used until soiled, then thrown on the ground and left to rot by the thousands.

Bradley's first step was to requisition woolen shirts and attend the Sunday-morning inspection with the officer. "On that damp and chilling day, on the banks of the Potomac in mid-winter," she found seventy-five men with nothing warmer than thin cotton shirts. That problem was easily solved. Next she requested hospital tents with floors and stoves for the sick. She installed a washhouse so clothing and linen could be cleaned and purchased a bathtub, evidently an amenity previously lacking in the camp. Recognizing the value of amusement for men forced to be idle, she brought in playing cards, backgammon boards, checkerboards, chess sets, dominoes, and Chinese checkers sets.

With the men adequately clothed and fed and the sick among them made as comfortable as possible, she turned her attention to "another wretched class": men who had "proved incapable of service on account of chronic ailments or feeble constitutions," but who had not yet received honorable discharges or their arrears of pay. In some cases their papers had waited for several weeks in the surgeon's office, "while they were too weak or ill-clad to go out in the cold and stand till their turn came." Bradley brought these men to her hospital tents, where they were warmed, fed, and clothed; she then applied for their papers, arranged their transportation orders, and sent them to Washington in her ambulance "where they could take the proper train, go home and die among friends."[49]

Between May 1 and the end of December 1863, she traveled to Washington with almost every discharged soldier, settled him in the Commission Home, and walked him through the process of "obtaining a prompt and satisfactory settlement of [his] account with the government," almost 2,000 soldiers in total. She also helped reinstate some 150 soldiers on the army's records so they could receive their back pay. She noted with justifiable pride that "the sum total of the moneys thus paid in settlement to soldiers whose accounts were placed in my hands during the years, is between seven and eight thousand dollars,"[50] the equivalent of between $136,000 and $156,000 today.

When Bradley was sent to Camp Misery, she was asked what she wanted to accomplish. Her answer was "Ultimately to break up the camp,"[51] and she succeeded. On January 14, 1864, thirteen months after she arrived, the army issued Special Order No. 20, which provided that "Camp Convalescent will hereafter be known as 'Rendezvous of Distribution' and the place from which all men fit for field duty arriving at the Department of Washington will be distributed to their regiments. In future, none but men fit for field service, and deserters, will be sent to Rendezvous."[52] Bradley's last task at Camp Convalescent was to organize the transfer of the remaining convalescents to hospitals or their homes.

Before Camp Convalescent was disbanded, its men and officers presented Bradley with a gold watch in appreciation of her services, an acknowledgement of her extraordinary accomplishment.

• • •

The newspapers of the time referred to Clara Barton as "the soldier's friend," but she was not the only nurse to deserve the title.

Soldiers and their families regularly thanked the "friends" who nursed them back to health or eased their way into death. Amy Bradley's receipt of a gold watch from grateful soldiers was unusual, but it was not unique; Cornelia Hancock received a silver medal from the wounded soldiers of Third Division Second Army Corps inscribed *Testimonial of regard for ministrations of mercy to the wounded soldiers at Gettysburg, Pa. —July 1863*.[53] Other nurses received smaller tokens: a hand-carved ring, a picture frame made from a cigar box, a spun-glass ornament, an ivory cross. In one case, a grateful father offered to take his son's nurse home with him to be his daughter.

The most common tributes, and perhaps the most valued, were the letters from the boys themselves: "To our soldiers' friend . . . You will please excuse a Soldier for writing a few lines to you to express our thankfulness for your kindness to our pour wounded comrades after the late battle."[54]

As far as their soldier patients were concerned, the nurses had become indispensable indeed.

Chapter 8

Leaving Mansion House Hospital

"I shall not come home, unless I get sick,
while this hospital lasts."
—Cornelia Hancock[1]

C ivil War–era hospitals were breeding grounds for contagious diseases, including smallpox, measles, pneumonia, influenza, tuberculosis, typhoid, and yellow fever. Typhoid and what Civil War doctors loosely termed "diarrhea and dysentery" were the most widespread. Malarial diseases came in a close third for Northern soldiers with no immunity against the malaria endemic to the Southern marshlands.

Of the three, typhoid was the most deadly and most feared. It accounted for 17 percent of patient deaths in 1861; by 1865 that percentage had increased to 56 percent.[2] The bacteria that cause typhoid, *Salmonella typhi*, live in the human bloodstream and digestive tract. The only way to catch the disease is to eat or drink something contaminated by the virus, which can happen if someone carrying it handles food, or if sewage contaminated with it gets into the water used for drinking or cooking. Once the bacteria are in the body, they spread into the bloodstream from the digestive tract. At first the body responds to the presence of the bacteria with fever and fatigue, accompanied by headaches, diarrhea, loss of appetite, and, in the most severe cases, intestinal perforation. Some patients have a rose-colored rash. The infection can also travel to the lungs, causing pneumonia. Intestinal bleeding and pneumonia were the cause of most typhoid deaths in the days before antibiotics.

Dysentery and related diseases were less deadly than typhoid. Today we use the word "dysentery" to describe two specific diseases caused by the bacteria *Shigella* or the amoebic parasite *Entamoeba histolytica.* Both forms of dysentery cause fever, abdominal pain, vomiting, headaches, delirium, and diarrhea with stools containing blood or mucus. Like typhoid, both types are transmitted by ingesting food or water contaminated by someone who carries the disease. During the Civil War, the word was used in a more generic sense to describe any condition that resulted in a loose or watery stool containing blood or mucus.

John Snow's groundbreaking work in tracing the source of a virulent outbreak of cholera in London in 1854 identified contaminated water as the source for cholera, and by the 1860s much of the European medical community had accepted his discovery and extended it to include dysentery and typhoid. A bacterial theory of disease was still some decades in the future.

American medicine was slower to accept Snow's work. The most progressive American doctors recognized the relationship between bad latrines, human waste, and diseases like dysentery. But because the mechanism of contagion remained unclear, they could do little more than attempt to keep regimental latrines and hospital wards "sanitary" within the contemporary understanding of the word. The prevailing theory of the period focused on clean air rather than clean water. Instead of disease being transmitted in some way from person to person, mias-matic medical theory held that diseases were spread through the poisoned atmosphere of "miasmas," including "crowd poison-ing," caused by soldiers sleeping packed together in unventi-lated tents. While proponents of this theory also advocated sanitary camps and hospitals, their concern was eradicating the source of foul smells, especially those caused by rotting vegeta-bles or meat. Other popular explanations for outbreaks of the "flux"—an old-fashioned term for all manner of gastrointesti-nal diseases—included eating unripe fruit or raw vegetables, wearing wet clothes, and sleeping on damp ground. No one understood that both typhoid and dysentery could be carried by an individual displaying no symptoms of the disease, mak-ing the use of convalescent soldiers as cooks and ward atten-dants an active danger to patients whose immune systems were already compromised. Think Typhoid Mary, the infamous asymptomatic carrier whose career as a domestic cook twenty years later resulted in multiple outbreaks of typhoid.

The sanitary arrangements in Civil War hospitals also made it easy for both typhoid and dysentery to spread. Many latrines and indoor water closets had to be flushed with buckets of water, carried some distance by hand, which meant they were not flushed out as frequently as required to keep them sanitary. In some hospitals, latrines were located too close to kitchens. Even when there was an adequate distance between the two, flies carried bacteria on their feet as they flew between latrines, kitchens, and patients' dinner trays.

Disease was the greatest danger for nurses as well as for wounded solders. Few who had regular contact with soldiers escaped infection. Nurses, worn down from the physical and emotional strain of their work, were often hit harder than the men they took care of.

Mary Phinney von Olnhausen lasted eleven months at Mansion House Hospital before succumbing to dysentery.

A High-Risk Environment

Civil War hospitals were battlefields in their own rights, where nurses fought to save lives and sometimes became casualties of war. In 1863, Hannah Ropes and Louisa May Alcott fell ill at Union House Hospital.

Ropes found the atmosphere in Union House Hospital difficult in the days following her confrontations with the steward and Dr. Clark's arrest and release: "The matter of food is bad enough," she wrote in her diary on November 6, 1862. "But I believe the depressing sphere of the house tells quite as much upon the men as anything else. Generally I have been able to bring a smile from the invalids, but now they curl their heads under the sheet and think it is of no use to try any longer to get well."[3] Dr. Clark, now back at the hospital, refused to visit the wards. Ropes thought it was just as well: "I fear the men would hiss at him if he did."[4] Holed up in his office like a wounded fox, he lashed out in irrational ways against his staff, countermanding other surgeons' orders for invalids' food and refusing Ropes access to either the room where surgeries were performed or the storeroom.

The tempest inside the hospital was matched by the weather outside when a severe snowstorm hit Washington. Icicles hung from the hospital's window sashes, and snow stood a foot deep on the roof. There was no coal on hand, thanks to the steward's depredations, and the men suffered needlessly in the unheated building. Ropes worried about the men in the camps, fearing that the next patients who came to the hospital would suffer from fever rather than wounds. Soon, though, the hospital would be overwhelmed with the wounded from the Battle of Fredericksburg, at which the Union forces suffered a bloody and spectacular military failure.

On November 9, 1862, President Lincoln replaced McClellan as the commander of the Army of the Potomac with General Ambrose Burnside, a West Point graduate who proved to be as impulsive in the field as McClellan was cautious. In mid-November, Burnside began the Union's next "drive to Richmond." He planned a massive direct attack on the Confederate capital. The first step was a rapid advance that would allow the Union troops to move across the Rappahannock River, seize the heights to the west and southwest of Fredericksburg, and march on Richmond before Lee could shift his troops north and prevent the Union's forces from crossing the river. Burnside's troops arrived at the river according to schedule, but a mix-up about the pontoon bridges they needed for the river crossing left Burnside, then General-in-Chief Henry "Old Brains" Halleck, and Quartermaster General Montgomery Meigs pointing fingers at each other while Lee entrenched his troops along the heights behind Fredericksburg. Burnside's troops outnumbered Lee's 100,000 to 75,000, but Lee held the stronger position, an eight-mile-long front anchored on the east end by a twelve-hundred-foot stone wall at the foot of Marye's Heights. If Burnside continued the attack as planned, his troops would have to cross the river, move through the town, and cross a wide plain under Lee's guns. Burnside decided to do just that.

On December 11, Union troops fired on the city while engineers put three pontoon bridges in place, and the battle began in earnest on December 13. Over the course of the day, Burnside flung his infantry in fourteen suicidal charges against the stone wall at Marye's Heights; none of them reached the wall, and few got within fifty yards of it. When the two sides declared a truce on December 15, so that the wounded of both armies could be removed from the field, the Union army had suffered 12,700 casualties, with 6,000 of them dead.

Dr. John Letterman, known as the "father of battlefield medicine" and then medical director of the Army of the Potomac, took advantage of the delayed arrival of the pontoon bridges to be sure his arrangements for treating and evacuating battlefield casualties were in order. With a storehouse of supplies at the nearby railroad depot at Aquia Creek, five hundred hospital tents, and almost a thousand ambulances, Letterman and his staff crossed the pontoon bridges with Burnside's troops on December 12, to identify undamaged buildings that could be used as temporary field hospitals and stock them for use. For the first time since the war began, the Medical Bureau was prepared for battle. Problems began when it was time to move the men from field hospitals to facilities more suited for long-term care.

In Washington, fifty-some miles away from the battlefield, the staff at Union House Hospital anticipated the arrival of the wounded. "All the week we have been getting ready for the expected battle," Ropes wrote in her diary on December 13, the same day Burnside's troops battered themselves against Lee's defenses. Every morning they sent those patients who were in the best condition to hospitals farther north in order to make room for the expected flood of patients; every evening their beds were full again with sick men from the camps around Washington.[5] The only bright point in the day was the arrival of "Miss Alcott from Concord," who showed the potential to be a really good nurse, something the hospital desperately needed as some of the current nurses seemed to consider keeping a patient from falling out of bed the full extent of their job.[6]

The transfer of some six thousand wounded soldiers from Fredericksburg to the hospitals in and around Washington began on December 16. In order to give them time to stabilize, Letterman had kept the wounded on site as long as possible, housed in canvas tents outside Fredericksburg even though they were less than a day's travel from Washington, and he intended to keep them longer. Burnside, however, insisted that it was necessary to transfer the men to permanent hospitals. The disorder of an unplanned evacuation replaced Letterman's careful planning for battlefield care. Those in the best condition were moved first. Soldiers walked or were taken by ambulance to the Falmouth railroad station, where they were loaded onto railroad cars. Many of the cars were open platforms with nothing to protect the men from the weather, not well designed for transporting wounded men at any time, but especially bad in midwinter. There was only a single railroad track between Falmouth and Aquia Landing, which served as the embarkation point for the river steamboats that carried the wounded to Washington. No one coordinated the arrivals and departures of the trains and steamers, so wounded soldiers were left on the landing in the winter cold without shelter for hours at a time, dependent on an improvised Sanitary Commission relief depot for food, medicine, blankets, and care. Only two of the steamers were equipped for the purpose; others had been pressed into service with no provisions made for the soldiers' comfort. Soldiers, already cold and worn, rested on the hard boards of the deck, without even food or drink.

Seventeen hours after they finally left Fredericksburg, the wounded soldiers arrived in Washington, where ambulances transported them to hospitals throughout the city. It was Christmas before the evacuation was complete.

The first seventy-one casualties from Fredericksburg reached Union Hotel Hospital on the evening of December 17. As soon as the nurses got them settled in, they received an order to send forty men, the least wounded, to a hospital farther north to make room for the next shipment of casualties. On December 21, Ropes told her daughter Alice that they were waiting for "a fresh supply of worse wounded from the Fredericksburg battles, or murder ground I might say."[7] Eight days later, the hospital was filled with seriously wounded men, including twenty who had suffered amputations, and the nurses had their "hearts and hands full."[8]

In addition to washing men, dressing wounds, and carrying trays, Ropes and Alcott worked together over the next ten days to take care of four dying men, who proved to be highly contagious. Alcott developed a cough almost immediately. Since many of the patients suffered from a similar cough, Ropes initially dismissed it as "purely sympathetic,"[9] the nineteenth century's equivalent of the medical student who diagnoses herself as suffering from each ailment she studies. By January 11, Alcott was sick enough that Ropes ordered her to stay in her room with a mustard plaster on her chest. The doctors visited her room daily to tap on her chest. After several days they began to raise their eyebrows ominously. Finally they told her to go home, but Alcott was determined to serve out her three-month commitment to the nursing corps. Her severe chills and the violent cough of typhoid-related pneumonia developed into delirium: "Hours began to get confused; people looked odd; queer faces haunted the room, and the nights were one long fight with weariness and pain."[10] In the third week of January, Alcott's father arrived in Washington, where he found her near death. "At the sight of him, my resolution melted away," Alcott admitted. "My heart turned traitor to my boys, and when he said 'Come home,' I answered 'Yes father.' And so ended my career as an army nurse."[11]

Ropes became sick with typhoid pneumonia at the same time as Alcott. She developed the characteristic rose-colored rash on her chest and suffered from sharp pains in her ribs, severe coughing, and uncontrollable diarrhea. On December 29, the new head surgeon placed Ropes "under arrest" in her room. He visited her twice a day. The entire hospital staff worked together to care for her. The surgeons swore the place would fall apart without her.[12] It wasn't enough. With two nurses seriously ill and the hospital full of the wounded from Fredericksburg, Ropes's Washington friends sent for Alice to help care for her. Ropes died the evening of January 20, the same day Bronson Alcott was preparing to take his daughter home.

Ropes worked at the Union Hotel Hospital as a nurse for six months; Alcott for less than forty days. Nursing was hazardous work.

On the Front Lines at Mansion House Hospital

In the six months from December 1862 through May 1863, the nurses at Mansion House were stretched trying to keep up with the flow of wounded in and out of the hospital.

Mansion House Hospital received an overwhelming number of wounded men after the Battle of Fredericksburg. Like their counterparts at Union Hotel Hospital, the nurses at Mansion House received orders to clear space in anticipation of the arriving wounded from the great battle. Anne Reading noted that they needed to do the best they could for the seventy-five patients who had just arrived from the convalescent camp because they would soon have to send them, as well as their own convalescent patients, to one of the hospitals farther north to make room for as many new patients as possible. When the time arrived, she made sure that her ward was ready. Beds made up. Sponges, soap, clean linen and towels ready. It was a good thing they were prepared: on December 21, seven hundred wounded men, rebel and Union alike, were brought into Alexandria, filling every bed in every ward at hospitals throughout the city.[13]

Reading looked back on her performance with satisfaction at a job well done. By contrast, von Olnhausen, worn out with excitement and fatigue, described the arrival of the wounded after the Battle of Fredericksburg with righteous indignation about the handling of the evacuation:

> To-day has been such an awful day . . . The whole street was full of ambulances, and the sick lay outside on the sidewalks from nine in the morning till five in

the evening. Of course, places were found for some; but already the house was full; so the most had to be packed back again and taken off to Fairfax Seminary, two miles out. I have been so indignant all day,—not a thing done for them, not a wound dressed. To be sure, they got dinner; but no supper. They reached town last evening, lay in the cars all day without blankets or food, were chucked into ambulances, lay about here all day, and tonight were put back into ambulances and carted off again. I think every man who comes a-soldiering is a fool![14]

In the weeks and months that followed Fredericksburg, the hospital received wave after wave of wounded, beginning with the Confederate raid on the Union supply depot at Dumfries on December 28 and ending with the great battle between Generals Hooker and Lee at Chancellorsville, which dragged on from April 30 to May 6 and left more than 30,000 dead on the field. For von Olnhausen and the other nurses, the days ran together in a patchwork of boredom, frantic activity, and exhaustion. Sometimes they were barely aware of what day it was or the place from which the men were evacuated.

Over and over nurses sent convalescent patients to hospitals farther north in anticipation of more wounded coming in: "We have been sending off this week everyone who could be moved," von Olnhausen wrote.

And you may believe it's been a pretty blue time with me, I have had so many of them so long under my care.[15]

On Friday last, we sent over fifty men from this hospital to Providence Rhode Island. As we are in daily expectation of another battle, we are clearing out as many as are convalescent in order that we may be ready for reception of the wounded.[16]

Tuesday night came another dispatch from head-quarters that every man who could be moved must leave next morning for Philadelphia; so before I had got interested or could distinguish one man from another I lost them all . . . wasn't it too bad when had got them all cleaned up and straightened out to have them go again? They left me only six of the new cases. I have eleven in all. It was harder to have them go than come, I think; they did not want to leave, either.[17]

Repeatedly, the nurses received the news that patients were on the way, hurried to prepare the wards to receive them, and resigned themselves to the strain of waiting:

We have just heard that by the last of the week every bed in the house will be full; the sick and the wounded are all to be sent from the front.[18]

We have been expecting some wounded all day from Fairfax Station . . . but they have not come yet; probably, as usual, they will come in the night.[19]

I hope before I write you again we have have our house filled up once more; I am so tired of this idleness.

Those wounded expected yesterday did not come, and we almost despair.[20]

On Monday morning news came that a boatload of wounded men were on the way for us. They arrived about five o'clock,—such a sick, neglected set as one could ever see.[21]

As each fresh lot of wounded arrived, Reading found it heart-sickening to see them. They were so dreadfully mutilated and suffered so badly. The head wounds were particularly bad. The ball went in the back of one young man's head and came out the front, carrying hair and brains with it; he lived just long enough to make it to the hospital and then died. In another case, the ball missed the man's brain, but tore out his left eye as it exited. She found such wounds more shocking than anything she had seen before.[22]

In one nightmarish repetition of the arrival of the wounded from Fredericksburg, sometime in March or April, von Oln-hausen struggled to deal with the newly arrived wounded without the help of attendants or supervision from the ward physician. Boatload after boatload of the wounded had arrived in Alexandria over the course of the day, so many that the city's hospitals could not take them all and two boatloads of men had to be reloaded and sent on to Washington. Seventeen hundred injured soldiers, ambulances, stretchers, crutches—everything and everyone jammed the streets. The ward attendants made multiple trips, lugging crippled men from the wharves to the hospital until they were too exhausted to carry another man. It was midnight before the last boat of suffering men arrived.

With the exception of two men detailed to wash the wounded as they arrived, von Olnhausen had no attendants to help her in the ward. The doctor in charge of her ward was the officer of the day and could not leave his post. He sent for her and told her to manage everything as she thought proper—a statement of trust that she valued, though in the moment she would have valued another set of hands more. She helped wash the men, then began to dress their wounds, make splints, and put up fractures. With no assistance, it took hours. The closest thing she got to surgical support was a a flying midnight visit from the chief surgeon, Dr. Page, who simply told her he was pleased with her work and moved on to inspect the next ward. It was nearly morning before she fell into bed, knowing that another round of dressing wounds awaited her in the morning.[23]

Several weeks later, von Olnhausen had only a few brand-new recruits as attendants to help her with a boatload of wounded who had been in rebel hands for more than a week: "I thought I never should get the patients washed and into bed . . . Until you could once be in a hospital and see the state of the men as they come in, especially of those who have the blood of three weeks upon them and the dirt of as many months, you can form no idea of the undertaking. But the satisfaction on their faces when all is done and they are finally at rest is very great. Especially when a woman is near to nurse them, they seem so grateful."[24]

In May, as the wounded rolled in from Chancellorsville, rumors flew around Alexandria that Confederate troops were poised to invade the city and liberate it from its Northern occupiers. Most people only half believed the rumors, but the military could not afford to ignore them; Alexandria was not only the major storehouse for the Army of the Potomac but the gateway to Washington. General John Clough, military governor of the city, ordered that preparations be made for its defense. Soldiers dug rifle pits across the streets leading to the commissary departments and rigged the bridge across the Potomac so it could be destroyed in an instant. Armed sentries patrolled the streets and the few secesh men in the hospital were put under guard. Von Olnhausen informed her correspondents in Lexington that a battery of four guns had been planted in a pit just under her window. Even as she wrote, the orderly was arming every man in the hospital able to shoulder a gun. She assured her correspondents, "I don't feel the least frightened for myself, but it's horrid to think of these poor wounded fellows and what they would suffer. The town is full of Secesh just waiting for a raid in order to come out openly; and they could fire every hospital at once."[25]

With the Confederate army reportedly only ten miles away, the front lines seemed very near.

Nursing the Enemy

Nurses fell into two camps on the question of caring for the enemy. Those driven by a religious need for service were generally willing to nurse the enemy, even if they couldn't manage to love him. Those who enlisted out of patriotic zeal were less sympathetic to wounded Confederates.

Amy Morris Bradley was clearly one of those who took to heart the dictum "If thine enemy hunger, feed him." When a surgeon advised her not to help a wounded Alabamian, she snapped back, "Doctor, that poor boy is wounded [and] suffering intensely—he was my enemy, but now he needs my aid. If I obey not the teachings of the Savior I am not a true disciple."[26] Hannah Ropes was a devout Swedenborgian; her response to the presence of a Confederate soldier with an amputated leg in Union Hotel Hospital was simple: "We take just as good care of him as of anyone."[27] (Louisa May Alcott, confronted with the same Confederate soldier, was not inclined to "deliver a moral sermon upon the duty of forgiving our enemies." Instead she promised herself she'd get soap in his eyes, and rub his nose the wrong way if she got the job of washing him.[28]) Anne Reading, whose Anglican faith was clearly an important part of her life, admired the patience and resignation with which one rebel officer who had been shot in the spine at Fredericksburg and was paralyzed from the waist down dealt with his sufferings. She claimed her sister, who was assigned to nurse him, couldn't have done more for him if he had been a Union officer.

Von Olnhausen was definitely in the patriotic zeal camp and not shy about expressing her feelings on the subjects of seceshes and "copperheads," a pejorative term for Northerners who opposed Lincoln's war policy and advocated restoring the Union through a negotiated settlement with the South. In May 1863, after the battle of Chancellorsville, where her hometown regiment the Second Massachusetts was hard hit, she snarled, "How I hate my Reb wounded."[29] She didn't think she could bring herself to dress their wounds anymore. It was a position she found hard to maintain when faced with a badly wounded Confederate. A few weeks later, sixteen men from the Forty-third Virginia Battalion, known as Mosby's Raiders, were brought to Mansion House Hospital. Four of them were placed in von Olnhausen's ward. She hated having them there and at first felt that she could not, would not, take care of them. But two of them were so badly wounded that she began to feel pity for them, even after she learned that one of them had killed a Union soldier after the man surrendered to him. He was only sixteen, with voice still like a child's, and had been in the army for just two months. In the end, "his sufferings were so terrible that [she] forgot for the time how wicked he was," and cared for him as best she could.[30]

Fighting for Their Rations

In the middle of this period of hard work and high stress, von Olnhausen led the other nurses in a revolt against the tyranny of the cooks and the steward.

In March 1863, Dr. Summers, with whom von Olnhausen had developed a good working relationship after a rocky start, was promoted and sent to another post. A new chief surgeon, Dr. Page, replaced him, and the steward and cooks took the opportunity to lash out at the nurses, who had cut off their ability to sell rations on the black market by fighting for the soldiers' rights. Instead of spoiling their food, the cooks attacked the nurses' rations, serving them nothing but bad coffee with no milk and dry bread for breakfast, bread and stringy meat for dinner, and coffee and bread again at night. Mrs. B., who seemed the logical person to address the problem since she managed the low diet, refused to go to Dr. Page and ask about their rations for fear he would think the nurses were selfish.

Sitting by the fire one night, tired, and so hungry she could have eaten cat's meat, von Olnhausen decided she had had enough. She went to Dr. Page, who called the steward, H., into his office and told him that in the future the nurses were to draw their own rations from the common store and have their own cook.

They waited for five days and received no rations, despite making repeated demands to the kitchen. Finally von Olnhausen threatened to appeal to Dr. Page again. Only then did the steward—described by von Olnhausen as "just the meanest, hatefullest (oh, help me to a word, I don't care if it *is* profane) man that ever lives"—send them rations for a ten-day period. The rations were so short the nurses were forced to buy half of what they needed. Sure that something was wrong, von Olnhausen asked soldiers from the quartermaster's department to check their rations; the nurses learned they had not received a third of what they were due. After another round with Dr. Page and the steward, von Olnhausen asked that the nurses be allowed to draw their rations directly from the quartermaster. No doubt happy to end the discussion, Dr. Page signed a requisition order for the eight nurses.

Von Olnhausen and Mrs. B. went straight to the quartermaster, taking a boy along to help them carry the rations. To their amazement they needed a cart, not a boy with a basket: eighty pounds of meat and eighty pounds of flour plus beans, rice, molasses, vinegar, salt pork, tea, coffee, and sugar. Even candles. When von Olnhausen and Mrs. B. called the other nurses down to see the bounty, they all went a little crazy with joy. The women immediately indulged in their own version of selling off rations. They sold sixty-two pounds of meat for $5.25 ($102 today), and used it to buy butter and milk, plus some cups and saucers to replace the standard-issue tin mugs. They traded their flour pound for pound to a baker in exchange for bread and an occasional cake or pie. In the short run, the revolt was a success. The nurses drew their rations every ten days, using the surplus to allow them to buy items that were not standard rations. They were overjoyed with how nicely they could live once they understood how the system worked; the luxury of drinking from a cup made an enormous difference.

Their triumph would be short-lived.

Phinney Comes Down with Dysentery

Von Olnhausen enjoyed her triumphs, small and large: a doctor's praise for her skill in splinting a fractured leg, a field trip to Mount Vernon with a group of convalescents, a venal steward thwarted. Nonetheless, confusion, overwork, and exhaustion are recurring themes in her letters and diaries during this period:

> I live in such a state of confusion all the time. There is always somebody new quartered upon me. I have had a "game" leg and so many bad sick ones.[31]

> I hardly know whether I have a head on my shoulders; since last summer I never saw such times here, sick coming and going all the time.[32]

> You can form no idea of our disturbed nights,— constant alarms and the backward movement of the army. The continual rattling of heavy wagons and the guard patrolling and challenging, one cannot sleep much. I have not felt fully awake in a fortnight; and

when the noise outside is a little less, comes the watch-
man with, "Somebody has a chill or a pain, or wants to
see me," so all nights are disturbed ones[33]

I shall give up, I cannot write; I have tried fifty
times since this was commenced. You can't know all I
have done these last two days; more patients have come
and gone, and now I have only ten left in my ward.[34]

When an epidemic of dysentery swept through the hospital
in June, she was already weakened by the long strain of work
and the heat and humidity of Washington's "evil climate." She
soon contracted a severe case of the disease. The other nurses
were too busy to care for her, so she lay in her room, half con-
scious and tended to by a small German convalescent, with big
round blue eyes that looked as large as cups to von Olnhausen
in her fever-induced delirium.

It was July before she was well enough to be moved, and
her sisters then took her home to Lexington to recuperate. Von
Olnhausen admitted, "After all the turmoil of that life, it was
so delightful to be quiet."[35] But as far as she was concerned, her
time in Lexington was nothing more than a leave of absence:
"I'm in it for the war until discharged; . . . I could never be
contented now at home remembering what I can do here and
how many need me. I know that all are not fitted for this life,
but I feel as if it were my special calling and I shall not leave it,
if God gives me strength, while I know there is a Union soldier
to nurse."[36]

• • •

Anne and Jenny Reading also left Mansion House Hospital in 1863, but for a much happier reason.

On October 30, 1862, Anne committed an unforgivable sin from Dorothea Dix's point of view and married one of her patients, Andrew Flurry. Not surprisingly, Reading chose to keep quiet about the marriage. In March someone told Miss Dix that Reading had gotten married. "Dragon" Dix was not pleased.

Reading was not the only woman to meet her future husband while nursing. Ellen Sarah Forbes and Nancy M. Atwood both married men they nursed. (Like Reading, Forbes married while part of the nursing corps and left as a result.) Amanda Akin, Georgeanna Woolsey, and Annie Bell all later married doctors they met during the course of the war. One Sister of Charity left her order to marry one of her soldier-patients. The numbers were small, but Dix feared the people who opposed female nurses in the army would use them as proof that women entered the nursing corps only to find a husband.

It was a common charge. Cornelia Hancock told her niece Sallie that she was sure most people believed that was the reason she'd joined the army. Hancock acknowledged that if she were interested, it would be a good place to look since there were many nice men, and since soldiers were required to show respect to women. There were a number of women who spent the evenings gallivanting in just that pursuit. As for herself, she declared, "I do not trouble myself with the common herd."[37]

Elvira Powers, somewhat older, took the suggestion that she might husband-hunt among her patients as a joke. "Once in my life did I have the audacity to pay special attention to a young corporal from Massachusetts by accompanying him to church one Sabbath evening, and came very near being discharged for the same. Shall never dare to repeat the heinous offense. Special attentions not allowed among Uncle Sam's nephews and nieces. It is my opinion that said corporal is not over fifteen years younger than myself, still there's no knowing what might have come of it." She concluded, tongue-in-cheek, "Ah, me! What a sacrifice am I making for the good of my country."[38]

Faced with Dix's strong disapproval of nurses marrying patients or doctors, Reading reached the conclusion that it was time for her to go. Jenny chose not to remain in Alexandria without her sister.

Reading planned to stay with her husband's family in Philadelphia until he was free to leave his regiment, but that changed when she got the news that he had been injured in a gun explosion and transferred to the convalescent camp. He expected it to be a year or more before he would be discharged. Rather than travel back to Alexandria to nurse him, she chose to stay in New York with her sister, where it would be easier to get work. She was unable to get her old job at St. Luke's; the matron, like Dix, disapproved of married nurses. Instead she found work in a factory in Yonkers, where she stayed through the end of the war, working her way up to a supervisory position over a female workforce made up primarily of Irish immigrants. Her nursing career, which had taken her to three continents and two wars, was over.

Chapter 9

Reporting Back to Duty

"One lady came here a few days since, who staid
[*sic*] only two days. She was 'not used to any such
fare, such cold rooms, and couldn't work for any such
pay.' There are others here who do not work for the
'pay,' but for something higher and better."
—Elvira Powers, *Hospital Pencillings*[1]

"Sometimes I think I cannot bear it another hour,
that I'll just leave here; but when I see these miserable
nurses and more miserable attendants who are here
merely for the poor pay, I think it cruel to go, for,
if anywhere, I can do some good here; these poor
fellows have at least someone to help them."
—Mary Phinney von Olnhausen[2]

Hundreds of women lasted little more than a month as
nurses in the Civil War, worn down by the physical
and emotional challenges, but others stayed for several years. Those who lasted were transformed by their experiences at the front and in general hospitals; fighting for soldiers
and with surgeons; facing the realities of dirt, disease, and
death; and the frustration of hospital politics and military protocol. Over time, they began to see themselves as veterans.

Though nursing would not become a profession until well after the war was over, when Mary Phinney von Olnhausen came back to Mansion House Hospital in September 1863, she returned with a renewed sense of vocation. She also found a new set of opportunities waiting for her. Doctors who "a year ago were all opposed to female nurses and 'poohed' at the idea of one being useful"[3] were now eager for her to work with them.

More Trouble at Mansion House Hospital

After a month of convalescence at home in Lexington, Mary Phinney von Olnhausen arrived back at Mansion House Hospital on September 3, 1863. The trip from Lexington to Alexandria was always long and complicated, and this time it had been particularly difficult. The boat from Boston was so full she considered herself lucky to find a spot to sleep on the floor of the main cabin, though it was next to the door and everyone who came in or out was forced to step over her. The boat became even more crowded at Newport, Rhode Island, where 150 women and children got on board; all of them suffered from seasickness when the sea got rough. Once on land, a "copperhead" sat next to her on the train ride to Philadelphia and made her so furious she couldn't sleep. She boarded the train to Baltimore at midnight, only to have the girl in the bunk beneath her talk for two hours until von Olnhausen's own bunk broke down, and she almost squashed the young woman. The fright silenced the girl. Von Olnhausen moved to another bunk and finally got some sleep. When she reached Washington, she barely had time to run to Miss Dix's office, report in, and catch the boat to Alexandria.

After such an eventful and exhausting journey, her arrival at Mansion House Hospital felt like a letdown. The chief surgeon, Dr. Page, was delighted to see her, but most of the nurses she had worked with were discharged during the month she was away, and the doctors had relocated to other hospitals. In fact, it soon turned out the only thing that hadn't changed was her former adversary, the steward.

Von Olnhausen found two letters waiting for her, both of which offered her options if she didn't want to stay at Mansion House. The first was from Dr. Summers. He had wanted nothing to do with her when she had arrived at Mansion House the year before, but now he begged her to join him in Chattanooga, Tennessee, where he needed a matron for the large hospital under his control. The second job offer was from her old ward surgeon, Dr. Bellangee, who was now in charge of a new hospital at Morehead City, North Carolina, and needed a surgical nurse.

At first, von Olnhausen wasn't sure what to do. Mansion House Hospital looked dreary compared to the plan for the new hospital in North Carolina, and though Dr. Page was pressuring her to stay, Miss Dix urged her to go to North Carolina. The choice wasn't any clearer when looked at in terms of how busy a nurse was apt to be based on surrounding military activity. In the late summer and early fall of 1863, Union and Confederate forces were struggling for control over Chattanooga, which was a key railroad center and the gateway to the Confederacy from the west. Several of the bloodiest battles of the Civil War would be fought in and around Chattanooga later that fall, including the Battle of Chickamauga, but in the first week of September, the campaign was still a matter of feints and skirmishes. The Outer

Banks of North Carolina were the site of continual armed encounters between blockade runners and the Union's navy, but had not seen a major battle since before McClellan's Peninsular Campaign the previous summer. Alexandria, on the other hand, was located in the Union's medical center.

Mansion House soon became a less appealing option. H., the steward with whom von Olnhausen had fought the "ration wars" in March, had taken revenge in her absence. He had reported the butcher to whom the nurses sold their excess meat ration, and the government fined both the butcher and the nurses $50. Mrs. B. had appealed the case, but it was decided against the nurses soon after von Olnhausen's return. Angry that she had to pay out of pocket for her share of the fine, back to the old ration of beef and bread for meals, and irate at the lack of justice in the system, von Olnhausen told Dr. Page she could not stay in the hospital if H. remained. Dr. Page did not try to change her mind, but made her promise she would come back to him if he ever had a hospital without H. The last thing he said to her when they parted was that he depended on her to keep that promise. With the Mansion House door closed, von Olnhausen allowed Miss Dix to make the decision. North Carolina it was.

Von Olnhausen's trouble with the steward was not quite over, however. Just as she and Mrs. B. got in the ambulance to leave for the station and the first leg of their journey south, an order came for their arrest. H. had informed Dr. Page, who was out of town, that the two nurses were absconding with large quantities of the hospital's stores. Dr. Page could not ignore the accusation, so he sent word to the officer of the day to arrest and search them. The officer in question, Dr. Barnes, found

Mrs. B., told her he would rather leave the service than follow the orders, and got the chaplain to back him up. The two nurses were halfway to Baltimore before Mrs. B. recounted this to von Olnhausen, who was disappointed she had lost the opportunity to bring H. to grief. If she had known, she would have insisted Dr. Barnes carry out the search and prove them innocent.

As she told her correspondents in Lexington, "There can never be an end to fusses in the Mansion House."[4]

Impatient in North Carolina

Von Olnhausen and Mrs. B. arrived at Morehead City, North Carolina, on September 14, 1863, to find that the town and hospital were as different from Alexandria and Mansion House as it was possible to be.

Morehead City was located thirty miles from the state's former capital of New Bern, which served as the Union's military garrison for the region, and the town, like the hospital, was very new. Developers with aspirations of building a new port city on the Newport River sold the first six hundred lots in 1857; but it was still little more than a fishing village at the terminus of the new Atlantic and East Carolina Railroad when it was incorporated on February 20, 1861, only two months before the war began.

The Union army occupied Morehead City in April 1862, as part of an amphibious campaign to gain control of the barrier islands and numerous inlets of North Carolina's Outer Banks, thereby plugging holes in the Union's blockade of Southern ports. The campaign was successful enough that

Lincoln appointed a military governor for the state in May 1862. Major operations in the region ended that summer with the withdrawal of troops for McClellan's Peninsular Campaign, but a force of Union troops remained garrisoned at New Bern under the control of Major General John G. Foster. While North Carolina seemed like a military backwater compared to Alexandria, New Bern served as the hub for regular raids against Lee's supply lines. The region would remain a contested area until February 1865, when Union forces captured Wilmington, the last open Confederate seaport. Casualties in the Outer Banks campaigns were small compared to those in Virginia or the western territories, but the need for military hospitals was real. Mansfield General Hospital at Morehead City was the last of three general hospitals the Union army built in coastal North Carolina. It was not yet finished when von Olnhausen arrived. Her initial impression was that the place "looked forlorn enough,"[5] though she admitted that Dr. Bellangee had accomplished wonders in the short time he had been there. Eight barracks, holding forty-five beds each, were completed and ready for patients, and another three to four were scheduled to be built. So far the hospital held only two hundred patients, but there was talk at the time of breaking up the hospital at New Bern and transferring its patients to Morehead City, a proposal von Olnhausen approved of because she felt New Bern was unhealthy—a sinkhole of bad smells and uncleaned cisterns. Rumors about which hospital should be closed and how patients should be moved among the general hospitals at Morehead City, New Bern, and Beaufort would be a regular and distressing part of von Olnhausen's experience in North Carolina.

Von Olnhausen would later declare that Morehead City was the best hospital she saw during the war, but she was slow to reach that conclusion. She spent her first several months there begging Miss Dix to relocate her because she felt she was underutilized. Only two weeks into her assignment, she complained that while she was a little less homesick, she was not happy. The setting was beautiful, only two miles away from the open sea and surrounded by green woods, and Dr. Bellangee was kind and supportive. But she had nothing to do. Anytime she got a patient, he recovered in only a few days thanks to the fine sea air. She ranted to a friend, "I certainly did not come into the service to play; and every walk I take I feel as if I were a real humbug."[6]

The only excitement she had in her first weeks at Mansfield Hospital was a tussle with an assistant surgeon protective of his rank and privileges. He threatened to have her discharged because had she not consulted him before performing what he claimed was a surgical procedure. She had applied a mustard plaster, a remedy familiar to nineteenth-century housewives, to a man who suffered from the colic in the middle of the night. (Today colic refers to an infant disorder, but in nineteenth-century medical terminology it was a painful abdominal spasming that usually occurred in adults; perhaps irritable bowel syndrome.) When the assistant surgeon complained the next morning, Dr. Bellangee wrote out permission authorizing her "to mustard" when necessary.

During this period, von Olnhausen was torn between frustration at Dix's refusal to relocate her and very real appreciation of the relative peace of the hospital in contrast to "the corruption and constant fusses of the Mansion House."[7] Her daily routine was as orderly as that maintained by Nightingale's nurses in the Crimea, with time for long walks after dinner and an occasional sail. She admitted that it was a very healthy life— and it drove her crazy. She complained loudly and often about both the low quantity and quality of the work that was asked of her. By December, she was so discouraged that she was tempted to "cut Miss Dix altogether and run away."[8] She had only two wounds to dress and feared she was forgetting all she knew. One was an injured rebel, who wasn't even wounded in battle, but had cut his hand making shingles, severing the artery. It kept bleeding, so she had to watch him night and day, finding it "pretty tedious to have to sit all day looking at the very dirtiest paw you ever saw." The other was a black freeman "who was shot, all for love."[9] At a time when there were thousands of wounded Union soldiers in other parts of the country who needed her, she felt she was wasting her time caring for Confederate soldiers and civilians.

She was distracted in mid-December by the unexpected arrival of some half dozen inspectors, sent by General Butler with what proved to be idle threats of closing the hospital; and again at New Years' Eve when the soldiers at Fort Macon, located across Bogue Sound from the hospital, invited the nurses to a ball. Dr. Bellangee insisted his nurses accept the invitation. Von Olnhausen went reluctantly, feeling shabby in a patched purple skirt, without the proper shoes or gloves. It ultimately didn't matter what she wore: "I was not first-best, but as there were only seven ladies, I had to be a belle, and so danced continuously."[10] It was a late night, even for nurses accustomed to long days. The weather turned so bad that they could not take the tug back across the sound until five in the morning. When they got to the station, they discovered the mule that pulled their cart to the landing had run off, so they had to walk the last mile on dance-weary feet. Just as von Olnhausen got upstairs, hoping to get an hour's sleep before beginning the inexorable routine of the hospital day, an orderly came to tell her that one of her patients was worse. When she checked on him, she was sure he wouldn't live long, so she threw off her "ball fixings" and stayed with him until he died, at about nine that morning.

On January 3, foreseeing another year at Mansfield Hospital, von Olnhausen reached the point of despair. Her ward had been full for the last fortnight, but all her patients were up for discharge or furlough. She was nursing two bad typhoid cases, but she didn't think they would live much longer. Then she would be out of a job, with nothing to do but loaf. She was ready to "darn" Miss Dix, who seemed determined to keep her in North Carolina for the rest of her life, particularly since Dr. Bellangee had told the nursing supervisor how useful she was. She wanted someone to need her somewhere else and to demand that she come, no matter who objected.

Dirty Line

To add insult to frustration, von Olnhausen was given responsibility for the laundry operation at Morehead City, a task that involved supervising as many as twenty laundresses in a demanding job. To most nurses, the laundry was the least prestigious and most annoying of all the jobs associated with nursing, and one that von Olnhausen had never been involved with at Mansion House.

Civil War–era laundry was a difficult job under any circumstance, one that most households undertook no more than once a week. Washing machines were a relatively new invention, first demonstrated at the 1851 Crystal Palace exhibition in London. They consisted of a ten- or twenty-gallon cylinder on top of a boiler that produced both hot water for the clothes and the steam that drove the engine. The operator would put clothes and soap in the cylinder, which then revolved for five to ten minutes. High-end versions had a second boiler for hot rinse water. The machines were expensive and found in only the wealthiest homes: in 1861 a basic machine cost $50—more than $9,000 today.[11]

Most people made do with wooden washtubs, soup-sized kettles for heating water, and elbow grease. The first step, one not thought of as part of the laundry process today, was mending and patching. Once she finished mending torn clothing and bed linens, the laundress or housewife moved on to stain removal, a time-consuming process that could involve applying lemon juice (a relatively expensive choice), exposing stained items to direct sunlight, or soaking them overnight in "blood warm water" (basically the same temperature as a baby's bottle). Washable clothing (made from fabrics such as cotton and linen as opposed to silk, leather, velvet, and some woolens), bed linens, and rags were then washed in hot water using soft soap and a scrub board, boiled to kill lice and insects, rinsed several times in hot water, allowed to cool, and then rinsed again in cool water. Wet laundry was hung out to dry on anything that would hold it off the ground: lines in a yard, bushes, porch railings. Once dry, clothing would be ironed using a cast-metal iron heated on a stove or run through a mangle, a device made up of two rollers and a crank that used pressure to smooth the wrinkles from the fabric.

This description masks the layers of physical work involved in the process. Water had to be brought from water sources that varied in degree of inconvenience: a stream or pond at some distance from a home, a shared pump in an urban neighborhood, a farmyard well. Once acquired, water was heated in large kettles on wood- or coal-burning stoves and carried from kitchen to washtub. Commercial soap was not yet widely available outside of major cities, though Procter and Gamble would transform itself from a struggling Cincinnati soap and candle maker to a national brand over the course of the war thanks to army contracts; many homes made their own.

From mending to folding, laundry was backbreaking work, and hospital laundry was done the same way on a larger scale. It was not unusual for a general hospital laundry to process two to three thousand pieces of laundry in one day.

Laundresses were employed directly by the army and entitled to the same housing, fuel, and rations as a soldier. Early in the war, they were often the wives or widows of enlisted men. As the war went on and the Union army moved farther south, the demographic makeup of laundry staffs shifted. Most of the laundresses who reported to von Olnhausen in North Carolina were free blacks or escaped slaves; not surprising since the region around New Bern was the principal refuge for escaped slaves on the North Carolina coast.

Von Olnhausen's relationship with the women who worked for her is troubling from a modern perspective, though typical for the period. Racism and abolitionism were not mutually exclusive positions at the time. (Louisa May Alcott, for instance, who claimed "the blood of two generations of abolitionists waxed hot in my veins,"[12] nonetheless described the black laundry and kitchen workers at Union House Hospital in less than flattering terms as "obsequious, trickish, lazy and ignorant, yet kind-hearted, [and] merry-tempered."[13]) Von Olnhausen refers to the laundry workers under her supervision as "nigs" and "darkies" and complains of their inability to use a handkerchief or properly fold a dressing gown. Yet, recognizing that the laundry staff were in rags and unable to provide clothing for themselves because the army was almost a year behind in paying salaries, she sewed night and day to make dresses and underclothing for them as Christmas gifts, an act of generosity that would be more impressive without her assertion that "it was no use to give them anything unmade, as they would botch it so."[14] In one horrifying scene, she slapped one of the women out of a hysterical fit, then followed it up by a "good shaking," "a right smart scolding," and "another dose of each" when the woman began to cry. When the rest of the staff broke out into sympathetic tears, von Olnhausen was so frustrated that she claimed, "If I'd been big enough and strong enough, I would have slapped them all."[15]

It was far from von Olnhausen's finest hour.

Under Attack

Von Olnhausen's wish for someone to need her was soon answered. In late January 1864, the Confederate army staged an attempt to recapture New Bern, which, as the major Union supply base in the region, held provisions that would be useful to the increasingly impoverished Confederate army. The news that New Bern had been attacked reached Morehead City on February 4; the next day they learned that a large Confederate force had attacked Newport Barracks, a Union supply depot only ten miles away on the railroad south of New Bern. Most of the forces garrisoned at Morehead City had already been sent to help defend New Bern. Now Colonel Jourdan of the 158th New York left for Newport Barracks with the few remaining men, mostly raw recruits, and two field pieces, leaving Morehead City almost defenseless for a brief time. The troops were forced back almost immediately, and Morehead City prepared to defend itself. "Such a scurrying time you never saw," von Olnhausen reported later. White men were armed, and black men were put to work digging entrenchments—a contrast to the response to possible attack in Alexandria, where all men not suspected of harboring Confederate sympathies, black and white, were armed to defend the city. Regimental stores were loaded on the gunboats to protect them from seizure by the Confederates, and everyone began to pack their belongings in case they had to flee. Von Olnhausen complained that "everything seemed to be thought of except the patients."[16] She refused to leave, or even pack, unless the patients went too.

That night they could see Newport Barracks burning. Cut off from all communications and "just waiting to be 'took,'" with only three hundred men to defend the city against a reported five thousand rebel soldiers, the residents were jumpy. Civilian women screamed in their houses with fear that their men might be forced to fight. Occasionally a terrified sentry fired his gun at nothing. Soldiers from Newport Barracks arrived throughout the night; some had been wounded in the attack on the depot, and all had alarming stories of Confederate forces on the move. A thousand rumors flew, but the feared Confederate force never arrived.

The main body of the defending force from Newport Barracks began to find their way to Morehead City the next day, arriving a few at a time. Even with more men to help defend the city, its residents spent another day and night of constant alarms, with everyone ready for instant flight. The hospital not only took care of all the sick and tired soldiers as they arrived, but also sheltered about a hundred black women and children from the surrounding countryside who had taken refuge in the city. Fires were visible in all directions. Parties of men could be seen moving on the other side of the river, too distant to tell if they were friend or foe. Hopeful citizens watched for reinforcements from the high places in the city. With the telegraph lines cut and bridges burned, no one knew whether New Bern had fallen or not. In the course of the excitement, von Olnhausen never lost focus on her main concern: "They talk of many wounded and killed, but they brought only three into Beaufort and one or two have straggled in here. All that came I have in my ward."[17]

Skirmishes continued throughout the region well into the spring. By February 25, von Olnhausen was able to report with satisfaction: "I have had my hands full of wounded at last." She was particularly excited about one case: a Confederate soldier with "a good Union ball through his lung." He was gaunt, haggard, and emaciated, a physical type she believed was peculiar to North Carolina, though it is probable that the poverty of the Confederate army was actually to blame. He was also filthy, very grateful, and very sick. She had him washed and clothed as the first step to tending his wounds, in his case having evidently made an exception to her prejudice against caring for Confederate soldiers.[18]

In May, Morehead City once again feared a Confederate attack. The train line and telegraph wires were severed. With no news, rumor claimed that the garrison at New Bern was fighting hard. Instead of being attacked by the dreaded Confederate soldiers, Morehead City was invaded by refugees driven from their homes by the fighting. Three hundred and fifty women and children occupied two of the hospital's barracks, giving von Olnhausen a new population to care for. They had received only an hour's notice of attack, and few of them escaped with as much as a change of clothes. Worse, they reported that the men who fell into rebel hands were marched out in squads, made to dig their own graves, and then shot. Von Olnhausen told the ladies of Lexington, "I never before knew anything of war horrors."[19] Quite a statement for someone who had been an army nurse for two years.

Yellow Fever

An epidemic of yellow fever swept New Bern in 1864. Spread by the bite of infected mosquitos, yellow fever is a viral disease that begins with the sudden onset of fever and chills, accompanied by headaches, muscle aches, nausea, vomiting, and fatigue. In severe cases of the disease, patients develop a high fever, jaundice (hence the name yellow fever), and eventual liver and kidney failure. The distinctive symptom is black vomit, a sign of gastrointestinal hemorrhaging. Even today, between 20 and 50 percent of the people who develop a severe case of yellow fever die, and there is no known treatment for the disease.

In the nineteenth century, people feared yellow fever for the rapidity with which it spread and its high death rate: an outbreak in New Orleans in 1853 claimed nine thousand lives, 28 percent of the city's population. More than 50 percent of those who contracted the disease died within a few days. Coastal cities in North America suffered epidemics of the fever every summer. Doctors inaccurately believed the disease was spread through direct contact with those already infected and attributed the annual epidemics to the arrival of infected seamen on ships from tropical ports. In the years before the Civil War, Southern ports established periods of quarantine for ships from tropical ports, often as long as three or four weeks, before crew and passengers were declared free of disease and allowed to come ashore. When the "Yellow Jack" appeared, anyone who could flee a town would run; entire blocks of houses were burned in an attempt to stop the disease from spreading. Whole families would lie dead in their homes, decomposing in the summer heat. Those who remained would pray for frost and the end of the disease.

The citizens of New Bern at first denied that yellow fever had hit the town, calling the cases of illness "congestive fever," an old term for malaria, another and less deadly mosquito-borne disease marked by fever.

Von Olnhausen first reported rumors of yellow fever in New Bern on September 18, noting that so far everyone who came down with the disease died quickly and that it seemed to be confined to the civilian population. A week later, Dr. Bellangee went to New Bern to take charge of the health department, where he began sweeping changes intended to correct the public health errors of his predecessor, whom von Olnhausen claimed had neglected his responsibility and allowed filth to accumulate to a horrifying degree. The cisterns and latrines had never been drained, not even those at the hospital. Dead animals drifted down the sluggish Neuse and Trent Rivers, got caught in the town's piers, and rotted away. The Union army not only did nothing to solve the problem, it contributed to it: the quartermaster filled a square of the dock with barrels of condemned beef, pork, and vegetables, covered them with three feet of dirt, and left them to contaminate the neighborhood around them. At a time when the cause of yellow fever was unknown it seemed entirely plausible that such conditions were the source of the epidemic.

In only a few days, Dr. Bellangee was stricken with the disease and brought back to Morehouse City, where von Olnhausen took personal charge of his nursing care. On September 30, von Olnhausen found his symptoms encouraging and took a moment to report to her friends back home. Her optimism proved to be unfounded; an hour after she mailed the letter, he was taken worse. He screamed with the pain, and nothing von Olnhausen did could ease the pain, not even large amounts of chloroform, which was used primarily for anesthesia in the mid–nineteenth century. His suffering went on for hours, until he finally died at three in the morning. Thinking later about Dr. Bellangee's death, von Olnhausen came to the conclusion that a patient's fear added a burden to the suffering caused by the disease itself:

> Till you are with it you can have no idea of this dreadful fever; nothing else approaches it except cholera. The effect upon the spirits would alone be distressing enough; but then the agony of the patient, and his consciousness of the danger add so much to the horror.

No one expects to live, and when the black vomit comes that look of despair with the "There is no show for me any longer" makes your heart just full.[20]

Though she had sat with many men while they died, and would sit with many more before the war was over, this was one death scene she would never forget.

Meanwhile, the news from New Bern grew worse each day. The disease continued to spread, and the weather remained hot. The army's regional medical director, Dr. Hand, was the only surgeon in New Bern who had not yet come down with the disease; he was so exhausted he could scarcely get upstairs to bed after the day's work was done. The port was closed except for gunboats, and Mansfield Hospital was filled with yellow fever victims from New Bern, though no cases had originated in Morehead City.

On October 14, von Olnhausen took the time to write a letter to her friends. It was the first time she had sat down all day, and she'd had no sleep the night before, so she felt "drowsy and stupid." With the port closed, she had no idea when she would be able to go home for a visit. She didn't even know when her letter would reach them, since mail from the stricken region was being quarantined in New York for twenty days for fear of spreading the disease. Even if it were possible to go home, she felt it was her duty to stay where she could help comfort so many. She assured them she was fine, only "a little weaker than usual from being over-tired."[21]

That little weakness turned out to be the first symptom of a serious case of yellow fever. Once again, von Olnhausen was one of the lucky survivors. As soon as she was strong enough to travel, her family took her home to rest in the "frosts and healing air" of Lexington.[22]

Sherman Marches on Mansfield Hospital

A month later, in December 1864, von Olnhausen returned to Morehead City, where she would remain through the end of the war.

During the final four months, Union troops fought in North Carolina in unprecedented numbers. In a two-part amphibious campaign, Union troops conquered Fort Fisher in January, and the port city of Wilmington on February 22, an operation that closed the last important seaport in the South to blockade runners and cut off a critical portion of General Lee's supply line into Virginia. In March, General William T. Sherman entered the state from the south in pursuit of the Confederate army under the command of General Joseph E. Johnston, fighting critical battles at Averasboro on March 15 and 16, and at Bentonville on March 19 and 20. On April 26, seventeen days after the war officially ended with Lee's surrender at Appomattox, Sherman accepted the surrender of Johnston and with him all the Confederate troops in Georgia, Florida, and the Carolinas.

During this period, von Olnhausen focused her attention on the day-to-day life of the hospital: the condition of the men under her care, the scarcity of rags and bandages, her gratitude for a box of food from the ladies of Lexington, a battle for supremacy between the two hospital chaplains, attending a black prayer meeting. She ignored the war being waged around her except when it intersected with her life. She admired the Union fleet in the harbor before it sailed against Wilmington, and wondered at the construction of the iron-clad warship *Monadnock:* 'I don't see how any thing could hurt her;—four

feet of wood, and seven inches of wrought iron, and such tur-
rets, and such guns!"[23] She reverted to her old hostility toward
Confederate wounded, refusing to allow them in her ward, and
speculated on the number of new patients they could expect
based on rumors that Longstreet has arrived at Goldsboro with
fifteen thousand men.

That sense of separation between military hospital and military action vanished when the Union army's Medical Bureau
began to shrink and consolidate its facilities in the region
around New Bern. The first change affected von Olnhausen's
hospital in Morehead City. On March 8, General Sherman's
chief quartermaster requisitioned the hospital buildings to serve
as Sherman's main supply depot, just as the Medical Bureau in
Washington had claimed Green's Mansion House for a hospital earlier in the war. Upon learning that Dr. Hand intended to
relocate Mansfield Hospital to nearby Beaufort and expand the
number of beds, she wailed, "Beaufort is such a flea-y,
dirty-smelling hole, and full of Secesh and rum-holes, and gam-
bling of all kinds going on there."[24] Military officers stood in
front of the hospital, asking when it would be vacated and
talking about what they would do when they got the quarters.
If anyone "remonstrated with them" they answered, "We're
from Sherman's army," as if that justified all actions. (And perhaps they thought it did, given the "total warfare" policy Sherman exercised on his March to the Sea.) "I am getting about
sick of Sherman's army," she grumbled in a letter, "if this is the
way we are to be treated by them."[25]

Worst of all, from her perspective, was the callous treatment of her patients by a system intended to see to their care.
Orders for their movement were issued, changed, and changed

again. She prepared her patients to leave at eight in the morning, only to be told at four in the afternoon that they would not leave until the next morning, if at all. Some were moved out of the hospital on such short notice that she did not have time to dress their wounds, only to lie packed in train cars for four hours without food or drink before finally leaving for New Bern. When they arrived, the wounded soldiers found there was no room for them in the New Bern hospital. They were left to sleep in churches or anywhere they could settle, most of them without even a blanket. Describing herself as more than discouraged, von Olnhausen railed against an army that would treat its own soldiers with such callous disregard. "If this is justice," she said, "I hate it forevermore."[26]

It's Not Over 'til It's Over

For most civilians the Civil War ended with Lee's surrender. But the war was far from over for the army's nurses. Thousands of soldiers remained in hospitals or convalescent camps, not yet strong enough to be sent home, and hundreds of female nurses remained at their posts to care for them.

In many ways, the disorganization in these final months reminded von Olnhausen of her early days at Mansion House Hospital. On April 9, she was at Mansfield Hospital's new quarters in Beaufort, cursing her fate. A month later she was relocated to a temporary hospital at Smithville, near Fort Fisher. Both towns were "cram-jam full of returned Secesh, all swelling about in their uniforms, swaggering as usual, saying the south is not beaten yet,"[27] a sight that roused her to sputtering fury. At Beaufort, the hospital was left in the hands of a "drunken, ignorant bad man"[28] who did not even bother to make the rounds of the wards. The steward tried to wrest the storeroom key from her control. There were no barracks and no blankets, only seventy tents pitched on sand. At Smithville, she once again faced problems finding a room to call her own. She lived in the hallway in the light-diet kitchen for several days, then moved to a tumbledown house with such a bad rat and bedbug problem that she was happy to return to the cook's hallway the next day. She shot three marauding pigs from the cookhouse door; the reputation she earned as a no-nonsense sharpshooter later protected her from a brigade of marauding Union soldiers who "broke into houses, smashed ever so many heads, insulted women, stole horses and everything else they could steal."[29]

Like the soldiers she nursed, von Olnhausen was ready to put down her burden and go home. At the same time, watching her patients assembled for roll call several weeks after the war's official end, she swore "I shall stay until the last gun fires if there is anything for me to do."[30]

Mary Phinney von Olnhausen stayed at the hospital at Smithville as long as there was need for her services. She received her discharge at the end of August 1865 and returned to her family in Lexington. A letter of commendation from the chief surgeon at Smithville had arrived shortly ahead of her, addressed to her brother-in-law. Dr. Palmer wrote at length about von Olnhausen's services, but it boiled down to one statement: "She was able to do more good than any nurse I ever knew."[31]

• • •

On September 11, 1865, Dorothea Dix received notice that the army's nursing corps was abolished, and all nurses were discharged, effective immediately. The nurses' war was finally over.

Chapter 10

After the War

"I wonder what I shall do with myself when the
war is over. I never can sit down and do nothing . . .
I never expect to live at home again, I shall always
be working somewhere or other, I hope. Work is my life.
I cannot be happy doing nothing."
—Emily Parsons[1]

"The war for the preservation of our Union evidently
did much to advance the best interests of women.
It created a necessity for her labor in new and untried
ways. It gave her an opportunity to prove her ability,
and also to cultivate that true courage without which
the most capable person may utterly fail of success."
—Vesta M. Swarts[2]

"Thank Heaven the War is over. I would
that its memories also could pass away."
—Dorothea Dix[3]

Speaking at a Memorial Day event in 1888, Clara Barton told her audience that as a result of the Civil War women had advanced at least fifty years beyond the position they would have held had the country remained at peace.[4]

The Civil War was a pivotal experience for many of the women who served as nurses, as well as their counterparts in the United States Sanitary Commission, whether they served for three weeks or three years. For many it was their first time away from family and home, and their first step outside the narrow framework of what society expected from them. They learned not only new skills but also new confidence. Whether in the immediacy of letters at the time or with the distance of memory, they expressed deep satisfaction with the work and the way of life, though they often groused about a particular detail. Katharine Prescott Wormeley, who served first on the hospital transport ships and later as the matron for a hospital for convalescent soldiers in Rhode Island, claimed to speak for the army nurses as a whole: "As for the ladies among whom my luck has thrown me, they are just what they should be,—efficient, wise, active as cats, merry, lighthearted, thoroughbred, and without the fearful tone of self-devotion which sad experience makes one expect from benevolent women. We all know in our hearts that it is thorough enjoyment to be here,—it is *life*, in short; and we wouldn't be anywhere else for anything in the world."[5] Emily Parsons, who served as a nurse for two years at a variety of hospitals despite being blind in one eye, partially deaf, and lame, took the sentiment one step further: "I should like to live so all the rest of my life."[6]

Parsons, like most of the women, and the soldiers they cared for, went home at the war's end. Nursing had been a temporary part of their lives, just like being a soldier was a temporary part of the lives of most of the men who served in the war. They stepped back into their old lives as daughters, seamstresses, schoolteachers, wives—and reformers. Some made a living writing. The most famous of these was Louisa May Alcott, whose account of her Civil War experience, *Hospital Sketches*, was the first work she published under her own name.

A few women who served as nurses during the war went on to earn medical degrees. Vesta Swarts, for instance, was a high school principal in Auburn, Indiana, before the war. She nursed at Louisville, Kentucky, from sometime in 1864 until March 1865, when she was honorably discharged, a fact she mentions with pride in an essay she wrote on her war work.[7] After the war, she became a physician, still a challenging proposition for women, and returned to Auburn, where she practiced medicine with her husband for the next thirty years.

Many of the middle-class women who volunteered as nurses or worked in some capacity for the Sanitary Commission were part of the large and varied community of American reformers before the war. Their wealthier counterparts often came from families who expected them to take part in high-profile charity work. After the war, both middle-class reformers and wealthy philanthropists used their newfound experience at organizing, political activism, and manipulating their way through male-dominated bureaucracies to expand their influence. Some took on new leadership roles at the local level. Parsons, for instance, organized a campaign to open a charity hospital for women and children in Cambridgeport, Massachusetts, where she then worked as matron and nurse—one of the few women to work as a nurse after the war. A few, particularly those who served as leaders of the larger branches of the Sanitary Commission, used their experience as a springboard to national leadership roles, founding groups such as the Women's Christian Temperance Union, the Women's Educational and Industrial Union, the American Social Science Association, and the American Red Cross. They involved themselves in opening schools, reforming prisons and asylums, improving conditions for women and children, "saving" unmarried mothers and their children (both in moral and practical terms), and providing vocational training for girls. Some became active in the labor, women's rights, and temperance movements, which expanded after the war to fill the political and emotional space previously occupied by abolition. Others spearheaded social welfare programs designed to alleviate the human misery left by the war. They formed relief funds for war widows and orphans, and programs to settle unemployed veterans on farmland in the West, and schools for former slaves. Cornelia Hancock, for instance helped found a freedman's school in Mount Pleasant, South Carolina, where she taught ex-slaves for a decade. At one point those who objected to the concept of education for black children riddled the schoolhouse with fifty bullets. Several decades after the war, they used those same skills to advocate for themselves. Arguing that they too had served their country, they successfully pushed through the Union Army Nurses Pension Act of 1892, which provided government pensions for army nurses similar to those given to Union soldiers.

Mary Phinney von Olnhausen Becomes a Hero

Unlike most of her comrades-in-arms, Mary Phinney von Olnhausen's career as an army nurse had an odd second act. She had barely recovered from the fatigues of her Civil War experience when she returned to the hard and monotonous duties of life on the Illinois prairie. During her absence, her brother's wife had died, leaving him with five children, including an infant boy. For the next five years, von Olnhausen lived a hardscrabble life on his farm, taking care of children and homestead and worrying about the grinding uncertainties of weather, water, crops, and markets.

In July 1870, Napoleon III declared war on Prussia. When news of the Franco-Prussian War reached the prairie some weeks later, von Olnhausen was overcome with the desire to once again volunteer as a nurse. Her official explanation was a combination of zeal for nursing and the wish to be of service to her husband's countrymen. She may also have simply wanted to leave the prairie.

Whatever her motivations, nursing on European battlefields was not an obvious choice. She spoke some French, but no German, and the Prussian army discouraged the participation of foreign nurses. She had no money and the German organizations in America could not support her. Von Olnhausen was not deterred. She begged and borrowed money from her friends, asked for recommendations from the doctors she had worked with, and began to study German. In October 1870, at the age of fifty-two, she set sail from Boston for Liverpool.

She had never been out of the country before, but she made her way without difficulty to Berlin, practicing her German every chance she got. Fellow travelers on the ship to Liverpool assumed she was "some forlorn German *Frau*" because she made a point of speaking only to German passengers. She laughed at their mistake, sure that if any of them spoke German they would have known better. She knew that she was anything but fluent, but the only way to learn was to plunge in and blunder along.[8]

In Berlin, she managed to get permission to go to the front, which was then not far from Paris, despite the fact that there were strict orders no civilians would be allowed to do so.

She attributed her success to her status as an American and the letters of recommendation she carried from Rev. Bellows and others, but it is probable that being the Baroness von Olnhausen also helped. As she would later note when she met an incompetent German nurse, a red-faced, hard-drinking "*Fraülein von* somebody," membership in the privileged class denoted by that "von" at the front of a name made it possible to keep a job—or gain permissions that plain Mrs. Olnhausen might not have received.[9]

With her permissions in hand, she set out from Berlin on November 10. On the way to the front she lost her trunk, which contained her letters of recommendation, credentials, and all her extra clothing. (The trunk turned up in Nancy, France, four months later.) For several months she moved through German-occupied territory in search of a place where she could put her skills to use, passed along from one German official to another. At times she was thwarted by officials who would not approve her passage to the next hospital until they received specific instructions from higher authorities. She served for a short period with various ambulance units, only to be shoved aside by the arrival of German nurses. (In one letter she gives in to a moment of professional pique and complains: "The way they dress wounds is abominable; they are not even where we were in '62."[10]) At the hospital in Meung—run by the Knights of St. John, a nineteenth-century variation of the medieval Knights Hospitalers—the other nurses were so hostile that they did not tell her they were preparing to evacuate before the French took the city. Luckily the knight in charge of the hospital insisted on waiting for von Olnhausen to join them.

Her letters from this period are once again "growlers." She was horrified by the condition of German hospitals, which she thought were worse than the worst field hospitals in the most disorganized days of the Civil War. The beds were abominable, the patients were dirty, and the rooms had no ventilation at all. As far as she could see, the staff did nothing but eat and drink all day long. In one hospital the matron drank red wine right out of the bottle all through rounds; von Olnhausen claimed that had she drunk in such a way she "would have had to occupy one of the beds before the first half-hour."[11]

She was saddened by the destruction the war had caused: "beautiful villas entirely destroyed; furniture, pictures, glass, all broken in pieces; trees and shrubs torn up; marble statues all in ruins."[12] Any house that had not been destroyed was occupied as a hospital or government office.

By early December she was thoroughly frustrated: "I can't get up the least enthusiasm. In the first place, I haven't enough to do, nor can I get it. I think there is one woman to every two wounded men—all with caps or some such costume, and calling one another 'Sister.'"[13] She briefly turned into a nineteenth-century ambulance chaser, following rumors of freshly wounded soldiers in need of help.

In January 1871, von Olnhausen finally found her place at an army hospital in Vendôme, in the Loire valley. She worked there through the beginning of March, pleased with the doctors, the sisters, the town, the food, and most of all the work. Her French and German had improved to the point where she no longer needed a translator, so she was able to explore the town in her little free time.

The German and French governments ratified a peace settlement on March 1, 1871, and German forces began to withdraw, taking their wounded with them. Von Olnhausen reconciled herself to leaving Vendôme with the army. On

March 9, just as she was getting into the carriage, the chief doctor informed her they had received badly wounded men from another hospital, and he hoped she would care for them. He didn't have to ask twice. She was delighted, not only by the compliment to her skills but by the opportunity to stay in France until the weather got warmer in Germany.

With the new patients in her care, von Olnhausen worked from early morning until nine each night. The men had received no care at all as far as she could tell. They had lain in the wet for weeks, so they had horrible sores as well as the "indescribable wounds" that had put them in the hospital in the first place.[14]

When the hospital corps prepared to leave Vendôme nine days later, several men were not strong enough to travel: three wounded, four with typhoid, and two with smallpox. Von Olnhausen volunteered to remain with them and to transport them to Berlin when they were well enough to move.

It turned out to be more hazardous duty than she expected. The working classes in Paris rose in revolt the day before the hospital corps left Vendôme, in part over one of the terms of the peace settlement, which provided for the German army to march through the Arc de Triomphe. The mood in Vendôme was ugly. Children yelled "Prussian, Prussian" whenever von Olnhausen stepped outside. Her patients were afraid of what the French might do to them.

The news from Paris grew worse every day. On March 24, she received a telegram saying they must leave the next morning. Two of her patients were too ill to travel, so she refused. One died soon after, leaving her with eight men in her care.

On the evening of March 30, the mayor of Vendôme arrived with a dispatch from the German Sanitary Commission agent at Orléans saying they must evacuate immediately. The mayor too was eager for them to leave because of the bad sentiment in the city toward Prussians. Von Olnhausen reached the hospital at six and got the men to the *diligence* (the French equivalent of a stage coach) by eight. It was market day and the town was full of people. She was afraid things could get violent when some people shouted and ran after the coach, "but the drivers were real good, and we were soon out of their claws."[15]

Transportation and housing arrangements failed at every stage of the trip, forcing von Olnhausen to beg for help and borrow money to keep her small crew of invalids fed.

When they reached Blois, they found they could not go on to Orléans, but must wait for three or four days. As far as von Olnhausen was concerned it was a relief. The men were already exhausted. The next morning she received another urgent dispatch: they had twenty minutes to get to the station. She scrambled to get the men dressed and packed while someone found them a carriage and men to carry the stretchers. When they got to the station she found only an open pack wagon without even straw for bedding in place of the ambulance train she expected. Due to the confusion of their packing, von Olnhausen didn't have enough blankets to cover all the men, so she removed her dress and skirt to use instead and "rode to Orléans without."[16]

At Orléans, she hired two armed guards on the advice of an official at the station. She was glad to have them when a crowd surrounded her charges while the men were transported on stretchers from the *diligence* station to the hospital: "They hooted and screamed, and one horrible old woman howled out all sorts of curses, kicked up the dust over us with her awful old wooden shoes and shook her head so that her gray hair fell over her face and shoulders . . . I could then understand what a revolution in France meant."[17]

The next morning the men were shuffled in and out of pack wagons at the Orléans station, waiting for an ambulance train they were assured would arrive at nine. Half a day passed with no train. The men were crying with cold and pain. The waiting room was full of French soldiers, who were vocal in their dislike of the Prussians. Von Olnhausen had just decided to take the men back to the hospital when the train finally arrived. Three doctors appeared at the station door and helped the men into the railroad cars, where they were fed and made comfortable. Von Olnhausen was given a bunk with the two Protestant Sisters who served as the ambulance's nurses.

They traveled with the train to Tours, where they picked up more patients, and then back to Vendôme, where the train had been scheduled to pick them up. They had been gone for a week; it felt like a month. The entire difficult and dangerous trip had been totally unnecessary, the result of panic on the part of the German Sanitary Commission agent.

After two days in Vendôme, they set out with the ambulance train for Berlin, where they arrived on April 19, 1871.

• • •

Two years later, von Olnhausen received an unexpected tribute for her courage in remaining behind with the Prussian soldiers. Kaiser Wilhelm I, the king of Prussia and newly elected emperor of Germany, presented her with the Iron Cross, the Prussian equivalent of the Medal of Honor.

Von Olnhausen's European nursing experience provided her with one last adventure at the end of her life. In March

1902, Prince Henry of Prussia, the brother of Kaiser Wilhelm II, visited Boston during a trip to the United States. Some German friends insisted von Olnhausen accompany them to a reception in his honor, and she decided to wear the Iron Cross for the occasion. She was so intimidated by the idea of meeting the prince that she just wanted it to be over, but Prince Henry noticed the decoration and broke away from the receiving line to speak to her. He shook her hand twice, "just as any other *feller* would." She was so flustered that she forgot to bow or address him by his title. He spoke first in German, but it had been almost thirty years since she used the language. Seeing that she was struggling to understand him, he switched to English and asked about her experiences in the war.

The newspapers dubbed von Olnhausen "the Little Madam of the Iron Cross," and her story appeared in papers from Maine to California. Visitors, known and unknown, crowded her rooms at Grundmann Studios in Boston. Writing to a friend in North Carolina on March 10, von Olnhausen admitted to enjoying both the experience and the subsequent "fuss": "Nothing like being the *fad* for a while. I've waited forty years, and now, when I'm so old it comes all at once."[18]

She died a month later, at the age of eighty-four.

Clara Barton Continues to Serve

Clara Barton, as founder of the American Red Cross, made the largest impact of any single Civil War nurse in the years after the war.

The International Red Cross had been founded several years before. In 1863, while the United States was locked in its internal struggle, Swiss businessman Henry Dunant, who had witnessed the aftermath of the Battle of Solfierno in the Italian War of Independence several years before, called a conference of thirty-nine delegates from sixteen nations to Geneva to discuss questions of battlefield relief and humanitarian aid. The group met again in 1864 and created the set of recommendations that would become the Geneva Treaty, now the Geneva Convention. The guidelines called for the humane treatment of wounded soldiers and universal recognition of the neutrality of medical personnel, ambulances, and hospitals in time of war. The convention adopted a reverse Swiss flag, a red cross on a white ground, as an emblem of medical neutrality that would be easily recognized. They also urged each country to create its own national society of volunteers to provide battlefield relief when needed. Twelve European governments ratified the treaty, but the United States initially refused to sign on the grounds that it was a possible "entangling alliance."

Barton first became aware of the International Red Cross on a visit to Switzerland in 1869. She had spent the years immediately after the Civil War locating missing soldiers. Women wrote to Barton asking for help in finding husbands and sons whom they feared had ended up in Southern prisons. The anguish in their letters convinced her that finding missing soldiers was the most important thing she could do in the peace. She put together lists of missing soldiers, organized by location and unit, posted them in army hospitals, and had them printed in local and national newspapers, with the request that any information about the missing men be sent to her to pass on to their families. Eventually she received official sanction for the task. President Lincoln wrote a letter to the public informing them to contact her with information about missing soldiers. When her own resources were exhausted, Congress appropriated $15,000 to complete the project—close to $3 million today. The search for missing soldiers led to an effort to identify graves, beginning with the unmarked graves of the 13,000 Union soldiers who died in the prison camp at Andersonville, Georgia. Between 1865 and 1869, she helped locate 22,000 missing soldiers.

She was already physically exhausted from her grueling work in the war, and her efforts after the war imposed a new kind of strain. In 1869, her doctors ordered her to Europe for a rest cure. She did not rest for long. Like Mary Phinney von Olnhausen, Barton felt called back into action by the Franco-Prussian War. She traveled to Strasbourg as a Red Cross volunteer, wearing a cross she improvised from a red ribbon and a Red Cross pin given her by the Grand Duchess Louise, daughter of Kaiser Wilhelm I. Barton's experience in the Franco-Prussian War was very different from her experience in the American Civil War. Instead of soldiers, she worked with civilian victims. For her first several days in Strasbourg, she dutifully served soup and distributed supplies to survivors. But as she spent more time in the burned-out city, she realized that more than soup and soap were needed. She organized women into sewing workrooms as a first step in reestablishing the city's economy. She organized a similar relief effort in Paris the following year.

When she returned home in 1873, Barton took on the task of lobbying for the United States to ratify the Geneva Treaty. It took her nine years and three presidents, but at long last President Chester Arthur signed the treaty in 1882, and the Senate ratified it several days later.

She founded the American Red Cross in 1881 and led it for the next twenty-three years. At her initiative, the American Red Cross proposed an amendment to the Geneva Treaty calling for the expansion of Red Cross relief to include victims of natural disasters. The so-called American Amendment, perhaps more accurately the "Barton Amendment," was passed in 1884.

Nursing Becomes a Profession

In 1868, the American Medical Association (AMA), founded in 1847 and still finding its role in a rapidly changing profession in the years after the Civil War, recommended that general hospitals open schools to train nurses. It was a two-edged response to the success of volunteer nurses in the Civil War. The AMA both acknowledged the value of skilled nursing in hospitals and hoped to avoid another flood of untrained and uncontrollable volunteer nurses in future wars.

The first nursing school in the United States opened during the war. The New England Hospital for Women and Children, founded in 1862 by Dr. Marie Zakrzewska, had its own nurses' training program, and the hospital's articles of incorporation included training nurses as one of its fundamental purposes. Zakrzewska modeled her training program on that of the secular school of the Charity Hospital in Berlin, where she studied both midwifery and medicine. The six-month program focused on practical experience rather than medical theory. After a one-month probationary period, students received a small wage, board, and laundry service. In the first years, the nursing program made little progress. The hospital had little space and fewer resources to devote to the school; at the same time, few women were prepared to devote the required six months to a program that offered no diploma at the end. Zakrzewska trained only thirty-two nurses between 1862 and 1872; those women found themselves in demand as head nurses at hospitals and as private-duty nurses.

After 1872, the New England Hospital had a new building and a new doctor in charge of the nurses' training program. Dr. Susana Dimock, a protégé of Zakrzewska's who had trained at the University of Zurich and done clinical work in Vienna and Paris before returning to Boston, created a more formal one-year training program, based on the methods used at Kaiserwerth, where Florence Nightingale studied twenty-one years before. Over the course of the year, nursing students rotated through the different departments of the hospital, spending three months each in the medical and surgical wards, the children's wards, the maternity ward, and on night calls. This practical training was supplemented by a course of twelve lectures on the theory of nursing given by staff doctors at the hospital. At the end of the year, the school required students to work at the hospital for four months before they received their diplomas. The program grew rapidly in response to an expanding demand for trained nurses, and by 1889 the school was successful enough that it required a separate building to house students, who had previously slept in small rooms next to the wards.

In the five years between 1877 and 1882, two hundred women applied for admission; one hundred were accepted. Dimock's requirements for admission were just as strict as Dix's requirements had been as for the nursing corps. Like Dix she demanded written character references, but unlike Dix, she wanted students between twenty-one and thirty-one. As she explained her reasoning, "Younger than this, neither physical health nor judgment are sufficiently developed, older, it is not easy to acquire new habits."[19] In short, she wanted women who were younger and less set in their ways than the Civil War nurses who made Americans aware of the need for trained hospital nurses.

In 1873, just as Dimock's first class of nurses graduated, three new nursing schools opened: the New York Training School, attached to Bellevue Hospital; the Connecticut Training School, attached to New Haven Hospital; and the Boston Training School, attached to Massachusetts General Hospital. All three offered programs based on Florence Nightingale's school at St. Thomas Hospital in London. Two of the three schools were founded by women who either nursed or worked for the Sanitary Commission.

The New York school was the first of the three to open, on May 24, 1873. The New York Training School for Nurses had its roots in Louisa Lee Schuyler's work as the chair of the New York branch of the Sanitary Commission. At the age of twenty-four, Schuyler was by far the youngest of the branch managers; in fact, she was chosen over her mother for the position. She would later claim her experience with the commission laid the groundwork for her long and successful career as a reformer, saying the commission "opened my eyes to the great value and the great power of organization."[20] After the war, Schuyler applied her skills as an organizer to reforming New York's state asylums, prisons, poorhouse, schools, and other loosely defined "charitable institutions." In 1871, she formed the State Charities Aid Association (SCAA), a formidable group of women who combined intelligence, education, and social position with practical experience from their days with the Sanitary Commission and the Woman's Central Association of Relief. Schuyler's organization used a combination of personal inspections by association committees and detailed statistics, sometimes derived from an institution's own reports, to push through reforms, often in the face of opposition from politicians and administrators.

One of these committees was assigned to investigate Bellevue Hospital and was horrified by what they found. The SCAA reached the conclusion that many of the hospital's problems were due to the nursing service, which relied on the infamous "ten-day" women serving out their parole for public drunkenness. Meaningful reform of the hospital would require more trained nurses than were available. Inspired by the success of Nightingale's school in London, the SCAA suggested forming a nursing school attached to the hospital. They received no encouragement from the local medical community, who rejected the idea on the grounds that the quality of the patients was too rough. One doctor said plainly, "I do not believe in the success of a training school for nurses at Bellevue. The patients are of a class so difficult to deal with, and the service is so laborious, that the conscientious, intelligent woman you are looking for will lose heart and hope long before the two years of training are over."[21] Not discouraged, Schuyler's ladies sent a young physician, Gill Wylie, to London to learn more about Nightingale's school firsthand. On his return, Wylie recommended to the SCAA that a similar school be established at Bellevue, and that the governing board invite Nightingale's school to send some of its nurses to New York to help. Doctors associated with the hospital resisted, despite the AMA's endorsement for training nurses. One of the concerns these doctors raised was the fear that, in the absence of medical licensing laws, women trained as nurses would go out into the country and set themselves up as doctors. Hospital wardens and politicians also opposed the proposed school, wardens because it threatened their control over hospitals, and politicians because they feared it would reveal instances of corruption and abuse. The existing "ten-day" nurses were not too happy about the new program either; they reportedly lived up to their rough reputation by cursing and throwing stones at the student nurses.

The SCAA prevailed. The group raised the money needed to start the school, rented a house near the hospital for nursing students to live in, and hired Sister Helen Bowden of the Sisterhood of All Saints to run the program. Admissions policies were stringent: only twenty-three of the seventy-three original applicants were accepted, and ten of them were dismissed within the first nine months.

The Connecticut Training School for Nurses at New Haven Hospital was also inspired by the absence of trained nurses. A group led by Georgeanna Woolsey met on May 21, 1873, with the purpose of appointing a superintendent of nursing for the hospital. They found it a difficult task because of the small number of experienced nurses available and decided they needed to train their own. They started with a smaller pool of applicants than their New York counterparts. Of the twenty-one applicants for the first class, they accepted six, two of whom withdrew before the school opened on October 6, 1873. The next year they received nearly a hundred applications.

The Boston Training School for Nurses at Massachusetts General Hospital opened in November 1873, and, like their counterparts in New York and New Haven, faced opposition from most of the staff physicians. The school began with six students, who were allowed to work in two wards as an experiment. Mary Phinney von Olnhausen served as the school's superintendent for a brief time after her return from Europe. She was not a success. Even her nephew, who was a child at the time, "could see that his aunt had not the qualifications essential for the post, which, with unflagging zeal, she was trying so enthusiastically to fill."[22] Von Olnhausen resigned in November 1874, to the relief of all concerned. After holding several other nursing-related positions, she returned to her roots as a textile designer, supporting herself as a designer and maker of embroideries.

Von Olnhausen was replaced by Linda Richards, one of the first women to receive a nursing diploma from Susan Dimock's program at the New England Hospital for Women and Children. Richards held the position for the next two and a half years. During her tenure, the school assumed responsibility for nursing for the entire hospital, and ten years after its founding, the school had forty-two students and twelve nurse-instructors.

By 1880, there were a total of 15 nursing schools in the United States; by 1900, there were 432. Nursing had become recognized as a skilled profession.

Dorothea Dix Lays Her Burdens Down

During the four years of the Civil War, Dorothea Dix butted heads with officialdom, quarreled with military surgeons and the men who ran the Sanitary Commission, lost weight, and suffered from a variety of ailments, including malaria and pulmonary disorders, but she never faltered. Even after Hammond's General Order 351, issued in October 1863, gutted her authority, she continued to work on behalf of nurses and hospitals for the duration of the war without a single leave of absence.

Discharged along with her nurses on September 11, 1865, Dix wrote to her lifelong friend Anne Heath that, though she resigned from the office of superintendent of women nurses, she had no intention of stopping work. She was eager to abandon what had become a thankless task and return to her life's work helping the helpless, but she recognized there was little point in resuming her role as an advocate for asylum and prison reform as long as state legislatures focused their time and resources on rebuilding their economies and institutions after four years of war. Instead she stayed in Washington, where she appointed herself a one-woman relief agency, putting in long days calling in small favors from her vast network of contacts. Her favorite task was helping disabled soldiers and nurses left invalided by their work in the war to find their way home. She also helped soldiers collect back pay, found food and clothing for poor veterans and their families, searched for homes for war orphans, and occasionally used her contacts to help families locate soldiers missing in action.

Her last war effort was a granite monument to the Union war dead at Fort Monroe. When a committee of war veterans asked for her help with the project, she not only raised a substantial amount of the needed funds, but played an active role in its design. She spent weeks visiting quarries in Maine in order to choose the perfect granite. A fence constructed of stone and armaments surrounds the sixty-five-foot-high obelisk. General Grant himself approved her request for "1,000 muskets and bayonets, 15 rifled guns, and a quantity of 24-pound shot, with which to construct my fence."[23] With the completion of the monument, she deliberately separated herself from her war experience, which had ultimately proven to be both frustrating and humiliating. She returned to what she considered her life's work, an assessment shared by her later biographers, who uniformly treat her war work as a footnote to her life.

Some months after the war ended, US Secretary of War Edwin Stanton asked Dix how she would like to have her service to her country honored, suggesting that her efforts be recognized with a grand public meeting or a congressional expression of gratitude. Dix asked for one thing: "the Flags of my Country."

On December 3, 1866, the War Department ordered a pair of flags made for Dix. They arrived at her home in Boston on January 25, 1867, along with an official order over Stanton's signature that read: "In token and acknowledgement of the inestimable services rendered by Miss Dorothea L. Dix for the Care, Succor, and Relief of the Sick and Wounded Soldiers of the United States on the Battle-Field, in Camps and Hospitals during the recent War, and of her benevolent and diligent labors and devoted efforts to whatever might contribute to their comfort and welfare, it is ordered that a Stand of Arms of the United States National colors be presented to Miss Dix."

She wrote in response: "No more precious gift could have been bestowed, and no possession will be so prized while life remains to love and serve my country."[24] She later bequeathed the flags to Harvard and arranged for them to be hung in the memorial hall built by Harvard to honor its Civil War dead.

Harvard lost the flags, perhaps a fitting end to the story of a woman whose contribution to the war effort has often been overlooked.

• • •

On June 10, 1903, the American Nurses Association met for its sixth annual convention. At one point in the meeting, the organization's president announced that by chance another group of nurses was meeting in the building, "an organization of nurses belonging to the Army and Navy of the Civil War." She suggested that it would be fitting that the convention pay tribute to them in some way. A nurse in the crowd suggested the older nurses be invited to join the afternoon session of the meeting.

Mary Livermore, a Civil War nurse who went on to become a national leader of the women's suffrage movement, was the next scheduled speaker. She rose to welcoming applause and began her address with a tribute from the older nurses to the new: "I find all that is within me rising up in this presence in a semi-reverential attitude. A congregation of trained women nurses! Something that in my earlier days I never expected to see, that I always thought of, and always felt that it was a desirable thing to accomplish." She went on to say what many of the younger women in the room were no doubt thinking: "The women whom you have just invited to meet with you are wrecks only, simply driftwood left from the Civil War, stranded here." Then she reminded her listeners, "They had a great work to do without any of the advantages that you would have if you were to take their places today . . . It was an impossible thing for those women to do all they had to do . . . Their own hearts' desire was that they should be successful, that they should mitigate the sufferings of the men and the community, and they came out from their work—some of them stayed the whole four years—very much better nurses, of course, than they went in."

Their legacy stood before her: trained nurses who could be called to duty in case of another war. Nurses "who know what to do and how to do it, who have learned to obey, and learned when they must depart from instructions, what rights they have, and when the occasion shall come that they fall back on their own trained judgment." She proclaimed it "one of the the best things that has happened in the advance that has come to womanhood generally during the last fifty years."[25]

A Different Viewpoint:
Nursing in the Confederacy

L ooking at the experience of Civil War nurses through the lens of Mansion House Hospital focuses the attention solely on the North, but it is important to remember that women in the South also volunteered as nurses in the war.

It is even harder to get a good estimate of the number of Southern women who served as nurses than it is to count their Northern counterparts, in part because a portion of the Confederate surgeon general's records, like those of many other departments of the Confederacy, was lost in the fires that accompanied the evacuation of Richmond in April 1865. In addition to women who worked for the Confederate Medical Department, estimated by one count at 1,666, unknown numbers of women worked in the hospitals as unpaid "visitors" and volunteers at wayside hospitals.[1] Others nursed wounded strangers in their own front parlor or the local church; these do not appear in official records at all, though they appear in anecdotal accounts.

Regardless of their numbers, Southern nurses shared some experiences with their Northern counterparts. The hostility of male surgeons to the "petticoat government" of female nurses in hospitals was not limited to the North. In 1862, when

Phoebe Yates Levy Pember, a thirty-nine-year-old widow, who applied for one of the newly created matron's positions to escape an unhappy living situation, arrived at her job at Hospital #2 in the enormous Chimborazo Hospital in Richmond, Virginia, she was greeted by a surgeon who noted "in a tone of ill-concealed disgust that 'one of them had come.'"[2]

The South had no equivalent of Dorothea Dix's selection criteria to limit who could become a nurse, but elite Southern women who wanted to volunteer still had to battle the familiar assumption that "such a life would be injurious to the delicacy and refinement of a lady—that her nature would become deteriorated and her sensibilities blunted."[3] That battle was made harder by an elevated sense in the South of what made someone a lady, including the belief that it was demeaning to work outside the home. Like their counterparts in the North, some elite women who volunteered as nurses not only showed no hesitation in stepping outside the stereotype, but also actively embraced the challenges of the job. Emily Mason, the matron at Camp Winder Hospital in Richmond, Virginia, described several Richmond belles who dragged wounded men from the ambulance, fresh from the battlefield at Petersburg, and set to washing and dressing them,[4] apparently close counterparts of the New York socialites who served on the United States Sanitary Commission's hospital transport ships.

Women on both sides faced the challenge of acclimating themselves to the grim realities of a military hospital. Cornelia McDonald of Winchester, Virginia, tells an anecdote of her first day on the job that in many ways typifies the experience of all the women who nursed in the Civil War: "I wanted to be useful and tried my best," she said. But the sight of one man's face was her undoing. The surgeon uncovered the man's wounded face and asked her if she would wash the wound. She tried to say yes, but the thought of touching it made her feel so faint that she staggered toward the door. As she went, she stumbled over a pile of amputated limbs heaped up near the door.[5]

As in the North, amputations were the most difficult thing for volunteer nurses to come to terms with. Some women, like Sara Agnes Pryor, who made the transition from lady visitor to volunteer nurse in Richmond during the bloody Seven Days' Battles of 1862, fought to overcome what one experienced nurse dismissed as "fine-lady faintness."[6] Others decided after their first fainting fits that their efforts at hospital work were best confined to raising supplies, not a trivial task, especially later in the war when there were shortages of many basic foodstuffs.

Despite these similarities, Confederate women's experience of nursing in the war differed in several significant ways, which reflected not only differences in the structure of Northern and Southern society but differences in how they experienced the war.

The South was largely untouched by the two events that combined to create the reform-minded class from which many of the Northern nurses came: the growth of industrialized cities with their attendant problems and opportunities, and the Second Great Awakening, a spasm of religious revivalism that spread from New York westward to the Mississippi and south toward the border between slave and free states. Consequently, the Confederacy had no equivalent of Dorothea Dix or Elizabeth Blackwell, with their backgrounds in reform leadership and hospital management. Perhaps more important, the South also had few equivalents of Mary Phinney von Olnhausen, Hannah Ropes, or Louisa May Alcott—members of the educated middle class with an inclination for reform and prior experience of working outside the home. Instead the region had its own breed of women with the habit of command: women who ran large plantation households that were effectively small, or even not so small, businesses.

The Confederacy's military leaders, trained in the same system as their Union counterparts, were equally unprepared to care for the flood of casualties that began with the first Battle of Manassas (known as Bull Run in the North). The situation was made worse by the fact that the state's rights ethos of the Confederacy meant that each state maintained control of its own troops' welfare. Throughout the South, women with social clout and experience in running their family estates stepped forward to organize care at the local and state levels. In Tennessee, Mary Rutledge Fogg, descendent of two signers of the Declaration of Independence, wrote to the Confederate president Jefferson Davis demanding help establishing hospitals in Nashville, Memphis, and Knoxville. She also informed him, almost as an aside, that she had recruited a corps of women through the Ladies Tennessee Hospital and Clothing Association to act as nurses, whom she was sending to Virginia the next day. In Virginia, Letitia Tyler Semple, granddaughter of former president John Tyler, descended on Williamsburg in the summer of 1861 with the intention of helping sick soldiers. Discovering that the "domestic arrangements" of the hospital were unacceptable, she took over the kitchen, pantry, and laundry. She later also wrote to President Davis and requested that he appoint her female superintendent of not only the Williamsburg hospital where she was already filling that role, but two others as well. Juliet Opie Hopkins, who managed her father's estate in western Virginia before her marriage to an Alabama judge, equipped and ran field hospitals near the front for the benefit of Alabama regiments, and took charge of both the provisioning and organization of the Alabama hospitals in Richmond. On a smaller scale, twenty-eight-year-old Virginia heiress Sallie Tompkins outfitted a Richmond house as a twenty-two-bed hospital where more than thirteen hundred men were cared for over the course of the war, with only seventy-three deaths—the lowest mortality rate of any military hospital in the war in either the South or North.

On September 27, 1862, the Confederate Congress passed an act intended to deal with the inadequacies of medical care for its soldiers. In conjunction with that act, a committee appointed by the Confederate senate to investigate complaints about military medical care reported an astonishing statistic regarding the impact of female nurses and female-run hospitals: investigators found that the mortality rate among soldiers nursed by men in male-run institutions averaged 10 percent, compared to a mortality rate of 5 percent among soldiers nursed in hospitals with a strong female presence.[7] These numbers created a major change of attitude about female nurses within the Confederate congress, if not within the Confederate medical community. Senator Thomas Jenkins Semmes of Louisiana summed up their shared opinion: "I will not agree to limit the class of persons who can affect such a saving of life as this."[8]

In response to the statistical evidence that patients fared better in hospitals run by women, the act created positions for women in the Confederacy's general hospitals. Each hospital would have two matrons and two assistant matrons who would be in charge of the "domestic economy" of the hospital. Responsible for the house-keeping, cooking, and nursing staffs, these women were hospital administrators rather than what we think of as nurses today. (Kate Cumming, perhaps the best known of the Southern nurses, worked in the field hospitals in Mississippi after the Battle of Shiloh and served as a matron in Chattanooga; she admitted that she was a nurse for more than two years before she ever changed a bandage or dressed a wound.) In addition, each ward would have two ward matrons, who were responsible for preparing beds for incoming soldiers, administering medicine, and supervising the nursing and cleaning staffs—the functional equivalent of the male ward masters in the Union's military hospitals.

The duties outlined in the 1862 legislation included little of what Mary Garland Holland considered "real nursing." In fact, the act did not deal with hospital personnel below the level of ward matron, ignoring the people who actually took care of the patients. At the beginning of the war, convalescent soldiers provided most of the actual nursing, a practice that Cumming railed against on the grounds that nursing was a skill that had to be learned, and that the soldiers were rotated through the job the same way they rotated through guard duty.

As the war continued, the South suffered a manpower crisis that made the continued use of convalescent soldiers as nurses increasingly difficult. The Confederacy desperately needed to fill noncombatant jobs with individuals ineligible for military service, of which women were the largest and most underutilized group. As early as June 1861, individual hospitals ran newspaper ads look-ing for nurses, but women did not volunteer for hospital work in the numbers needed in the face of mounting casualties.

Hospitals soon turned to a group of noncombatants who did not have the choice of saying no: slaves. Brigadier General John Bankhead Magruder argued for the employment of female slaves as nurses on functional grounds, claiming that they combined the qualities needed for the perfect nurse: female tenderness, no aversion to menial labor, and the habit of subservience. The largest number of women who performed front-line nursing and other hospital work in Confederate general hospitals were black slaves, either impressed into service or hired out by their owners.

• • •

The nurses who worked at the Confederacy's official hospitals were only a small part of the Southern nursing story.

With the war right on their own doorsteps, Southern women did not necessarily have to travel to one of the large hospitals to volunteer. With easy access to hometown hospitals, women often volunteered on a casual basis, just as women in Washington, DC, did after the First Battle of Bull Run. Some women who were unwilling to brave the hospital environment nursed a few soldiers at a time in their own homes.

Not everyone who volunteered for what could be more broadly described as "hospital work" actually nursed soldiers in the sense of providing medical services. "Lady visitors" were the most common variation: women from the community who brought comfort to the soldiers in the form of food and entertainment. They read the Bible to patients, helped them write letters, and occasionally washed their faces, "soothing a fevered brow" being an approved action for a lady. Emma Crutcher, a young Mississippi wife who served as a lady visitor while her husband was at war, outlined the distinction between a lady visitor and a nurse when she promised her husband, "I shall never take on myself anything that a servant can do as well, and never do anything that a lady may not with perfect propriety do."[9] In short, no mopping up bloody floors, no emptying bed pans, and definitely no bathing of strange men. (Crutcher found it hard to hold to this lofty standard in the face of the realities of hospital life. Even though she did not touch the patients, she became infested with lice, which apparently were unable to distinguish ladies from other women.)

The most important contribution to medical care in the war made by Confederate women was the wayside hospital, an innovative combination of infirmary and travelers' aid station for wounded soldiers as they traveled home from the front. By the end of 1861, women's organizations had opened such hospitals across the South and served thousands of soldiers. A group of fourteen women in Union Point, Georgia, provided hot meals and nursing care to more than 20,000 men in their wayside medical facility over the course of two years. Louise Medway of North Carolina estimated the Soldiers' Aid Society in Wilmington fed and dressed the wounds of six to eight thousand soldiers a month in a similar facility. The wayside hospitals provided a substantial contribution to the war effort by any standard.

• • •

The experience of nursing did not have the same post-war impact in the South as it did in the North either.

The war destroyed the Southern economy, and the types of jobs many Northern nurses took after the war, such as teaching and social work, were scarce. Even women eager to work could not find jobs. Previously wealthy women, caught between the need to earn a living and the social stigma attached to working for pay, found it difficult to translate the skills they utilized during the war into work.

There was no great surge of reform. Women who played philanthropic roles before the war seldom had the funds or the opportunity to do so in the postbellum South. No one founded nursing schools.

The main vestige that remained of Southern women's work in the war was the transformation of the hospital and ladies' aid associations that collected supplies and ran wayside hotels into groups dedicated to building memorials for the Confederate war dead, another way to tend to the wounded South.

Acknowledgments

It's been a privilege to write about the nurses who served during the American Civil War. I'm grateful for the chance to tell their story and to the people who helped me do so:

My editor at Little Brown, Malin von Euler-Hogan, whose suggestions and questions made *Heroines of Mercy Street* a better book.

Lisa Wolfinger and Lisa Goodfellow Bowe of Lone Wolf Media, who graciously shared their research for PBS's *Mercy Street*. That jumpstart was invaluable.

Rick Richter from Zachary Shuster Harmsworth, who put the team together and kept the lines of communication open.

Melissa Totten, who tracked down the photos with patience and imagination.

Jay Kreider who produced the index.

David Wilk, who gently nudged when needed, made sure nothing was forgotten, and transformed the computer files into a book, with the help of the team from Booktrix, including Barbara Aronica-Buck, Gray Cutler, David Kessler, and Rare Bird's Tyson Cornell and Alice Elmer.

And last but never least, my husband, Sandy Wilson, who read drafts, asked questions, listened while I talked through the tough spots, suggested improvements, and provided pizza and a beer when needed.

Appendix A

Circular No. 8

Washington, July 24, 1862

No candidate for service in the Women's Department for nursing in the Military Hospitals of the United States, will be received below the age of thirty-five years, (35) nor above fifty.

Only women of strong health, not subjects of chronic disease, not liable to sudden illnesses, need apply. The duties of the station make large and continued demands on strength.

Matronly persons of experience, good conduct, or superior education and serious disposition, will always have preference; habits of neatness, order, sobriety, and industry are prerequisites.

All applicants must present certificates of qualification and good character from at least two persons of trust, testifying to morality, integrity, seriousness, and capacity for care of the sick.

Obedience to rules of the service, and conformity to special regulations will be required and enforced.

Compensation, as regulated by Act of Congress, forty cents a day and subsistence. Transportation furnished to and from the place of service.

Amount of luggage limited within small compass.

Dress plain—colors brown, grey, or black, and, while connected with service, without ornaments of any sort.

No applicants accepted for less than ~~three~~ six months' service; those for longer periods always have preference.

D. L. Dix,

Approved:

William A. Hammond

Surgeon General.

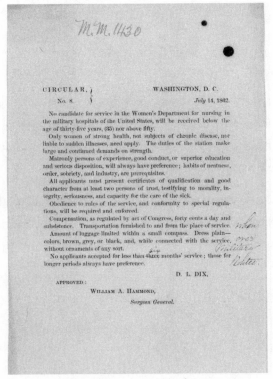

Circular No. 8 Regarding Requirements for
Female Nursing Applicants, 7/14/1862. *National Archives*

Appendix B

Letter of Commendation for Mary Phinney von Olnhausen's Service in the War

This letter was addressed to Mary Phinney von Olnhausen's brother-in-law:

> U.S.A. Gen'l Hospital
>
> Smithville, NC, July 4, 1865

Sir, I have recently received from the office of the Surgeon General, U.S.A., a Circular Order, directing me to forward to him "the names of those ladies who have rendered valuable services, gratuitously, for more than three years past, in attendance upon sick and wounded soldiers in Hospitals."

This Order was designed, I suppose, to secure some public and striking recognition of the services alluded to. I think this is right.

But there is a class of ladies who have rendered extremely valuable services to the sick and wounded Union soldiers in hospitals, but who do not come within the terms of the Order above mentioned. The Volunteer Nurses, who worked under the supervision of Miss Dix, received, from the Government, twelve dollars per month. Many of the women were so self-sacrificing and faithful and efficient, that we who live to enjoy

Freedom a second time won, and, I hope forever won, can scarcely manifest adequately, our gratitude to these women.

And among all the female nurses whom I have known or heard of, not one is better entitled to eminent and substantial notice than is Mrs. Mary Von Olnhausen of Lexington, Mass.

From my own observation, and from the statements of our lamented friend, Surg. J. B. Bellangee, I conclude that the services rendered by this lady to the sick and wounded soldiers, and thus to the Government, and to us all, have been quite equal in value to those afforded by any other person in her sphere of labor.

Her whole soul has been in the work. She very early acquired a marvelous dexterity in the management of the wounded. Thus, with her wonderful physical endurance, she was able to do more good than any nurse I ever knew. She was literally untiring in her labors. By her zeal and usefulness and general deportment, she entitled herself to the respect of us all.

Soldiers who owe their lives to her skillful attention are scattered, now, over nearly all the Northern States. They will remember her with gratitude. I presume that is all she will wish for. I suspect that Mrs. Von Olnhausen is not ambitious for notoriety or fame. But I take the liberty to suggest that the citizens of Massachusetts may with propriety, and honor to themselves, offer to Mrs. V. O. some substantial testimonial, which shall manifest their appreciation of her services and at the same time do her good. She is in every way entitled to all she will receive, and ought to feel no delicacy in accepting it.

This statement of mine is prompted in part, by hearing that the friends of Mrs. George, a Female Nurse, who "died at her post" in Wilmington a short time since, and purchased, for presentation to her, a home in the State in which she had been a resident. To me this is suggestive. A fee simple, in a piece of land, is worth a thousand golden trinkets.

I suppose you know Mrs. V. O. and are her friend. So, without apology for writing to a stranger, I simply hope that you and her other friends may some time act upon the suggestion given. I know many who you will never see who will gladly take part with you.

Yours respectfully,

J. M. Palmer

Surg., 3d N.Y.V. In Charge Hosp.

Endorsed:

Med. Dir's Office

Newburn, NC, July 17, 1865

Mrs. M. Von Olnhausen has served in hospitals under my direction for nearly two years past, and I take pleasure in endorsing all the statements of Surg. Palmer. This lady has won the respect and confidence of all brought in contact with her; and by her devotion to the sick and wounded soldiers has deserved all a grateful country can do for her.

D. W. Hand

Colonel and Med. Dir., Dept. N. C.

August 2, 1865

I most cheerfully endorse all that has been said herein of Mrs. Von Olnhausen. I believe that this lady has done more good in the hospitals than any other female nurse I ever saw or of whom I have ever heard.

I. N. Palmer

Bt. Maj. Genl. U.S.A. (late Comdg Dept. of NC)

Notes

Introduction

1. Quoted in Drew Gilpin Faust, *Mothers of Invention: Women of the Slaveholding South in the American Civil War* (Chapel Hill: University of North Carolina Press, 1996), 100.
2. V. M. Francis, *A Thesis on Hospital Hygiene, for the Degree of Doctor of Medicine in the University of New York* (New York: J. F. Trow, 1859), 145.
3. Quoted in Susan M. Reverby, *Ordered to Care: The Dilemma of American Nursing, 1850–1945* (Cambridge: Cambridge University Press, 1987), 22.
4. Kate Cumming, *Journal of Hospital Life in the Confederate Army of Tennessee from the Battle of Shiloh to the End of the War: With Sketches of Life and Character and Brief Notices of Current Events During That Period* (Louisville: John P. Morton, 1866), 28.
5. Jane E. Schultz, *Women at the Front: Hospital Workers in Civil War America* (Chapel Hill and London: University of North Carolina Press, 2004), 20.

Chapter 1

1. Quoted in Thomas J. Brown, *Dorothea Dix: New England Reformer* (Cambridge, MA: Harvard University Press, 1998), 301.
2. George Templeton String, *Diary of the Civil War, 1860–1864,* ed. Allan Nevins (New York: Macmillan, 1962), 173–74.
3. Quoted in Maury Klein, *Days of Defiance: Sumter, Secession and the Coming of the Civil War* (New York: Alfred A. Knopf, 1997), 176.
4. Quoted in James M. McPherson, *Battle Cry of Freedom* (New York: Ballantine Books, 1988), 269.
5. Quoted in McPherson, 275.
6. Quoted in David Gollaher, *Voice for the Mad: The Life of Dorothea Dix* (New York: Free Press, 1995), 391.
7. Quoted in Gollaher, 397.
8. John G. Nicolay, *With Lincoln in the White House: Letters, Memoranda, and Other Writings of John G. Nicolay, 1860–1865*, ed. Michael Burlingame (Carbondale, IL: Southern Illinois University Press, 2000) 36.
9. Brown, 278.
10. Quoted in Frank R. Freemon, *Gangrene and Glory: Medical Care During the American Civil War* (Cranbury, NJ: Associated University Presses, 1998), 52–54.
11. Brown, 282.

12. Quoted in Mary C. Gillett, *The Army Medical Bureau, 1818–1865* (Washington, DC: Center of Military History, US Army, 1987), 154.

13. Quoted in Brown, 290.

14. From Circular No. 8, July 24, 1862, quoted in Philip A. Kalisch and Beatrice J. Kalisch, *The Advance of American Nursing*, third ed. (Philadelphia: J. B. Lippincott), 1995), 40.

15. J. H. Brinton, *Personal Memoirs of John H. Brinton, Major and Surgeon U.S.V., 1861–1865* (New York: Neale Publishing, 1914), 44.

16. Cornelia Hancock, *Letters of a Civil War Nurse, Cornelia Hancock, 1863–1865,* ed. Henrietta Stratton Jaquette (Lincoln, NE: University of Nebraska Press, 1998), 3.

17. Quoted in Julia Boyd, *The Excellent Doctor Blackwell: The life of the First Woman Physician* (Stroud, Gloucestershire: Sutton Publishing, 2005), 184.

18. Quoted in Stephen B. Oates, *A Woman of Valor: Clara Barton and the Civil War* (New York: Free Press, 1994).

19. Quoted in Gollaher, 415.

20. Quoted in L. P. Brockett and M. C. Vaughan, eds., *Woman's Work in the Civil War: A Record of Heroism, Patriotism and Patience* (Philadelphia: Zeigler, McCurdy & Company, 1867), 103.

21. Quoted in Brown, 308.

22. Ibid., 315.

Chapter 2

1. Ira M. Rutkow, *Bleeding Blue and Gray: Civil War Surgery and the Evolution of American Medicine* (New York: Random House, 2005), 4.

2. Stephen Oates, *A Woman of Valor: Clara Barton and the Civil War* (New York: Free Press. 1994), 4.

3. Quoted in George Worthington Adams, *Doctors in Blue: The Medical History of the Union Army in the Civil War* (New York: Henry Schuman, 1952), 19.

4. Quoted in Hannah Ropes, *Civil War Nurse: The Diary and Letters of Hannah Ropes*, ed. John R. Brumgardt (Knoxville: University of Tennessee Press, 1980), 40.

5. Quoted in Ropes, 40–41.

6. Quoted in Freemon, 35.

7. Ken Burns and Geoffrey C. Ward, *The Civil War: An Illustrated History* (New York: Alfred A. Knopf, 1990), 62.

8. Quoted in Kenneth C. Davis, *Don't Know Much About the Civil War* (New York: Avon Books, 1997), 188.

9. *New York Times*, July 22, 1861

10. *Saint Paul Daily Press*, July 30, 1861

11. Rutkow, 5.

12. Quoted in Freemon, 35–36.
13. S. Smith editorial, "Rank of Civil and Military Surgeons," *American Medical Times*, 3 (1861), 56.
14. Quoted in Horace H. Cunningham, *Field Medical Services at the Battles of Manassas (Bull Run)* (Athens, GA: University of Georgia Press, 1968), 13.
15. Edwin S. Barrett, *What I Saw at Bull Run* (Boston, n.p., 1866), 26.
16. *New York Daily Tribune*, July 26, 1861.
17. Barrett, 24.
18. Rutkow, 36.
19. Mary A. Holland, *Our Army Nurses. Interesting Sketches, Addresses and Photographs of Nearly One Hundred of the Noble Women Who Served in Hospitals and on Battlefield during Our Civil War*, ed. Mary A. Gardner Holland (Boston: B. Wilkins, 1895), 167.
20. Quoted in Oates, 52.
21. *New York Times*, July 26, 1861.
22. Stephen Smith, "The Profession and the Crisis," *American Medical Times* 3 (1861), 73.

Chapter 3

1. Mary Phinney von Olnhausen, *Adventures of an Army Nurse in Two Wars* (Boston: Little Brown, 1904), 29.
2. John Matteson, *Eden's Outcasts: The Story of Louisa May Alcott and Her Father* (New York: W.W. Norton, 2007), 265.
3. Schultz, 63.
4. Ibid., 63.
5. Holland, 207.
6. Ibid., 125.
7. Amanda Aiken Stearns, *The Lady Nurse of Ward E* (New York: The Baker & Taylor Co., 1909), 116; 60.
8. Von Olnhausen, 8.
9. Ibid., 13.
10. Ibid., 13–14.
11. Ibid., 21.
12. Ibid., 22.
13. Ibid., 23.
14. Ibid., 26.
15. Ibid., 29.
16. William Howard Russell, *Times* (London), September 15 and 22, 1854.
17. British National Archives, catalogue reference: WO 33/1 ff.119, 124, 146–47 (February 23, 1855), http://www.nationalarchives.gov.uk/battles/crimea/popup/medical.htm. Retrieved 8/30/15.

18. http://www.nationalarchives.gov.uk/education/resources/florence-nightingale/source-4/. Retrieved 10/7/15.

19. Anne Reading, *The Journal of Anne Reading: From Florence Nightingale to Dorothea Dix and Beyond.*, ed. Margaret Garrett Irwin (Bloomington, IN: Trafford, 2006), 1.

20. Ibid., 5.

21. Ibid.,10.

22. Ibid., 23.

23. Ibid., 24.

24. Ibid., 26.

25. Ibid., 44.

26. Louisa May Alcott, *Hospital Sketches* (Bedford, MA: Applewood Books, 1993), 7–14 *passim.*

27. Holland, 19–20 *passim.*

Chapter 4

1. Katharine Prescott Wormeley, *The Other Side of the War with the Army of the Potomac: Letters from the Headquarters of the United States Sanitary Commission During the Peninsular Campaign in Virginia in 1862* (Boston: Ticknor and Company, 1889), 105.

2. Reading, 50.

3. Elizabeth Blackwell, *Pioneer Work for Women* (London: J. M. Dent and Sons, 1914), 189–90. Quoted in Judith Ann Giesberg, *Civil War Sisterhood: The U.S. Sanitary Commission and Women's Politics in Transition* (Boston: University Press, 2000), 32.

4. *New York Herald*, April 30, 1861. Quoted in Giesberg, 33.

5. Quoted in William Quentin Maxwell, *Lincoln's Fifth Wheel: The Political History of the United States Sanitary Commission* (New York: Longman's Green, 1956), 5–6.

6. Quoted in Giesberg, 36.

7. Maxwell, 8.

8. Giesberg, 5, 79.

9. Georgeanna Woolsey Bacon and Eliza Woolsey Howland, *Letters of a Family During the War for the Union 1861–1865* (London: Forgotten Books, 2015), vol. 1, 48.

10. Quoted in Schultz, 43.

11. Frederick Law Olmsted, *Hospital Transports: A Memoir of the Embarkation of the Sick and Wounded from the Peninsula of Virginia in the Summer of 1862,* (Boston: Ticknor and Fields, 1863), 37.

12. Quoted in Giesberg, 54.

13. S. G. "Correspondence. Duties of the Army Surgeon—Females Not Suitable for Nurses," *American Medical Times*, July 18, 1861, 30.

14. Reading, 49.
15. Ibid., 50–51.
16. Quoted in Giesberg, 122.
17. Reading, 59.
18. Ibid., 53–54.
19. Ibid., 57–58.
20. Quoted in Diane Cobb Cashman, *Headstrong: The Biography of Amy Morris Bradley 1823–1904, A Life of Noblest Usefulness* (Wilmington, NC: Broadfoot Publishing, 1990), 119.
21. Quoted in Giesberg, 130.
22. Giesberg, 123.
23. Ibid., 122.
24. Ibid., 120.
25. Ibid., 121.
26. Ibid., 129.
27. Reading, 60–61.
28. Ibid., 63.

Chapter 5

1. Alcott, 24.
2. *Alexandria Gazette*, July 31, 1860; quoted in George G. Kundahl, *Alexandria Goes to War: Beyond Robert E. Lee* (Knoxville: University of Tennessee Press, 2004), 3.
3. *Alexandria Gazette*, May 24, 1849; quoted in report by Fauber Garbee, Inc., "Restoration of the John Carlyle House, Alexandria, Virginia," July 1980, 111–19.
4. Anne S. Frobel, *The Civil War Diary of Anne S. Frobel* (McLean, VA: EPM Publications, 1992), 15.
5. *Alexandria Gazette*, May 16, 1861; quoted in Kundahl, 15.
6. Von Olnhausen, 33.
7. Joseph Spafford to Marianne Spafford, University of Vermont Libraries, Center for Digital Initiatives, http://cdi.uvm.edu/collections/search.xql?rows=1&start=6&term1=Mansion%20House%20hospital&field1=ft [downloaded 9/10/15]).
8. Brinton, 198.
9. James G. Barber, *Alexandria in the Civil War* (Lynchburg, VA: H.E. Howard, 1988), 9.
10. Joseph Spafford to Marianne Spafford.
11. Von Olnhausen, 32.
12. Joseph Spafford to Marianne Spafford.
13. Von Olnhausen, 32.

14. Quoted in Oates, 58.
15. Ropes, 63.
16. Robert E. Denny, *Civil War Medicine: Care and Comfort of the Wounded* (New York: Sterling Publishing, 1994), 139.
17. Von Olnhausen, 36.
18. Quoted in Oates, 66.
19. Von Olnhausen, 32.
20. Ibid., 33.
21. Ibid., 35.
22. Reading, 64.
23. Ibid., 65–66.
24. Von Olnhausen, 44.
25. Ibid., 43.
26. Ibid., 44.
27. Ibid., 44–45.
28. Bacon and Howland, 142.
29. Correspondence, "Duties of the Army Surgeon—Females Not Suitable For Nurses," *American Medical Times*, 3 (1861), 30.
30. Sarah Coster, "Nurses, Spies and Soldiers: The Civil War at Carlyle House," *Carlyle House Docent Dispatch*, March 2011, 2.
31. Quoted by Schultz, 124.
32. Ibid., 125.
33. Brinton, 199–200.
34. Ibid., 294.
35. Von Olnhausen, 61–63.

Chapter 6

1. Mark Twain and Charles Dudley Warner, *The Gilded Age* (New York: Random House, 2006), 173–74.
2. Elvira J. Powers, *Hospital pencillings: Being a diary while in Jefferson General Hospital, Jeffersonville, Ind, and others at Nashville, Tennessee, as matron and visitor* (Boston: Edward L. Mitchel, 1866), 123–24.
3. Von Olnhausen, 33.
4. Ropes, 52–53.
5. Alcott, 26.
6. Quoted in Thomas Neville Bonner, *To The Ends of the Earth: Women's Search for Education in Medicine* (Cambridge, MA: Harvard University Press, 1992), 11.
7. Bacon and Howland, 79–81 *passim*.
8. Von Olnhausen, 17.
9. Powers, 124.
10. Ropes, 58.

11. Mary A. Newcomb, *Four Years of Personal Reminiscences of the War* (Chicago: H. S. Mills, 1893), 116.
12. Stearns, 287.
13. Jane Hoge, *The Boys in Blue; or, Heroes of the "Rank and File"* (New York: E.B. Treat, 1867), 111.
14. Von Olnhausen, 76.
15. Bacon and Howland, vol. 2, 594.
16. Von Olnhausen, 38–39.
17. Lucy Campbell Kaiser in *Our Army Nurses*, 181.
18. Adams, 16.
19. Elizabeth D. Leonard, *Yankee Women: Gender Battles in the Civil War* (New York: W.W. Norton, 1994), 88.
20. Brockett, 633.
21. Stearns, 266.
22. Brockett, 322.
23. Bacon and Howland, vol. 2, 402.
24. Ropes, 61.
25. Alcott, 29.
26. Von Olnhausen, 50–51.
27. Alcott, 41.
28. Von Olnhausen, 141.
29. Ibid., 61.
30. Ibid., 54.

Chapter 7

1. Quoted in Schultz, 107.
2. Ibid., 74.
3. Powers, 137.
4. Wormeley, 89.
5. Cornelia Hancock, *Letters of a Civil War Nurse, Cornelia Hancock, 1863–1865*, ed. Henriette Stratton Jaquette (Lincoln, NE: University of Nebraska Press, 1998), 5.
6. Hancock, 10.
7. Alcott, 52.
8. Schultz, 107.
9. Reading, 87.
10. Wormeley, 136.
11. Newcomb, 33–34.
12. Von Olnhausen, 50.
13. Wormeley, 69–70.
14. Stearns, 36.
15. Von Olnhausen, 40.

16. Powers, 52.
17. Alcott, 63.
18. Powers, 157.
19. Von Olnhausen, 40.
20. Ibid., 38–39.
21. Bacon and Howland, 137.
22. Von Olnhausen, 72–74.
23. Lucy Campbell Kaiser in *Our Army Nurses*, 180.
24. Hancock, 14.
25. Ibid., 9.
26. Ibid., 14.
27. Von Olnhausen, 38.
28. Ibid., 50.
29. Ibid., 49–50.
30. Reading, 79.
31. Ropes, 55.
32. Von Olnhausen, 47–49.
33. Ibid., 101.
34. Ibid., 74.
35. Schultz, 134.
36. Ropes, 17.
37. Ibid., 51.
38. Ibid., 74.
39. Ibid., 73.
40. Ibid., 75.
41. Ibid., 79.
42. Ibid., 82–83.
43. Ibid., 85.
44. Ibid., 87.
45. Quoted in Oates, 95.
46. Von Olnhausen, 52–53.
47. Cashman, 91.
48. Ibid., 91–92.
49. Ibid., 143–44.
50. Ibid., 144–45.
51. Ibid., 149.
52. Ibid., 148–49.
53. Hancock, 12.
54. Ibid., 13.

Chapter 8

1. Hancock, 14.
2. Adams, 15.
3. Ropes, 91.
4. Ibid., 91.
5. Ibid., 112.
6. Ibid., 112.
7. Ibid., 114.
8. Ibid., 120.
9. Ibid., 121.
10. Alcott, 77.
11. Ibid., 78.
12. Ropes, 122.
13. Reading, 79.
14. Von Olnhausen, 56.
15. Ibid., 59.
16. Reading, 83–84.
17. Von Olnhausen, 75–78.
18. Ibid., 69.
19. Ibid., 83.
20. Ibid., 85.
21. Ibid., 86.
22. Reading, 88.
23. Von Olnhausen, 77.
24. Ibid., 86–87.
25. Ibid., 89–90.
26. Quoted in Schultz, 78–79.
27. Ropes, 120.
28. Alcott, 32.
29. Von Olnhausen, 81.
30. Ibid., 91–92
31. Ibid., 81
32. Ibid., 7.
33. Ibid., 75–78.
34. Ibid., 78–79.
35. Ibid., 103–4.
36. Ibid., 79–80.
37. Hancock, 18.
38. Powers, 158.

Chapter 9

1. Powers, 121
2. Von Olnhausen, 41
3. Ibid., 174
4. Ibid., 112
5. Ibid., 118
6. Ibid., 120–21
7. Ibid., 105
8. Ibid., 124
9. Ibid., 124–25
10. Phinney, 130
11. See www.measuringworth.com for a discussion of the different ways monetary values can be compared over time.
12. Alcott, 76
13. Alcott, 74.
14. Von Olnhausen, 161.
15. Ibid., 191.
16. Ibid., 133.
17. Ibid., 137.
18. Ibid., 138–39.
19. Ibid., 14–42.
20. Ibid., 150.
21. Ibid., 153–54.
22. Ibid., 155.
23. Ibid., 162.
24. Ibid., 173.
25. Ibid., 181.
26. Ibid., 180.
27. Ibid., 180.
28. Ibid., 182.
29. Ibid., 206.
30. Ibid., 193.
31. Ibid., 213.

Chapter 10

1. Emily Parsons, *Memoir of Emily Elizabeth Parsons* (Boston: Little, Brown, & Co., 1880), 125–26.
2. Vesta M. W. Swarts in *Our Army Nurses*, 146.
3. Quoted in Brown, 323.

4. Quoted in Margaret Humphreys, *Marrow of Tragedy: The Health Crisis of the American Civil War* (Baltimore: Johns Hopkins University Press, 2013), 48.
5. Wormeley, 43–44.
6. Parsons, 40.
7. Swarts, 146.
8. Von Olnhausen, 223.
9. Ibid., 225.
10. Ibid., 231.
11. Ibid., 225.
12. Ibid., 229.
13. Ibid., 232.
14. Ibid., 251–52.
15. Ibid., 258.
16. Ibid., 260.
17. Ibid., 261.
18. Ibid., 341.
19. Quoted in Virginia G. Drachman, *Hospital with a Heart: Woman Doctors and the Paradox of Separations at the New England Hospital 1862–1969* (Ithaca: Cornell University Press, 1984), 80.
20. Quoted in Giesberg, 60.
21. Quoted in Kalisch and Kalisch, 71.
22. Von Olnhausen, 332.
23. Quoted in Gollaher, 422.
24. Quoted in Charles Schlaifer and Lucy Freeman, *Heart's Work: Civil War Heroine and Champion of the Mentally Ill, Dorothea Lynde Dix* (New York: Paragon House, 1991), 133–34.
25. Mary Livermore, "Report of the Sixth Annual Convention," *American Journal of Nursing*, 1903, vol. 3, 834–35.

Afterword

1. Libra R. Hilde, *Worth a Dozen Men: Women and Nursing in the Civil War South* (Charlottesville, VA: University of Virginia Press, 2012), 3-4.
2. Phoebe Yates Pember, *A Southern Woman's Story: Life in Confederate Richmond*, ed. Bell Irvin Wiley (Saint Simons Island, GA: Mockingbird Books, 1974), 17.
3. Pember, 16.
4. Quoted in Schultz, 50.
5. Quoted in Faust, 106, Cornelia Peake McDonald, *A Woman's Civil War: A Diary, with Reminiscences of the War, from March 1862*, ed. Minrose C. Gwin (Madison: University of Wisconsin Press, 1992), 38.
6. Pember, 16.

7. Drew Gilpin Faust, *Mothers of Invention: Women of the Slaveholding South in the American Civil War* (Chapel Hill, NC: University of North Carolina Press, 1996), 97.
8. Quoted in Faust, 97.
9. Ibid., 103.

Suggestions for Further Reading

Alcott, Louisa May. *Hospital Sketches*. Bedford, Mass: Applewood Books. 1993. Originally published 1863.

Giesberg, Judith Ann. *Civil War Sisterhood: The U.S. Sanitary Commission and Women's Politics in Transition*. Boston: Northeastern University Press, 2000.

Hancock, Cornelia. *Letters of a Civil War Nurse: Cornelia Hancock, 1863–1865*. Ed. Henrietta Stratton Jaquette. Lincoln, Nebraska: University of Nebraska Press, 1998.

Hilde, Libra R. *Worth a Dozen Men: Women and Nursing in the Civil War South*. Charlottesville, Virginia: University of Virginia Press, 2012.

Humphreys, Margaret. *Marrow of Tragedy: The Health Crisis of the American Civil War*. Baltimore: Johns Hopkins University Press, 2013.

Leonard, Elizabeth D. *Yankee Women: Gender Battles in the Civil War*. New York: W.W. Norton, 1994.

Oates, Stephen B. *A Woman of Valor: Clara Barton and the Civil War*. New York: Free Press, 1994.

Ropes, Hannah. *Civil War Nurse: The Diary and Letters of Hannah Ropes*. Ed. John R. Brumgardt. Knoxville: University of Tennessee Press, 1980.

Rutkow, Ira M. *Bleeding Blue and Gray: Civil War Surgery and the Evolution of American Medicine*. New York: Random House, 2005.

Schultz, Jane E. *Women at the Front: Hospital Workers in Civil War America*. Chapel Hill and London: University of North Carolina Press, 2004.

Index

About the Author

PAMELA D. TOLER is a writer with a PhD in history from the University of Chicago and a fascination with historical figures who step outside the constraints of their time. She is the author of *Mankind: The Story of All of Us* and *The Everything Guide to Understanding Socialism.* She lives in Chicago.